D1567089

Forged Architectural Metalwork

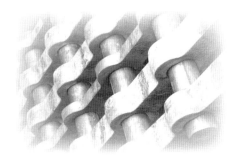

Peter Parkinson

The Crowood Press

First published in 2006 by
The Crowood Press Ltd
Ramsbury, Marlborough
Wiltshire SN8 2HR

www.crowood.com

British Library Cataloguing-in-Publication Data
A catalogue record for this book is available from the British Library.

ISBN 1 86126 817 3
EAN 978 1 86126 817 4

Acknowledgements
Crown copyright material is reproduced with the permission of the Controller
of HMSO and the Queen's Printer for Scotland.
   My thanks to The Arts Council England for financial assistance in funding
research undertaken for this book.
   I would, in particular, like to thank all those blacksmiths who have lent me
illustrations – and not complained about the length of time I have kept them –
and whose commitment and enthusiasm, along with others, have provided the
impetus to complete this book.

Front cover and back cover bottom right-hand image: Bigg Market gates,
Newcastle, by Alan Evans, under construction.

Back cover top image: Morton's Bond access gate, Exchange
Street, Dundee. P. Johnson and Company, designed by Phil Johnson and Jois
Hunter.

Back cover, bottom left-hand image: Swindon Dance Theatre, forged mild
steel and stainless steel railings, by Avril Wilson.

Typeset and designed by D & N Publishing
Lambourn Woodlands, Hungerford, Berkshire.

Printed and bound in Singapore by Craft Print International.

CONTENTS

Introduction 4

Chapter 1 Working and Workshop 7
Chapter 2 Basic Forging Processes 13
Chapter 3 Assembly Technique 27
Chapter 4 Surveying the Site 39
Chapter 5 Design and Regulations 49
Chapter 6 Handrails 67
Chapter 7 Balustrades 75
Chapter 8 Railings and Fences 89
Chapter 9 Screens and Grilles 99
Chapter 10 Gates 107
Chapter 11 Materials and Finishes 133
Chapter 12 Installation 153

Glossary 173
Further Reading 174
Index 175

INTRODUCTION

The surge of interest and activity in artist blacksmithing, which began in Britain in the very late 1970s, was a renaissance overdue. At that time, British blacksmithing was still to a large extent anchored in styles deriving from the seventeenth century, while ironwork in the rest of Europe had long since sailed on through the arts and crafts movement, art nouveau and art deco, to develop contemporary expressions of the craft. Other arts and crafts in Britain – ceramics, silversmithing, jewellery, graphic design, glass and textiles – had all been influenced by these movements, but blacksmithing remained virtually untouched.

One exception was metalwork designed by Charles Rennie Mackintosh in Scotland, at the very beginning of the twentieth century, which sadly had remarkably little influence in Britain at the time. Significantly, he was an architect. It was the architects in Europe whose art nouveau buildings involved ironwork as such a vital element, while in Britain there was simply no art nouveau architecture. So British smiths were perhaps more deprived of the opportunity, than blind to it.

Against this background and two World Wars later, it was to the credit of a few workshops, CoSIRA (the Council for Small Industries in Rural Areas) and Herefordshire Technical College that blacksmithing skills had survived at all. Indeed in 1979 and 1980, the Crafts Council organized two Forging Iron Conferences at Hereford – the first national, the second international – with the object of trying to revive what they had identified as a dying craft. These proved to be pivotal events, which with the advent of BABA (the British Artist Blacksmiths Association), initiated by Richard Quinnell in 1978, began an extraordinary period of development for blacksmithing. By 1982 several art colleges included blacksmithing in the syllabus and in 1989, some ten colleges contributed to a major exhibition of forged metalwork by students, which I curated as part of the First International Festival of Iron in Cardiff. Blacksmithing had become a challenging, expressive and creative activity. Smiths were taking on a new role, designing work as well as making it. Architecture was changing too. Modernist glass and concrete were giving way to a more craft-conscious approach, using good brickwork, stone, timber and metalwork. In this context, forged ironwork suddenly looked exciting, new and different. This had happened before, at the beginning of the eighteenth century: the period from the end of the seventeenth century to the middle of the eighteenth century saw a flowering of architectural ironwork in Britain, a creative golden age for blacksmithing. Jean Tijou, who produced dramatic metalwork at Hampton Court for William and Mary, directly or indirectly influenced a generation of other smiths. Just a few are known by name, including Robert Bakewell, Robert Davies, William Edney and Thomas Robinson. These blacksmiths worked with architects – Tijou worked with Wren on St Paul's Cathedral in London. The fact that they developed their own characteristic styles, suggests that they were commissioned as much for their design abilities as their making skills, but the lack of surviving documentary evidence makes this point ultimately hard to resolve.

More importantly in the context of this book, almost nothing was recorded by blacksmiths themselves about their working methods. We can be sure that fundamental forging processes have not changed, but how they worked – what judgements they made, how they surveyed, designed and progressed the work, how their workshops were arranged, how they transported and installed the work, how many people they employed – is all essentially conjecture. Perhaps little has changed. Compared with many other crafts, the literature of contemporary blacksmithing is distinctly thin, not least because smiths themselves still write very little.

My intention in this book is to record something of the creativity, craftsmanship and technical expertise that has informed the contemporary practice of the artist blacksmith's craft, and to describe the breadth of skills, techniques and considerations involved in the design and making of forged architectural metalwork – before yet another generation of smiths retire and it is too late to ask.

Blacksmiths make a wide range of products, including hinges, handles, locks, latches, push plates, hooks, brackets and so on, which in the sense that they are attached to a building, could all be categorized as 'architectural metalwork'. But for the purposes of this book, and to limit it to a manageable size, I have taken architectural metalwork to mean larger structural pieces.

Railings at Glasgow School of Art, by Charles Rennie Mackintosh, installed 1897–99.

1 WORKING AND WORKSHOP

SAFE WORKING

Every aspect from the design and layout of the workshop, through to the use of tools and to your personal conduct, should be guided by safe working principles. Making forged architectural metalwork involves handling pieces of red hot metal, moving heavy objects, the use of a wide range of hand and electric tools and equipment, inflammable fuels, compressed air and pressurized gases. There are a multitude of ways of burning, crushing, spiking, deafening, electrocuting or asphyxiating yourself, getting something in your eye, tripping, or even blowing yourself up in a blacksmithing workshop. The important point is to be aware of the hazards and build safety into the way you work. Never think of it as an optional extra.

Like putting on a car seat-belt, working safely should become such an integral part of the process that it is habitual. Much of it is common sense and good housekeeping – like wearing appropriate clothing and protective equipment, not leaving materials or electric cables all over the floor to trip you, putting tools away when you have finished with them and so on. Other aspects are to do with the way you operate and maintain each piece of equipment, how you start it up and close it down. Never, for example, leave machines switched on or running unattended, always de-pressurize the reducer valves of gas cylinders at the end of each day's work. There are established safety procedures for each piece of equipment, which should be well understood by everyone who uses them.

Clothing and Safety Equipment

Wear suitable clothing, made of cotton or wool – not synthetics, which can melt and stick to the skin. Since hot forge scale, dropped tools or pieces of metal fall downwards, bare arms are less vulnerable than bare legs, so you need a pair of jeans or

OPPOSITE PAGE: Jim Horrobin, hot ribs, work in progress for the Winston Churchill Memorial Screen. (Photo: Jim Horrobin)

heavy cotton work trousers to protect them. A T-shirt can be more comfortable in hot weather but, when necessary, even a long-sleeved shirt can offer a useful amount of protection from radiant heat or welding flash.

Good safety spectacles are essential to protect your eyes against hot forge scale, grit and fragments of grit, thrown out by the forge fire. It is a good habit to wear them all the time you are in the workshop.

Steve Lunn bending metal, wearing protective apron, gloves and boots. (Photo: Steve Lunn)

While ear-plugs or ear-defenders are obviously needed to protect your hearing when using noisy equipment like grinders or power hammers, the cumulative effect of hand hammering can also damage hearing. Custom-moulded ear-plugs are now available that offer a high level of protection, but do not significantly affect normal hearing. As with spectacles, these can be comfortably worn all the time you are working.

Safety boots with steel toe-caps and polyurethane soles, are essential to protect your feet should you drop something heavy, stub your toe on a sharp edge or stand on a piece of hot steel. Leather, or cotton and leather, gloves are important to protect your hands from hot, abrasive or sharp pieces of metal. Many smiths prefer to forge with a hammer held in a bare hand, but wear a glove on the hand that holds the hot metal. A traditional, blacksmith's leather apron provides excellent body protection against heat, sparks and general abrasion.

Specialist protective equipment is required for gas or arc welding and for gas or plasma cutting. The uses of oxygen, acetylene, propane and the shielding gases

Andy Quirk drawing a taper at the power hammer, wearing ear defenders. (Photo: Andy Quirk & Robert Kranenborg)

used in MIG and TIG welding (*see* page 35) are all covered by safety regulations and procedures, detailed by the suppliers and manufacturers, who are usually only too happy to sell you the requisite non-return valves, flash-back arrestors, gas economizers, safety goggles, helmets, face masks and gloves. The most important practical advice is perhaps not only to make sure that you use these things, but also to cover up exposed skin against flash burns. Doing the odd, casual little bit of arc welding in summer while wearing a T-shirt, can result in badly 'sunburnt' arms, far quicker than you might think. If you do not want to put on another shirt or jacket, elasticated welding sleeves are available to slip on over bare arms.

Electrical Safety

Electrical safety is a crucial consideration in a workshop full of metal, where you are invariably working with a good electrical conductor in your hand. The workshop wiring should provide reliable earth continuity, even though most hand electric power tools are double-insulated. Miniature circuit breakers (MCBs) in the workshop fuse board are easier to reset than conventional fuses, but may prove to be more of a problem than a help with circuits running arc welders, since the varying load can cause them to trip unnecessarily, making a conventional wire fuse a better alternative.

Residual current circuit breakers (RCCBs), either as part of the fuse board, integral with or plugged into socket outlets, are very effective and offer a high level of protection should the power lead to (say) a drill or grinder be severed. Routinely checking the trailing leads and plugs fitted to welding equipment, hand power tools and the fixed wiring to machinery, is a worthwhile precaution. In Britain there is a safety argument for wiring a workshop circuit to provide socket outlets at 110V (rather than the normal 240V) in order to operate hand electric tools more safely at the lower voltage. Low-voltage power tools are routinely required on building sites, so adopting this approach can avoid too much duplication of equipment.

Finishing

Using a rotary wire brush to clean rusty steel, or to strip old paint surfaces, calls for both eye protection and a face mask, not least because old paint may well contain lead. Preparing and finishing metal can produce airborne dust particles, so it makes sense to wear a breathing mask as well as safety goggles. Grinding steel tends to throw heavy particles away from the user but, depending on the ventilation in the workshop, lighter dust particles can build up in the air. It is a matter of judgement when and what kind of mask is needed, but it is fair to say that it cannot harm you to use one too often.

For general dust protection, the disposable, moulded paper masks may be adequate, but if galvanized steel, non-ferrous metals or lead paint is involved, a fitted respirator mask with the correct filter cartridge is essential. Non-ferrous metal particles are not good to breathe. Burning off galvanized surfaces with a torch, welding galvanized metal or plasma cutting non-ferrous metals, provides a similar toxic hazard.

Paint spraying also requires eye protection and a breathing mask. The mask required depends on the type of paint being sprayed and the environment in which it is being used. Many paints contain harmful solvents. Some two-pack paints – polyurethanes, for example – are distinctly harmful and in most cases, due to the nature of the paint, the spray particles are light. It is important to realize that you may well be working in a toxic fog, even out-of-doors. Specialist sub-contractors are equipped to apply these finishes, so it can make sense to use them.

Jim Horrobin's large assembly workshop, with the Winston Churchill Memorial gates erected and part complete.

round for access. Clearance on all sides is particularly important if the construction uses tenons or other details that need to be riveted, requiring a hammer to be swung horizontally.

The height of the workshop is an important consideration. Usually, at some point during the assembly of a grille or gate, it will need to be turned over, so height must be available to allow this to happen. Mechanical handling, whether with a chain hoist, crane or fork-lift truck, requires a larger working area and height to accommodate these facilities. Like the cartoon of the bemused boat-builder who has just finished assembling a sailing dingy in his front room, it is crucially important to think ahead and plan how the finished structure will be taken out of the workshop. Each component may seem easy enough to move individually, but the accumulated weight and size of the finished work can still sometimes come as a

WORKSHOP SPACES

Architectural metalwork makes greater demands on workshop space than other kinds of blacksmithing, because the work is of a large scale. Due to its variable nature, it is impossible to be specific about workshop requirements, except to suggest that the space can hardly be too big. Having said this, many smiths work in relatively small workshops and improvise, rent or borrow a larger space when the need arises. After all, if you are only likely to undertake a commission requiring a large workshop once or twice a year, why maintain a space you do not really need for the rest of the time?

While you can forge and fabricate numbers of components in a relatively small area, you need much more space to manoeuvre and assemble them. Even a gate or grille, the size of a domestic door, commands a large space when lying horizontally on trestles, allowing room all

RIGHT: A window grille being turned over on trestles, using a chain hoist in my workshop.

surprise to handle. A good, solid, load-bearing flat floor, can be a great asset. Good internal height, large access doors, a level access and, ideally, some outside yard space, are all important.

Assembling staircase balustrading or an entire staircase may call for sufficient height to accommodate a complete flight in the position it will assume when installed. Curved or helical staircases may require the fabrication of a 'drum' or setting-out jig representing – either wholly or in part – the form of the stair string or the stair well in which the metalwork is to be fitted. A run of curved railings will need to be set out using some form of beam compass, line or improvised radius bar. Ideally the workshop should be big enough to accommodate the centre of the radius.

Workshop Layout

Planning the ideal workshop suggests that dedicated areas are necessary for particular purposes, such as forging, metal storage, welding, flame-cutting, grinding, machining, bench work, assembly, painting and so on. The logic of this is to avoid one process contaminating another. You do not want showers of grinder sparks and grit all over a precision lathe or a wet paint surface. It is also important to try and avoid the unnecessary movement of heavy materials. The making of individual pieces of architectural metalwork cannot be expected to proceed in a neat, linear, production-line fashion. The pattern is perhaps more one of radiating lines converging on the assembly area. Making an effort to analyse the local workflow can help both efficiency and safety. It makes sense to site the metal storage where material can be off-loaded from the delivery truck and racked up without too much carrying, then removed to a cut-off saw nearby, when needed.

In practice, workshop layout is invariably a compromise. Some processes, like metal storage or machining, are essentially

fixed; others, like welding or grinding, are mobile. Siting particular fixed machines needs some thought, so that access is available, for instance, for long lengths of metal to be worked under a power hammer or fed through the headstock of a lathe. If space is limited, it can be helpful to use outside areas or lines of access within the building by, for example, feeding lengths of material through an open door. This may not be necessary very often, but when it is, you are glad you thought of it. In many workshops the layout is changed as needed. Equipment that does not have to be bolted down is made movable by fitting castors or can be moved with a fork-lift. If the demands on the workshop are variable, flexibility is crucial.

My small workshop, looking remarkably clean. To make best use of the floor space, everything is movable except the power hammer and the coke forge.

2 BASIC FORGING PROCESSES

The design and making of forged architectural metalwork demands skills of which hot-forging metal is just one. It is not the intention of this book to describe forging skills in detail, so just a summary is provided here.

Hot forging is a process that exploits the property of metals to deform plastically under the effect of impact and pressure. Rather than taking a piece of metal and removing unwanted parts – cutting them away, for example, by machining – forging does not remove material but causes it to flow into shape, as a potter might form a piece of clay. The hammer's blow or the squeezing of a press, moves the metal, providing forms and textures with a character quite unlike those produced by other metalworking processes.

HEAT SOURCES

The traditional method of heating iron and steel is in a coal or coke fire – the blacksmith's forge. Air is blown into the fire, traditionally with bellows, to provide combustion air and to control the fire. Solid-fuel forges are still widely used but are now almost invariably blown by electric fans, fitted with some form of air valve or speed control. The greater the air flow, the hotter the fire. Iron or steel can overheat, melt and literally burn, so it is a matter of judgement to withdraw the workpiece at the correct moment: take it out too late and it can be ruined. These fires are economical and efficient, provide largely unrestricted access, but can only heat a short length of the bar at a time, typically the span of a hand. This length is called 'a heat', and is convenient for most

hand forging, but if a long curve or taper is required, it would need to be forged in several heats, working a short length at a time.

Power hammers can work a far longer length of hot metal, so it is more convenient to forge long tapers using one long heat. The development of propane-fired forges, which can heat long lengths of material – up to a metre (39in) or more – has gone hand in hand with the increasing use of power hammers. A gas forge is essentially a chamber, like a potter's kiln, but usually with doors at front and back, so the end of a bar can be heated, or it can be passed right through the forge to heat some intermediate length. Gas forges are now commonplace in the artist blacksmith's workshop, where particularly in architectural work, there is often the need to make large numbers of similar components. Quantities of bars can be loaded into the forge and worked in sequence, with the heat regulated to avoid the risk of burning the metal. However, due to the height and width of the chamber, once a bar has been curved or bent, it may not fit back through a gas forge, for another heat.

OPPOSITE PAGE:
Forged components, Jim Horrobin.
(Photo: Jim Horrobin)

Hand forging; heating metal in a gas forge in my workshop.

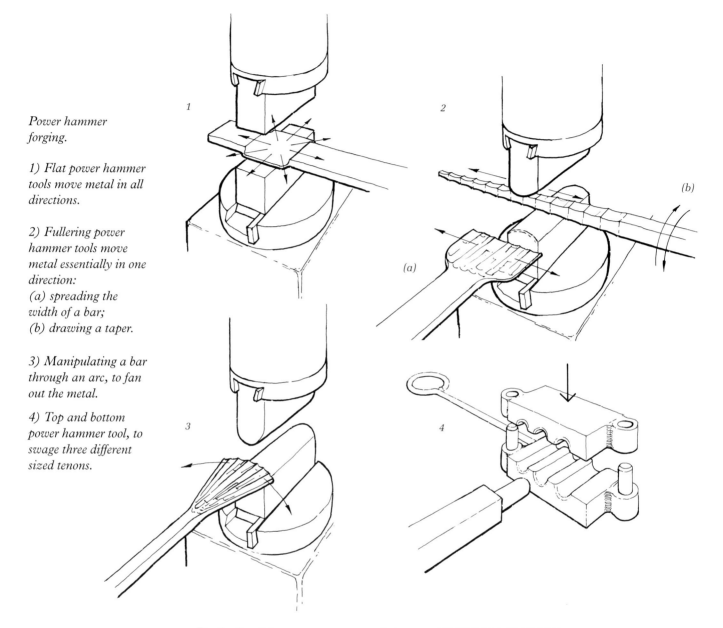

Power hammer forging.

1) Flat power hammer tools move metal in all directions.

2) Fullering power hammer tools move metal essentially in one direction:
(a) spreading the width of a bar;
(b) drawing a taper.

3) Manipulating a bar through an arc, to fan out the metal.

4) Top and bottom power hammer tool, to swage three different sized tenons.

Partly for this reason, most workshops today use coal or coke forges, as well as gas forges. Historically, blacksmithing has absorbed new tools and processes because they offer capabilities that add to, rather than substitute for, older methods. Gas torches – oxy-acetylene or oxy-propane – also provide a vital heat source, most often for local heating in processes such as bending, riveting or wrapping, or to allow a piece to be adjusted after assembly.

HOT FORGING

Much work is achieved on an anvil using a hand hammer and hand tools. For some processes, the smith may also work with the help of a 'striker' – whose job is to place accurate blows with a sledge-hammer – often to drive tools such as punches, chisels and swages. Power hammers are in widespread use and they can forge far larger masses of metal than can reasonably be forged by hand. The fundamental difference in technique between forging by hand and by power hammer, is that, whereas the angle and position of hand-hammer blows can be rapidly changed, the blows of a power hammer are strictly vertical. So the free forming of metal relies on the shape of fixed or hand-held tools and the manipulation of the bar under the hammer. Fly presses and hydraulic presses are also used for hot forming or bending, and sometimes for punching. The shapes that can be achieved by forging are – as the saying has it – limited only by your imagination. But no matter what the source of impact or pressure, at root there are a limited number of ways that hot metal may be made to move, and these give rise to core processes that, like the notes in a musical scale, provide the basis for endless possibilities.

The flat of the hammer moves metal in all directions.

The pein end of the hammer moves metal essentially in one direction, spreading the width of a bar.

Fundamental to all forging is the effect of the tool on hot metal. The shape of both the hammer and anvil contribute to the way the metal moves under impact. A vertical blow with the flat face of a hammer on a flat anvil will crush a bar, causing it to spread both in length and width. A vertical blow using a hammer with a cylindrical face (a cross pein hammer), on a flat anvil, will dig into the bar, creating a notch and displacing metal essentially in one direction. Aligning the hammer face with the long axis of the bar will increase its width, aligning it across the bar will increase its length. In both cases, the other dimension of the bar is much less affected. This directional emphasis is very important in providing control when forging a wide variety of forms. Moving metal in this way is described as 'fullering', since it is also achieved using special tools known as 'fullers'.

LEFT: The free-forming of metal relies on careful manipulation of the bar under the hammer. Charles Normandale at work. (Photo: Charles Normandale)

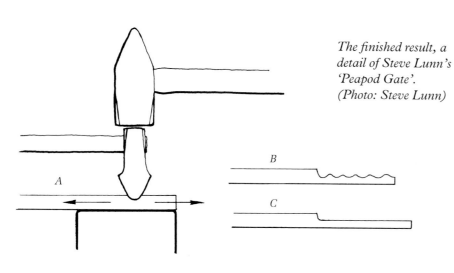

The finished result, a detail of Steve Lunn's 'Peapod Gate'. (Photo: Steve Lunn)

Fullering: A. a top fuller driven into the bar creating a notch;
B. the bar stretched by further fullering;
C. the bar forged flat. Note the increase in length.

Spreading the middle of a bar using a hand-held top fuller. Steve Lunn at the power hammer. (Photo: Steve Lunn)

Using a hand-held fuller to forge a notch under a hydraulic press, in Phil Johnson's workshop.
(Photo: P. Johnson & Company)

Fullers and Swages

Fullers, which have convex or cylindrical working faces, may be categorized as 'bottom tools' or 'top tools'. Bottom tools are made with a shank to fit in the square hole – the hardie hole – of the anvil. Top tools are usually fitted with a handle and struck with a sledge-hammer, or used under a power hammer. In combination, top and bottom tools act on both sides of the bar simultaneously, and hence stretch or 'draw' the metal more quickly. Fullers are also important in providing a notch that may be a decorative detail in its own right or the starting point for a stepped taper. Smaller power hammers have interchangeable tools (also called pallets), which may have flat or convex working faces and correspond to the flat hand hammer or the cross pein hammer and fuller.

Fullers spread metal, but the opposite effect is achieved by swages, whose working faces are concave. Like fullers, these tools may be used separately or in combination as top and bottom tools. The action of a swage is to mould and form the metal to a controlled shape and size. Often some initial forging is necessary to prepare the bar for finishing between swages. Standard swages are open-ended, so that a length of metal can be passed straight through and formed to a particular section – the precise diameter for a round tenon or a handrail section with a convex upper surface. More specialist, closed top and bottom tools may be used, for example, to create a ball-shaped finial or to make a spearhead on the end of a bar.

Special versions of top and bottom tools – fullers and swages – are linked in pairs and held in alignment by guide plates or pins. Some are linked by a U-shaped flat spring, which acts as a handle and holds the two faces of the tool open, to allow the workpiece to be easily inserted in between. These are intended for use under a power hammer, and are often made specially by the smith.

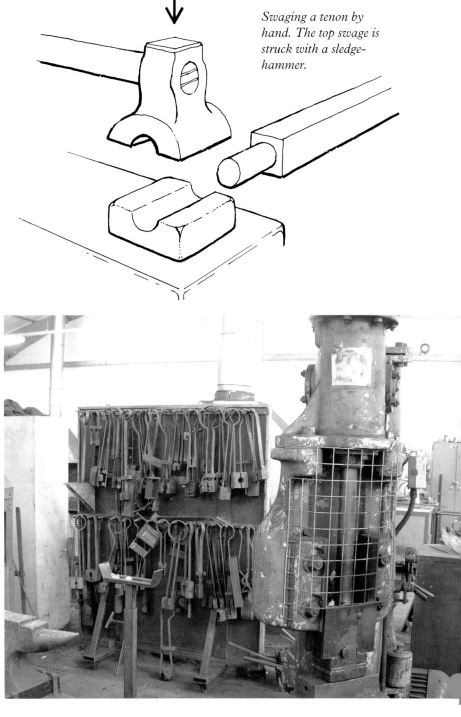

Swaging a tenon by hand. The top swage is struck with a sledge-hammer.

Power hammer and a rack of typical, spring top and bottom tools – mostly swages – at Hereford College of Technology.

Tapering or Drawing Down

Tapering is achieved by hammering two adjacent faces of a bar, rotating the bar backwards and forwards through 90 degrees between blows. The bar is gripped in the hand and rotated by twisting the wrist. In effect the hammer works on two faces, while the anvil works on the other two. The spreading caused by hammering one face, is crushed back by blows to the other face, the net result being to lengthen the bar and reduce its cross-section. Making an abrupt taper, completing the point first, either by hand or power hammer, is good practice, since it avoids the end of the bar folding and forming a crease that, when forged further, develops into a longitudinal crack. Split ends are not just a hair problem!

Flat or square bars are tapered in the way described. Tapering can produce a chisel (flat point) or pyramidal end (square point). The flat point calls for less hammering in one plane than the other, retaining the original width of the bar in one plane, while tapering it in the other. Tapering a round bar to produce a conical end (round point), calls for two additional stages: forging the metal from a square section to octagonal, then rotating the bar gently backwards and forwards under the hammer to 'round it up'. The change of cross-section from square to round does not add a great deal to the length of the bar, so it can be forged close to its finished length before rounding up. It is important to appreciate that the bar does *grow* in length. Forging a taper on the end of a bar is not like sharpening a pencil, or turning a taper in a lathe, where material is discarded. One of the great joys of blacksmithing is the sense that in forging metal you throw nothing away – you simply rearrange it. This also gives rise to an aesthetic, which celebrates the transformation. The appreciation of a forged form is often enhanced if it can be seen what it started from.

LEFT BELOW: Forging a square taper, turning the bar alternately through 90 degrees.

Forging a round taper:
A. forge a square taper;
B. turn 45 degrees and forge to an octagonal section;
C. twist left and right while hammering gently to 'round up' the taper.

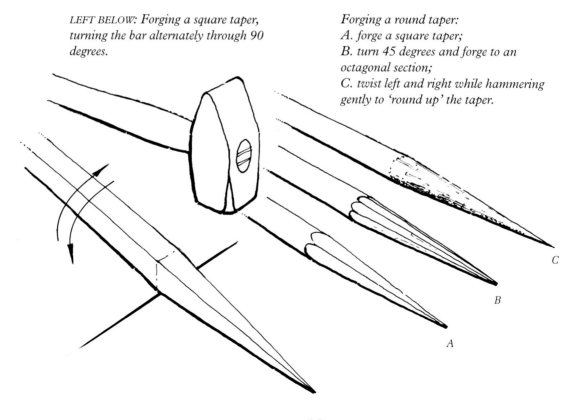

Measuring Forged Lengths

The length of material required for a taper (or for other forms) can be calculated by considering its volume. For tapers this results in a rule of thumb. A round point on a round bar, or a square point on a square bar, can be forged from metal one-third the length of the taper. A flat point on a square bar can be forged from a piece of bar half the required length. However, these rules derive from a geometry that assumes perfectly straight lines and needle-sharp points. Tapered forms seldom need to be geometrically perfect to look good. Indeed the classic architecture of Ancient Greece used 'entasis' – a slight convex curve to correct the illusion that the straight sides of a column curve inwards. If you establish a taper by eye, then check it with a straight edge, it is very likely to be convex. For these reasons it will be necessary to add an allowance to the theoretical length of the blank. Allowing also for the loss of metal through scaling in the fire, suggests that 5 or 10 per cent should be added. The pragmatic approach is to use the calculated length simply as a guide. It is normal practice to make a trial piece using a known length of metal, forge the required taper – or any other detail – and measure the length of the bar again, to establish the length of the blank needed to forge the component.

The fact that the bar grows in length when hammered, means that this can be used to adjust the length if it is a little too short. For architectural metalwork, precision of fit is crucial, so adjusting a length by even a millimetre or two – let alone five or ten – can be important. A small increase can be achieved by hammering carefully along the bar while it is cold, or hammering hot for a larger adjustment.

Upsetting

Upsetting is effectively the opposite of tapering. Metal is driven back into the bar, reducing its length and increasing its thickness, at a point determined by a short heat. The bar is upset by blows struck directly on its end, along the axis of the bar or, if it is heavy enough, by pounding it down on to a block on the floor, or the face of the anvil. Very short lengths of thick bar can be upset under a power hammer or vertical press; while, suitably gripped and

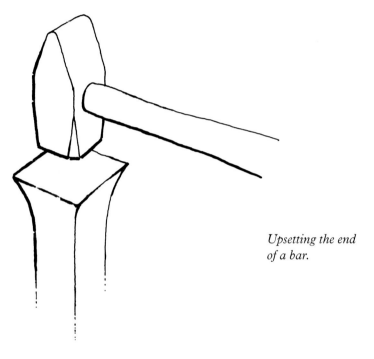

Upsetting the end of a bar.

supported, longer lengths can be upset in a horizontal hydraulic press. In all cases, the heat must be short and intense and, when working by hand, it helps to rotate the bar between blows to even out its tendency to bend. Any bending must be corrected immediately. Thick bars are easier to upset than thin ones. For this reason, very thin bars are better secured in a vice, heated very close to the vice jaws with an oxy-acetylene torch and hammered in that position.

Upsetting may be used for its own effect, or to gather more material in preparation for forging some other feature. Upsetting the end of a bar will provide more material for spreading a wide 'fish-

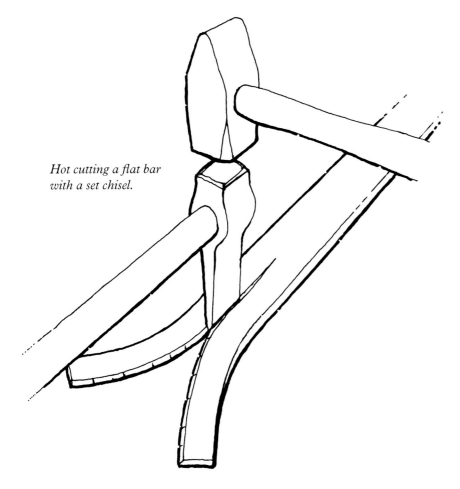

Hot cutting a flat bar with a set chisel.

others are forged solid and fitted with a steel rod handle, wrapped round a groove. Hand chisels are struck with a hand hammer, while set chisels are intended to be driven by a sledge-hammer. They may also be used under a power hammer, in which case they are made with a very short body, in order to make the most of its relatively short stroke.

A fundamental and often-used hot cutting tool is the 'hardie'. This is a short chisel with a shank that locates in the square hole – the hardie hole – of the anvil. Hot metal is positioned over the cutting edge and hammered down, either to make a cut all round a bar, or to almost sever it from one side. Since the cutting edge of the hardie would be damaged by the hammer, the remaining skin of metal is twisted or bent to break it. It is routine practice for components to be forged on the end of a bar, cut off with a hardie and the bar returned to the fire – still hot – to be heated again, ready to forge the next piece.

Chisels may be designed to make a straight or curved cut and can be ground on both faces or on only one. Ground on both faces, a chisel will leave a bevelled edge on both sides of the cut. Ground on only one surface, it will leave a vertical edge on one side and a bevelled edge on the other. Hot cutting can offer an alternative to joining parts, by splitting two or more 'tails' out of one piece. It can be used as a means of making slits or holes through bars, or for profiling forms out of flat bar or plate.

tail', making a knob, forging a 'leaf' form or any number of other details. An upset in the middle of a bar can provide more metal for a punched hole, a forged bend, or a thicker junction at the end of a hot cut line. Upsetting may also be used to make adjustments to the length of a bar, if it is found to be too long.

Hot Cutting

A variety of hardened steel chisels are used to hot cut steel. Some may be directly hand-held, like a builder's cold chisel. Others have a handle and are known as 'set' chisels or 'hot sets'. Some hot sets are punched with an eye like a hammer and similarly fitted with a wooden handle,

Punching

Punches are hardened steel tools used to mark, shape or make holes through hot steel. Some are directly hand-held like a chisel and are driven by a hand hammer. Others have handles mounted in much the same way as hot sets and are similarly used under a sledge or power hammer. Specially short punches are needed for power hammer use. For large architectural work, special punches are also used in a fast-

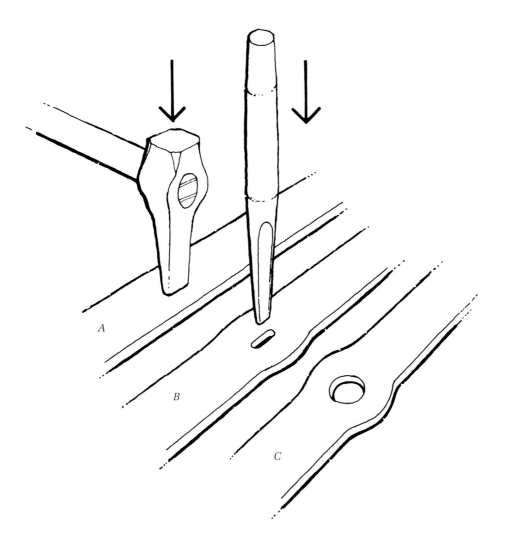

Punching a hole by hand:
A. punch located and driven as far as possible into the hot bar, which is then flipped over and the punch driven back in where the bar has chilled on the anvil, completing the slot;
B. bar located over a suitable hole in the anvil, and a round drift driven through;
C. finished round hole.

acting hydraulic press, to make large holes through heavy bars.

The action of a punch is much like pressing the flat end of a pencil vertically into a layer of clay, on a hard flat surface. The clay is displaced in all directions as the pencil passes through, until it can go no further and a thin skin of clay is left under the end of the pencil. A hot steel bar is placed on the flat of the anvil and the punch driven most of the way through with a hammer, until it can go no further and leaves a thin skin of metal at the bottom of the hole. The punch is pulled out, the bar turned over and the punch located carefully over the dark mark, where the

thin skin has chilled against the anvil, and driven in again, severing the skin and completing the hole. This skin is the only material actually removed. Most of the hole is created by the plastic displacement of metal around the punch, causing a characteristic swelling in the bar.

The shape of the punched hole is determined by the shape of the punch. A round punch will produce a round hole, a square punch a square hole. Whatever the shape of the hole, there is a limit to the size that can be punched in this way because, despite the swelling caused by the punch, there comes a point when the thickness of metal left at either side of the hole is insufficient for

A wrought-iron balustrade by Chris Topp, showing square punched holes. (Photo: Chris Topp)

strength. For this reason, holes are more often punched in a two-stage process. The initial hole is made with a slot-shaped punch or a chisel aligned with the long axis of the bar. This narrow, slotted hole leaves the maximum width of metal at either side. A 'drift' is then driven through the hole to give it its finished shape, which might be round, square, hexagonal or indeed slot-shaped. The drift need not be hardened and is usually made from mild steel with a long taper at one end and a short taper at the other. A slot punch and drift can be combined in one tool, for use by hand or in a hydraulic press. There must be a dimensional relationship between the slot punch and the drift. In theory, the periphery of the slot punch and, for example, the circumference of the corresponding round drift, should be the same. In practice, a fractionally smaller slot that is slightly stretched by the drift, is better than too big a slot that is not completely shaped.

Combined slot punch and drift, for use in a press. The plan drawing shows an example of the theoretical relationship between the size of the punched slot and the round hole. The periphery of the slot equals the circumference of the circle.

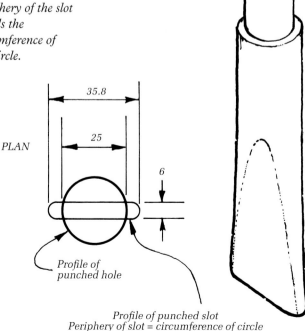

PLAN

35.8

25

6

Profile of punched hole

Profile of punched slot
Periphery of slot = circumference of circle

If a punch is not driven all the way through the metal, an impression will be left, with the same profile as the punch. So a round punch will leave a round recess, a square one a square recess and so on. Punches can be specially made to produce a wide variety of decorative marks, and are often used by smiths to provide an identifying 'signature' or maker's mark, to a piece of work.

22

Twisting

Bars are twisted by holding one end rigidly and rotating the other end, the position and length of the twist being determined by the heated part of the bar. For the twist to be even, the bar must be at the same heat – the same colour – throughout the length to be twisted, or the hotter part will twist tighter. If the entire bar is to be twisted, the easiest way to achieve an even temperature may be to leave the bar cold. Bars can be twisted using either hand tools or a twisting machine, which resembles a crude lathe, and holds the bar between a chuck and a movable tailstock. The tailstock end of the bar is held still, while the chuck rotates the required number of times, to create the twist. The rotation of the chuck is considerably geared down to deliver sufficient power to twist whole lengths of metal cold.

Bars to be twisted by hand are normally heated, either using a forge fire and quenching back at either end to provide a precise length of heat, or by heating the bar with a torch. The bar is held in a vice, a wrench applied to the other end and the bar twisted. It is important to maintain the straightness of the bar while twisting. A bend can be straightened without damaging the twist by hammering the hot bar with a rawhide mallet on a timber block.

Square, flat and hexagon bars, tubes, angle sections and so on, can all be twisted. Round bars can be twisted but the result is hardly visible, providing a useful means of offsetting other features of a bar, for example, through 90 degrees. The principle of twisting is simple but, by applying it in different ways, the outcomes can be surprisingly varied. The bar may be pretreated in various ways, by cutting, punching or tapering, before twisting: the twist itself may be reversed, clockwise and anti-clockwise, at intervals along the length of the bar. Groups of thinner bars may be twisted together, some of which may have already been twisted, to produce composite twists.

Examples of twisted bars.

Bending

Bars are usually tapered, upset, punched, split, twisted or otherwise forged, before any bending takes place. For practical reasons it is easier to position and forge these kind of features while the bar is kept straight. Bars may be bent or curved by impact, pressure or leverage. If the bends do not require a high degree of accuracy, or if only a few bends are needed, they can be achieved with hand tools at the anvil. Larger numbers of repeat bends and the need for greater accuracy will require some form of bending tool or jig. This may be hand-operated, or be fitted to a fly press or hydraulic press. Hand-operated bending machines are available, which can be set up to produce numbers of accurate bends in hot bars at 90 degrees or some other angle.

A bar can be bent hot, by resting it over part of the anvil and striking it with a hammer where it is unsupported, in effect using the anvil as a fulcrum. In this way the bar can either be formed freely, or dressed down over the edge of the anvil or beak, to reproduce a right angle or a particular radius. Bent over the edge of the anvil or in a vice, a right-angle bend will have an outside corner radius determined by the thickness of the bar. Forging the bend – upsetting metal into the corner – can provide a bend with sharp corners.

Bars may be bent in anvil 'horns', a U-shaped tool that fits the hardie hole. Leverage can be applied freehand or through a variety of bending wrenches. Free forging the same bent component repeatedly is not easy and usually requires reference to a master drawing, template or component. But, if precision is not a priority, forming over the anvil does have the virtue of producing curves and bends with a quality of freedom and spontaneity, hard to achieve any other way.

The quantities of components required by architectural work often demand the use of bending jigs or formers, which are purpose-made tools, enabling large numbers of curves and bends to be reproduced accurately. At the simplest, these involve a bar or pieces of bar, carefully formed so that one face of the bar corresponds to the required curves in the finished piece. It is easier to pull a bar over the convex side of a former, rather than push it into the concave side. So for choice, bending formers should operate in this way. Where this is not possible, the workpiece will need to be pulled into a concave bend, using bending wrenches levering over the former. Depending on the nature of the component, this kind of tool can be elaborated by the addition of stops, guides, built-in clamps and so on.

Bending and forming can be achieved quickly and accurately using top and bottom tools made to fit a fly press or hydraulic press. Because the tools are held in alignment, and the depth of movement of the top tool can be accurately controlled, even simple tools can be very precise and effective. As ever, it is a matter of trading the time needed to make this kind of tool against the gain in speed and precision they can produce. Very simple tools can be highly effective.

Forge or Fire Welding

Welding might be considered an assembly process, more relevant to the next chapter but, as such a defining blacksmithing technique, it seems appropriate to describe it here. From the Iron Age until the beginning of the twentieth century, the *only* available method of welding iron was in the fire. Since that time, blacksmiths have benefited from an increasing number of welding devices and methods that have provided alternatives, but have not rendered fire welding obsolete. Old and new methods all have their place.

Fire welding consists essentially of raising the temperature of the metal to a point where the surface becomes molten, placing two surfaces together and striking the

Using a fly press tool in Phil Johnson's workshop to make one of many joggled joints in a flat bar component for a gate. (Photo: P. Johnson & Company)

metal with a hammer, causing them to 'stick'. The impact of the hammer is not heavy but sufficient to eject the molten oxide from the joint, so that clean metal surfaces are in intimate contact and fuse together. At welding temperature, the metal is very soft and can easily be thinned down by too much hammering, so to counteract this, it is normal practice to prepare the metal by upsetting – thickening – the metal at the point where it is to be joined. In this way, for example, two pieces of bar may be joined end to end, first upsetting the ends of both pieces and forging them to an angled scarf. The two scarfed faces provide a larger surface area in contact, and the overlap provides the additional thickness, which will be reduced by the action of the hammer in closing the weld. In Britain, fire welding is traditionally undertaken after cleaning the hot metal with a wire brush. In America it is usual to treat each joint with a borax flux. Wrought iron is somewhat easier to weld than mild steel because it will tolerate a higher temperature and contains silicates, which act as fluxes.

It is important to appreciate that fire welding causes the metal to be fused across the entire internal joint surface, so the two pieces of bar become a single piece, carefully hammered to finish the surface and provide an invisible joint. Arc-welding methods are essentially line of sight and the weld only penetrates a few millimetres into the surface of the metal. Placing two bars together end to end, and electric welding all round, will only join the external surfaces. Making a joint by electric welding, equivalent to the fire weld described, requires that the ends of both bars be ground back to a blunt conical end, then butted together, providing a 'V' section in profile to accept the weld metal, which when completed needs to be dressed flush.

Fire welding lends itself traditionally to joining scrolls in a smooth line, to welding a pair or a group of branching bars together, or to weld a larger detail on the end of a thinner bar.

Specially curved pieces of bar welded to a back plate to make a neat and effective batch production bending tool, in Steve Lunn's workshop. (Photo: Steve Lunn)

Imaginative use of a fork lift truck. Steve Lunn hot bending one of a series of heavy bars. (Photo: Steve Lunn)

3 ASSEMBLY TECHNIQUE

It is perhaps difficult to make a clear distinction between making and assembling – they tend to fade into each other. But assembly refers to the final phase of production when light begins to shine at the end of the tunnel and all the parts of a structure have been forged, checked and trued up, so that they can be fitted together and finally joined.

A great deal of architectural metalwork provides a barrier or a boundary, and as such is often constructed as a panel, or a series of panels, secured directly to a building or by supporting posts. Although a fence, railing, balustrade, grille, screen or gate has its own particular place and function, their general methods of construction share a great deal. A gate can be seen as a grille with hinges. However, while the word 'gate' defines a well-understood object, this is less true for terms such as grille, screen, railing and balustrade, which, depending on their situation, can be hard to apply as a clear and unambiguous label. One may blur imperceptibly into another. For the purposes of this book, I have tried to distinguish and to define – perhaps not always successfully – each of these categories in separate chapters and to deal with their particular concerns. This chapter deals with some of the generalities of assembling all kinds of panel structures.

LAYOUT DRAWING

Invariably, right at the beginning of the project, it is necessary to make a full-size layout drawing in the workshop. This enables the entire structure to be accurately defined, and can sometimes help details to be worked out, which were too small to be determined on a scale drawing. It also provides the reference, against which components are checked as they are forged.

OPPOSITE PAGE: Detail of Winston Churchill Memorial Screen gate by Jim Horrobin on its assembly jig. (Photo: Jim Horrobin)

BELOW LEFT: Alan Evans's drawings for two huge screens, incorporating gates, laid out in a borrowed riding school. (Photo: Alan Evans)

BELOW: The finished gates and screens at Broadgate, London, designed to enhance a large open space between the buildings of a large new office development. (Photo: Penny Davies)

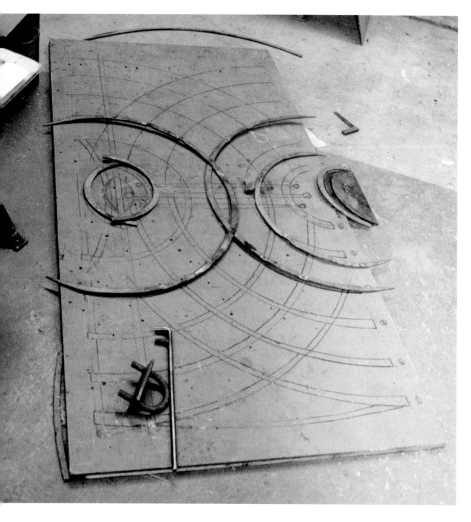

Gate layout drawing on the floor of Phil Johnson's workshop. (Photo: P. Johnson & Company)

Depending on the nature of the work, drawings might be made on a piece of building board or steel plate, a steel layout table or the floor, or a combination of these. Flat panel structures like gates, railings or grilles, can be laid out on plywood, blockboard, MDF or particle board, which is painted on both sides to prevent warping. A new clean board can be fine as it stands, but a coat of light-coloured, household vinyl emulsion paint provides a better drawing surface for a graphite pencil or felt pen, and can be repainted for the next project. A steel plate has the advantage that hot components can be laid on the drawing for checking, without burning the surface.

Lines can be drawn in French chalk (soapstone) directly on the mill scale or, more effectively, on a smooth rusted surface. Straight lines are best 'snapped' with a chalk line and, if necessary, sealed with pastel fixative or hair spray, to protect them. Alternatively, the plate can be painted with matt vinyl emulsion, and a durable drawing produced in pencil or felt pen. Used on steel, this paint will stand a surprising amount of heat and rough treatment in the workshop.

As making proceeds, components need to be tried on the drawing to check shapes, sizes, clearances and so on, and if the back of the piece is flat, the structure can be assembled directly on the drawing. If there are small projecting details, it will be necessary to raise the frame on packing pieces – small scraps of square or flat bar – kept for the purpose. For structures with components that project a long way at the back, use collars, wrapped joints or some other detail requiring access from both sides, assembly is better undertaken on trestles. If space permits, the layout drawing can be placed flat on one table or set of trestles and, after components have been forged and adjusted to fit, they can be transferred to another assembly surface alongside. In a smaller workshop, one table or set of trestles may necessarily have to serve both purposes.

For some structures such as curved or spiral stairs, a plan drawing on the floor of the workshop can be projected vertically to plot the position of each tread in three dimensions. The structure is assembled in the position it will assume when installed, extruded, as it were, vertically upwards from the drawing. If the drawing is set truly level on the ground surface, a plumbline and spirit-level can be used to locate vertical and horizontal points above the drawing. For other curved structures, the drawing itself may need to be set out on a curved surface, which is also the assembly former. Most pieces of architectural metalwork can be categorized as either flat or curved panel structures.

FLAT PANEL STRUCTURES

If these are assembled on a heavy layout table or levelling plate, the flatness is built in, but trestles require careful setting up, to provide a truly flat datum. To achieve this, they must be levelled up individually and to each other, with a spirit- or laser-level. It is arguable that the important thing is a flat, rather than a level datum. But if it is truly flat *and* level, a plumb-line or spirit-level can be used to check vertical and horizontal faces of components during assembly. Whether the trestles have adjustable feet or are levelled with packing pieces, their positions should be marked on the floor to ensure – crucially – that they are not moved during use. Choosing how far apart the trestles should be placed, whether more are needed to prevent sagging, how exactly the metalwork should be supported, all need some planning. It can be a frustrating experience to begin assembling a piece of work and reach a particularly delicate stage, before realizing that actually, it should have been the other way round.

Using trestles offers flexibility, particularly in a small workshop. Unlike a heavy layout table, they can be removed to release the floor space for other work. They are best used for supporting structures that have longitudinal members, capable of bridging between the supports. Structures comprising numbers of short elements will need a continuous supporting surface. Once set up, a heavy cast-iron levelling table or plate provides a solid and dependable assembly surface, but care must be exercised when using heat on a thick steel plate table. I recently saw the 40mm (1½in) thick, steel plate top of a layout table, which had been severely warped by the over-enthusiastic use of a large propane heating torch.

ABOVE: *Stringers of a stair assembled vertically over a layout drawing on the floor, in Phil Johnson's workshop. (Photo: P. Johnson & Company)*

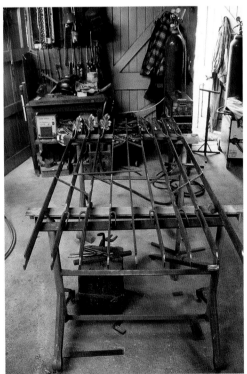

Assembling a gate on trestles in my workshop.

CURVED PANEL STRUCTURES

Elements derived from children's drawings laid on a curved assembly jig, ready for welding in my workshop.

BELOW: The completed railings, comprising six different panels creating a semi-circular entrance to a park in Harlesden, London. Designed by Lara Sparey in collaboration with the author.

The assembly of curved panels depends very much on their construction and detail.

Railing panels, constructed with curved, top and bottom rails and simple uprights, may not present any special assembly problems. The rails can be set up and secured with the curve in a vertical plane, on trestles or a table, to allow the uprights to be inserted and fixed. I have been told of, but have never tried, the idea of fully assembling a panel as a flat structure, then passing it through a rolling machine, sandwiched between two sheets of steel to produce the required curve. Given a well-jointed structure and a large machine, I see no reason why this should not work. Usually components must be formed to the required curvature before assembly, either at the anvil as they are forged, or using a hydraulic or fly press. It is crucial, therefore, to have an accurately curved, reference surface, on which to check the components and to assemble the structure.

A curved former is needed on which to assemble a series of curved railing or balustrade panels. A piece of plate, perhaps 6mm (¼in) or more thick, machine rolled to the required radius, will serve with minimal support. Or the former can be fabricated in thin plate, supported on profile-cut, steel plate ribs. So long as there are sufficient ribs to stop the skin sagging laterally between them, 3 or 4mm (⅛ or ⁵⁄₃₂in) plate can be used. Across a 2m length, this will sag into the curved ribs under its own weight and, with the encouragement of few clamps, can be welded in place. Whether the former should be convex or concave depends to a degree on the nature of the job. In my experience, there is some advantage in working on a concave surface, in that components placed on it tend to fall against each other, rather than sliding off.

Curved formers or 'drums' are often the only way of setting out curved panels and handrails or stair balustrading, either as they turn a corner from one straight flight to another (a wreath) or if the whole stair is curved. For a wreath, a piece of large-diameter steel pipe might provide the drum or, at the other extreme, it may be necessary to fabricate a sizeable and expensive structure, replicating the curved face of a wall or the cylindrical datum at the inner or outer line of a staircase. Drums can be constructed in steel, either as heavy rolled plate, a fabricated skin structure or built from timber. A former that mimics the wall, allows dimensions taken on site to be transferred directly to

its surface and, for example, the line of the stair string and the curve of a handrail or balustrade to be plotted. This kind of former comes into its own, both as a three-dimensional drawing and a jig, enabling a complex form to be visualized and components to be fitted to its surface. Handrail

brackets can, for example, be bolted to the drum and the handrail formed and fitted in between.

ASSEMBLY JIGS

A flat or curved surface controls the metalwork in one plane, but there is nothing to control it in the other two planes. The squareness – or angle – of the structure depends on careful checking and measuring as it lies on the plate or trestle. Once a structure is sitting truly square, or at its proper angle, temporary diagonal bracing bars can be clamped, bolted or tack welded in place to maintain the geometry, before all the joints are completed. This is usually perfectly adequate for a one-off piece of work but, if several railing panels, grilles or gates are to be produced, then making an assembly jig can be time well spent. The more units to be assembled, the more useful the jig.

Assembly jigs can take many forms, but their purpose is to hold the components in accurate alignment while they are welded, collared, riveted, wrapped or otherwise joined. Bars can be retained by bolts, screw clamps, cams, wedges or over-centre clamps, bolted to the jig. There are elements of most pieces of metalwork – like

LEFT: 'Drum' jig for the construction of a curved stair balustrade, in Jim Horrobin's workshop. The timber structure is assembled like the frames and cladding of a carvel-built boat. (Jig and photo: John Hesp)

BELOW LEFT: A simple and effective fence panel jig in Charles Normandale's workshop. The jig locates forged uprights, while they are welded to the cross-rails.

BELOW: One of sixteen finished fence panels in the workshop. Note the dramatic effect produced by bringing the flat bars away from the flat plane of the panel. (Charles Normandale.)

the position of fixing holes and hinges or the frame uprights of a panel – which need to be located very accurately. So it is important that the jig locates these positively and with a high degree of precision, while other elements – perhaps purely decorative – can, as it were, take care of themselves. Designing and making a jig is an interesting challenge and it is a matter of judgement how much elaboration, or time spent, can be justified in the light of the assembly time saved.

JOINING TECHNIQUES

It should be noted that even the most accurate jig will not, in itself, totally prevent the assembly distorting under the effect of heat. Since one of the most important considerations is to avoid distortion, heating for wrapped joints, to set rivets or caused by welding, should be planned and undertaken with care, working alternately across the structure to balance the heat input. No joint in a structure should need to be strained into place. If it does, the component should be removed and adjusted.

Rivets and Tenons

Riveted joints can be aligned and held temporarily by fitting the corresponding diameter bolts, nuts and washers, or, if they will stay in place, a combination of loose rivets and bolts to fill every hole. The rivets can then be headed in an appropriate sequence, replacing the bolts. If holes need to be drilled, it is good practice to pre-drill them through one component, then fit and clamp it to the structure, before drilling through the second component. Since the holes are marked and drilled *in situ*, a 90-degree drilling attachment and shortened drills may be required to give access in narrow spaces between bars.

Riveted joints need solid 'backing up', to avoid movement of the structure under the impact of a hammer, particularly if the blows are horizontal. This can call for some ingenuity in using a sledge-hammer, the side or end of a heavy piece of bar, an anvil or a heavy steel block, particularly if you work alone. If a shaped heading tool is needed, a cavity can be punched into a piece of bar, for the purpose. To set a series of rivets horizontally, a heavy

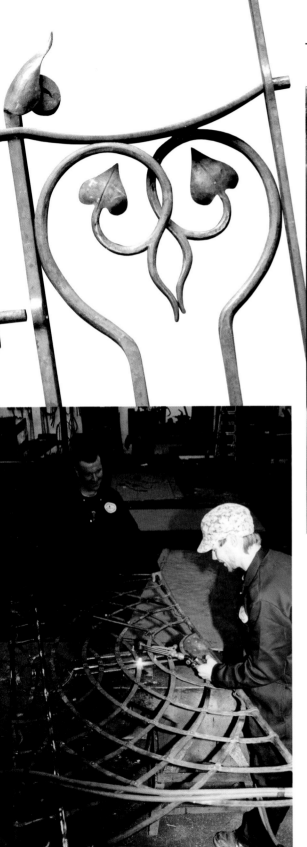

sledge-hammer can usefully be hung by a rope from the workshop roof, moving it from place to place and steadying it with one hand, while hammering the rivet head with the other.

Mortise and tenon joints comprise a projecting pin – the tenon – forged on the end of a bar, designed to fit a hole – the mortise – in another component. They are headed in much the same way as loose rivets but are likely to present greater demands in backing up, since they are often part of the frame or main bars in the structure; so the tenons may be large and require considerable upsetting. To absorb more of the impact, heavy pieces of bar can be clamped to the sides of the bar in question, or a loose leg vice can be laid on top and tightened to grip it.

ABOVE: David Tucker and assistant, riveting tenons to secure the uprights of a gate. (Photo: David Tucker)

TOP LEFT: Detail of a gate by Steve Lunn showing tenons, before they are riveted over. (Photo: Steve Lunn)

LEFT: Riveting a gate in Phil Johnson's workshop. The rivet heads are being supported on an anvil while their shanks are heated with a gas torch. (Photo: P. Johnson & Company)

WELDING SYSTEMS

Welding is the joining of metals by fusion. In the context of assembly, four main methods are usually employed for different purposes. All require the appropriate protective goggles or mask, clothing and gloves.

Gas-welding equipment consists of cylinders of oxygen and acetylene, connected through reducer valves to hoses that supply gas to the torch. Gas welding requires some time to learn and apply with skill. A welding torch can be used to make joints by simply fusing metal edges together or, more usually, with the addition of metal from a filler rod. The torch is held in one hand and a thin, compatible wire filler rod is held in the other hand and fed into the weld pool. Gas is effective in welding sheet metal up to perhaps 3mm (⅛in) in thickness. For this reason its use for welding is limited in a blacksmithing workshop, but oxy-acetylene torches are widely used for cutting and providing local heat, enabling rivets to be set, joints to be wrapped, or components to be adjusted.

Arc welding is available in a number of forms, which share the principle of a low voltage, high amperage spark, struck between the torch and the workpiece, to provide the heat source, but vary in the way they deliver the molten metal to the joint and shield it from the air. Their advantages and disadvantages, can be summarized as follows:

MMA (manual metal arc or stick welding) uses a chemical-coated, wire rod (or stick) of the same metal as that being welded. An arc is struck at the end of the rod to melt the joint and to add filler metal, while the chemical coating fuses to provide a protective slag, covering the molten weld pool and preventing oxygen or nitrogen contamination.

Advantages:
◆ low-cost equipment, simple and versatile;
◆ the thin rod permits welding in cavities or narrow spaces;
◆ tolerant to dirty metal surfaces;
◆ works effectively out of doors and in windy conditions;
◆ air-cooled sets offer a portable welding source.

Disadvantages:
◆ needs some skill and practice to use neatly;
◆ the arc is initiated by 'striking' the rod on the work, which is difficult for very short welds;
◆ requires the slag to be chipped or brushed off finished welds;
◆ slow in operation;
◆ needs skill to weld vertically or overhead;
◆ difficult to weld thin material.

Oxy-acetylene economizer valve. The torch is being placed on the arm, which shuts off the gas. It can then be relit from the pilot light on top of the valve.

If no assistant is available to heat the rivet with a gas torch, the kind of economizer valves that shut off the gas supply when the torch is hung on a hook are an invaluable help.

It becomes a simple and safe operation to heat the rivet shank with a torch in one hand, drop the torch back on its hook and hammer the rivet head to shape. The alternative of hastily planting the burning torch on the metalwork and watching it fall to the floor as you hammer, is not to be recommended. It should be remembered that the whole length of the rivet shank needs heating, so that it is upset in the hole and its length contracts on

◆ often produces weld spatter, which must be cleaned off with a chisel or wire brush.

TIG (tungsten inert gas) uses a non-consumable, inert gas-shielded tungsten electrode, to strike the arc. A thin wire filler rod, compatible with the metal being welded, is fed into the gas-shielded weld pool, with the other hand. The arc is usually started by a button on the torch, which initiates a high frequency spark, jumping the gap to provide a path for the main current.

Advantages:
◆ joints can simply be fused without adding filler rod;
◆ quickly adaptable for welding different metals;
◆ very clean with no slag or spatter;
◆ intense heat causes less distortion;
◆ inverter machines are physically very small and offer a portable welding source;
◆ precise current-control allows the same machine to weld thin or thick materials.

Disadvantages:
◆ expensive machine;
◆ welding needs both hands;
◆ can make poor welds if the metal is not clean;
◆ slow and needs some skill and practice to weld neatly;
◆ not suitable for outdoor use in windy conditions.

MIG (metal inert gas) uses a thin wire of the same metal as that being welded, fed from a reel through a flexible sheathing, which also feeds power and inert gas to the torch. The arc is initiated by a trigger on the torch, causing the wire to advance and touch the workpiece under the gas shield, striking an arc and depositing metal.

Advantages:
◆ medium-cost machine, fairly easy to learn;
◆ welds quickly and effectively when properly adjusted;
◆ vertical or overhead welding is relatively easy compared with stick welding.

Disadvantages:
◆ current and speed can be difficult to set correctly;
◆ not reliable out of doors, since wind blows away the inert gas shield;

cooling, to tighten the joint. For this reason, it is worth taking a little time to heat the exposed shank, to allow the heat to penetrate.

Screw Fixing

Holes for screw fixings should, like rivet holes, be pre-drilled in one-half of the joint, assembled, clamped and drilled through, however tempting it might be to mark out holes on both components and drill them separately. A drill press is always easier to use than a hand electric drill, but unless both components are drilled through the same jig, discrepancies tend to occur, leading to misalignment. A large clearance hole in one part may provide sufficient tolerance to allow the screw to fit, but is less precise in providing alignment. If a joint is to be drilled and tapped, the initial hole should be the tapping drill size, which can be aligned and drilled through both components. One hole is then tapped and the other drilled out to a clearance diameter. Holes drilled during assembly may need the use of a right-angle drilling attachment and a ratchet tap wrench. As a familiar engineering component, standard hexagon-headed bolts or nuts look completely out of place in hand-made blacksmithing work, and in my view should be made or reforged to some other

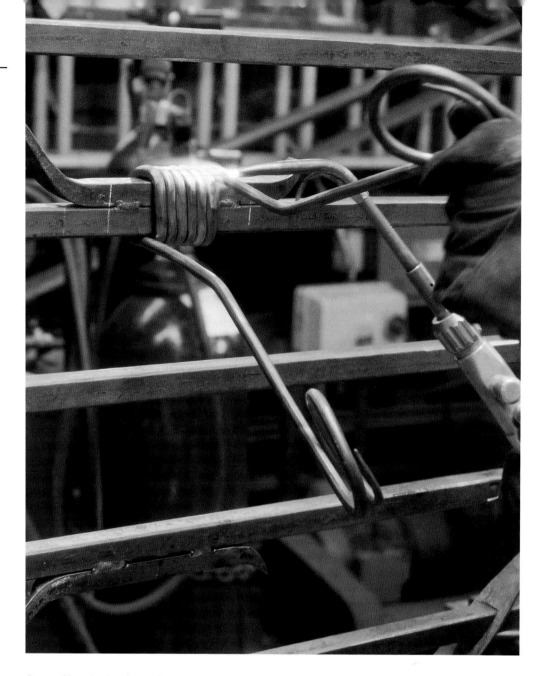

Wrapping a joint. The round, silicon bronze rod is coiled at both ends to allow it to pass between the square bars, which have been tack welded to hold them in place.

form. Simply forging a hexagon bolt head to a square can make a big difference. Hexagon socket screws can be less obtrusive, particularly with countersunk heads, which fit flush into the metalwork.

Arc-Welded Joints

Arc-welding techniques provide a reliable means of joining metals, but the heat input to a large structure can cause distortion unless care is taken. Since there are many welding handbooks that describe practices to minimize distortion, it is not

appropriate to offer much detail here. The crucial principle is to tack weld the entire structure initially, using small welds to minimize heat input, then to make the heavier welds in a carefully balanced pattern across the structure.

In the context of forged architectural metalwork, my feeling is that arc welding should either be invisible – placed where it cannot be seen, or blended in by grinding – or it should present a clean, neat, honest weld bead. It should never be visible by accident. In an appropriate context, I see no need to apologize for a neat weld, but a bad, ugly weld is unforgivable.

Collaring and Wrapping

Tack welds can be useful to hold components in alignment while a permanent fixing is achieved by collaring or wrapping. Tacks can be placed in pockets, ground into both sides of adjacent bars to be held by a collar. Any projecting weld bead can be ground flush before the collar is fitted. To work effectively, a collar must be carefully shaped and be at a good red heat when clinched into place, to gain the most from the contraction of the metal as it cools to grip the bars. It can be quickly dressed down with a hammer, or two hammers, to ensure a good fit, but over-hammering will spread the collar and loosen it. A wonderful creaking noise, as the metal cools, indicates a good fit.

In a similar fashion, a tack weld can be used to secure a wrapping bar to the parent bar. In most instances the wrapping bar only needs to be held temporarily with a clamp or a pair of tongs until a full turn has been made. After this it can be wrapped without difficulty. But the first turn of a bar as it wraps over another can sometimes slide a little, so if its other end is already restrained, it can exert a powerful pull. Preventing this movement is important in avoiding distortion, so a carefully placed tack weld can lock the bars together and be hidden under the wrap. This kind of distortion can also be avoided by careful clamping of the adjacent bars, or by a solid spacer wedged temporarily between the bars to prevent their movement.

Friction Joints

There are many joints that rely on friction for their effect and employ what engineers call an interference fit. A simple example is a plain parallel pin driven into a precisely drilled hole. A more blacksmithing equivalent is to drive a cold pin into a hole in a red hot bar, allowing the contraction of the metal to retain the pin. C-section, rolled pins are commercially available, which can be driven in cold and contract to be held by spring pressure. Taper pins are similarly available or can be forged and can be driven in to wedge in a tapered hole, shaped by an appropriate reaming tool or drift. The ends of pins may be left visible as a tiny visual accent, or ground and filed off flush to provide an invisible fixing.

Tapered pins or flat tapered wedges can be used through slotted, transverse holes in the projecting ends of tenon joints to draw them tight. With some design ingenuity, any joint where one component passes through another can be secured with a wedge, or two opposed wedges. In the context of architectural metalwork these kind of joints can look interestingly expressive.

The finished joint in my workshop. Part of a window grille.

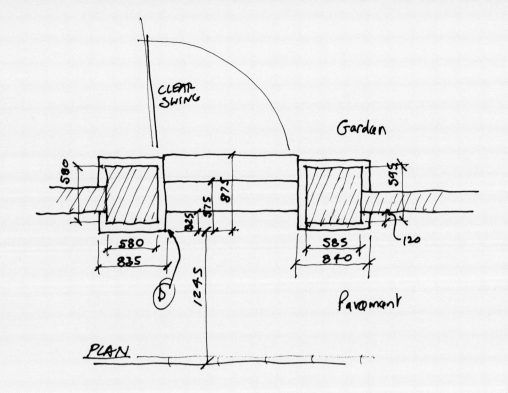

CLEAR SWING

Garden

580

835

580

375

625

875

1245

585

840

595

120

Pavement

PLAN

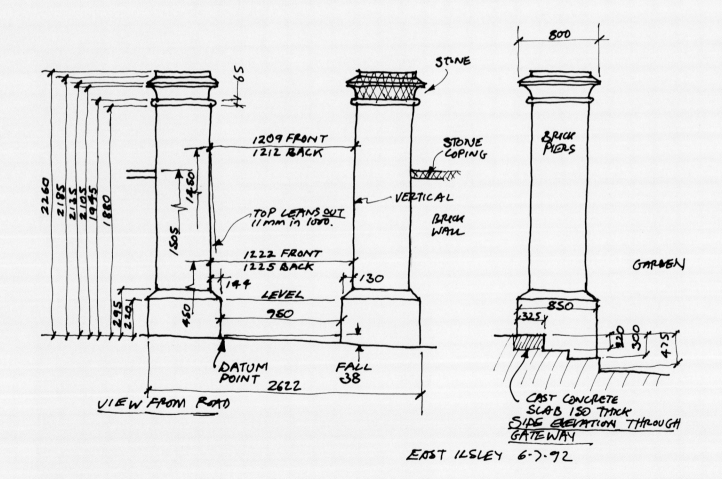

STONE

800

59

2260
2185
2135
2105
1945
1880

1209 FRONT
1212 BACK

1505

1460

TOP LEANS OUT
11 mm in 1000.

1222 FRONT
1225 BACK

144

LEVEL

950

275
220

450

DATUM
POINT

2622

FALL
38

130

STONE COPING

VERTICAL

BRICK
WALL

BRICK
PIERS

GARDEN

850

325

220

300

475

CAST CONCRETE
SLAB 150 THICK

VIEW FROM ROAD

SIDE ELEVATION THROUGH
GATEWAY

EAST ILSLEY 6·7·92

4 SURVEYING THE SITE

LOOKING AT THE SITE

The purpose of a site visit should not be simply to take a few measurements, but to examine, survey and gain some personal impressions of the place. Go with an open mind and allow time to really look. Time spent then, to ensure you have all the information you need, can save a great deal of time later. Where possible, talk to the client. What do they expect? What do they think is important? What are they interested in? Crucially, what kind of budget do they have in mind?

Take a good look at the whole area where the work is to be sited and make some judgements about its character and quality. The context is important. Be open to your impressions, and on the basis that it is always better to have a short pencil than a long memory – make notes. At its simplest, a city-centre location will have a different feel from a rural one, and each city is different. A public building is different in character from a private house. The particular use of materials, finishes and details go a long way towards defining the character of the place. Analysing the location is important in beginning to establish the nature and character of the proposed metalwork.

Partly for this reason, it is worth looking at, and taking photographs of, not just the site itself but the approaches to it. If the finished metalwork will be seen from a distance, look from that distance. Consider every viewpoint. A digital camera can be as useful as a tape-measure, not least because – despite your best endeavours – it notices things you overlooked. While your eye is

caught by a particular detail, some way behind, above or to either side, there may be another that would provide an inspirational design element. Back on the drawing board, this can provide the answer to a question you did not think of asking while you were there. Or, from a practical viewpoint, there may be a moulding in the stonework, a projecting brick course or some other feature that did not seem important at the time but which the photograph records. So long as you have noted the dimensions of something in the picture – the height of a doorway, for example – it is often possible to work out the measurement you forgot. Measuring as a matter of routine the size of a repeating element like the brick or stone in a wall, or a tile or flagstone on the ground, can be a good habit to develop.

It goes without saying that measurements should be taken with care but, while doing so, it is easy to take for granted *what* is being measured. Look carefully at the concrete, stone, timber, brickwork or whatever, will ultimately provide support for the metalwork. Check the quality of the material. Is it solid? Is it rotten? Is it cracked? Is it soft? Is it hard? Is the mortar falling out of the brick joints? Poking about with a hammer and chisel can be crucial in determining the kind of fixings that might be needed. I mention this as someone who has had the thought-provoking experience of arriving on site to install a heavy pedestrian gate, to discover that the brickwork was so soft that I could have drilled deep holes anywhere with a screwdriver. Testing with a chisel when I first visited the site would have told me that. At the other extreme, I designed a screen gate

OPPOSITE PAGE: *Typical site survey, sketch drawing.*

Chris Anstey drilling unexpectedly hard stone, with a hand-held core drill.

Fixing a gate to soft brickwork.

for a Norman church and commented to the architect that the masonry – a local sandstone – looked distinctly delicate and crumbly. I needed to drill this to provide deep pockets for grouting in the hinges. Since we both had doubts, she arranged for a stonemason to help with the installation. In the event, under a flaky surface, the stone was so hard and crystalline that drilling each 60mm (2½in) diameter hole took an hour with a core drill.

The lesson is to take nothing for granted. Do not assume that surfaces are hard and strong, flat and straight, vertical, horizontal or at right angles to each other. Do not assume that all the steps are the same height and depth. Do not assume that the sides of the doorway, window or gateway are parallel, or that the symmetrical arch is truly symmetrical. Do not assume that the ground is level. Do not assume that between the line of brick piers, the spaces for the railing panels are all the same length. All these things need to be checked and measured individually. Finally you *do* need to make your own

survey. Never trust an architect's or interior designer's drawing, after all – they do not. Why else would it say, 'Check all dimensions on site'?

EQUIPMENT

There is a wide variety of surveying equipment available, from a spirit-level, plumb-line and steel tape-measure to optical-levels, laser-levels and electronic angle- and distance-measuring devices. Doubtless we will all be using these before long, but as someone who can still recall the advent of the electronic pocket calculator, which it took me months to begin to trust, I still prefer a steel tape with marks on it. Much can be achieved with simple tools. A basic kit might consist of a steel tape-measure and steel rule, for measuring lengths; a square and an adjustable square for measuring angles; a builder's spirit-level and a combination square with spirit-level for levelling and measuring vertical angles; a plumb-line to provide a vertical, and some silicone putty to hold the line where needed; masking tape, which can be stuck as necessary to provide a surface on a wall or floor, for marking with a pencil; chalk or a silver pencil for marking on concrete or brick; sketchbook, notebook, clipboard and paper; pens/pencils for drawing and note taking; digital camera for record photography; and a torch because you never know. All this, except the builder's level, will fit in a tool box, briefcase or small rucksack.

Other items may be necessary depending on the nature of the site and the measurements to be taken. A long straight-edge can be important to extend the range of a spirit-level. A rigid surveyor's telescopic rule can be better than a steel tape to reach up high. A line, or trammels and a straight-edge, may be needed to measure curves.

A water-level is a simple and flexible way of measuring a series of levels across an area, where the distances are too great for a long straight-edge and a spirit-level, or out of sight of a laser-level. Crucially, points do not need to be in sight of each other. All that is required is a length of clear PVC tubing containing water, with the ends held up to prevent spillage. The water will find the same level at both ends. One end is set up and left fixed, the dimension from the water to the ground, providing a reference level, or datum, at this point. The other end of the tube can be moved wherever required and the distance from the level of the water to the ground measured with a steel rule or tape. For convenience this end can be fixed to a portable stand or be taped along the face of a steel rule and dimensions read off directly.

It is always worth checking the accuracy of a spirit-level by setting it so that it sits solid at both ends, reading horizontal. If it is now reversed, the bubble should be centred in precisely the same position. If it is not, the mean of the two positions will indicate a true level. Unless they are self-levelling, similar considerations apply to setting up an optical- or laser-level. Be aware that the measurements taken are only as good as the initial setting.

DRAWING AND MEASURING

It is important to think and measure in three dimensions. If you arrive completely focused on noting the width and height of a gate opening, it is easy to overlook other crucial factors. Each site, however apparently simple, needs to be considered and recorded at the very least as a front elevation, a side elevation and a plan. Considering the side elevation could, for example, reveal a slope through the gateway, and the design problems that might create.

The first thing is to draw the elevations and plan, and consider what information is required. Since it is always better to have too much information than too little, it is usually worth drawing additional sections or details to illuminate particular features. It is also better to draw more than the immediate area of concern. For example, include a wider area than just the gap between the brick piers where the gate is to go. In the case of a gate, the swing is important. Will it hit anything? Are there tree branches or overhead wires

Basic surveying equipment.

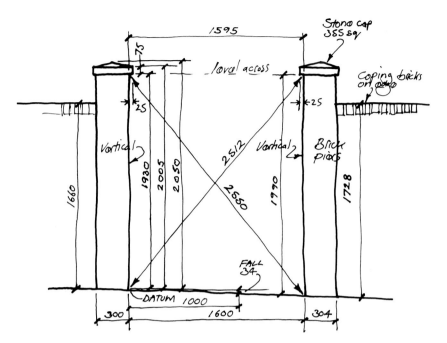

Sketch survey drawing, showing use of diagonal 'check' dimensions.

that might impede the installation? It is vital to anticipate this and note details on the plan and side elevation. In any case, you may want to make a drawing showing the metalwork in a wider context.

It is crucial to draw clearly and mark dimensions legibly. If possible, use two thicknesses or colours of pen or pencil, to avoid confusing an outline with a dimension line. The object is to gather information to be used back on the drawing board or computer, to make an accurate site drawing; or in the workshop to produce a full-size layout drawing. So, wobbly lines, out of scale details or odd proportions do not matter. The important thing is that you understand it and it contains all the information you need. If a drawing becomes so crowded that one set of dimensions threatens to obscure another, draw that view again and mark the rest of them on the second drawing. Do not trust your memory. Be clear where each dimension applies. There is nothing worse than getting back to the office and wondering what you meant.

There are basic principles that apply to taking and recording measurements,

irrespective of the means used to take them. Measure critical dimensions or angles at least twice, to be sure they are correct. Use 'check' dimensions. These may be overall dimensions to confirm the sum of those already taken or, conversely, dimensions of smaller elements within an overall length. Check dimensions might also be diagonal measurements taken to confirm angles already measured directly. Since the length of the sides of a triangle also define its angles, triangulation measurements provide a very accurate way of surveying. Repeated units or symmetrical features like columns or holes normally have their centrelines marked on a drawing and are located by dimensions to their centres.

Where possible, dimensions should be taken and noted on the drawing from a particular reference point or 'datum'. In the case of heights, this might be a convenient ground point close to the wall or other feature being measured. Part of the purpose of this is to avoid 'chaining' dimensions – measuring each feature from the previous one – which can result in an accumulation of errors. It also means that the end of a steel tape can be planted on the datum point, kept there and the various heights read off the tape, without needing to move it. Where the feature to be measured is a little distance from the tape, a square or spirit-level can be used to relate the point to the tape. Having an assistant to write down the dimensions can help. The datum point can also be transferred elsewhere with a level, horizontally across to the other gate pillar, for example, so that height measurements taken there will correspond to the first set. (*See* drawing at the beginning of this chapter.)

A vertical datum can be provided by a plumb-line. If necessary, its string can be chalked and 'snapped' to mark a line on the wall and measurements taken horizontally from the line. A plumb-line also provides a means of transferring dimensions in a vertical plane. The positions of the nosing of a flight of stairs can, for example, be measured along the horizontal line of the floor above, or referred from the side of the stair down to the ground level, using a plumb-line.

Never approximate dimensions on a survey drawing. Dimensions in Britain and Europe are expressed in metric units. The engineering and architectural convention is to use millimetres and metres, not centimetres (which seem to be used almost exclusively by antique dealers and art galleries). Millimetres give rise to large numbers, e.g. 5in is 127mm. Using millimetres (and equally using fractions of inches), there is a temptation to round dimensions up or down, but the time to do this is not while taking them. Always record the true length as measured, on the sketch drawing. You can decide whether the discrepancy is trivial later, at the drawing board. After all, if the measurement really is 127mm, it does not save any time on site to write '125' or '130'. If several dimensions are approximated, errors can accumulate.

Surveying Angles

Angles can be surveyed directly in degrees of arc using an adjustable square or protractor. Or they can be measured as a series of linear dimensions, from which the angle can be calculated. Reference books on geometry or engineers' handbooks contain formulae for 'the solution of triangles'. These set out all the combinations of lengths and angles of a triangle, from which the unknown value can be calculated.

A builder's spirit-level will have vials to check both true horizontals and verticals. It can also be used to measure angles in a vertical plane. The angle of a sloping ground surface can be measured using a spirit-level of known length, packed up truly level and the height of the raised end measured with a steel rule square to the

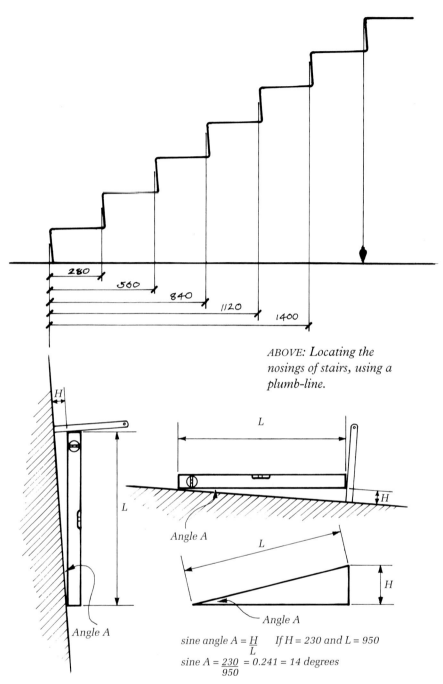

ABOVE: Locating the nosings of stairs, using a plumb-line.

$$\text{sine angle } A = \frac{H}{L} \quad \text{If } H = 230 \text{ and } L = 950$$
$$\text{sine } A = \frac{230}{950} = 0.241 = 14 \text{ degrees}$$

Calculating an angle using a spirit-level.

ground. This information may be used to set out the angle directly in the workshop or on a drawing board, or can allow it to be calculated. In the same way, small departures from the vertical – the lean of a wall, for instance – may be measured. Larger vertical angles – the angle of a stair

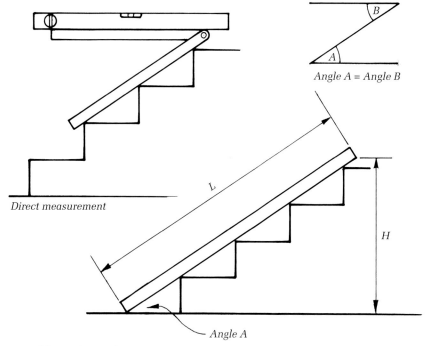

Direct measurement

Measuring and calculating vertical angles.

sine angle A = $\dfrac{H}{L}$ *If H = 770 and L = 1400*

sine A = $\dfrac{770}{1400}$ = 0.55 = 33 degrees 22 minutes

Angle A = Angle B

Angle A

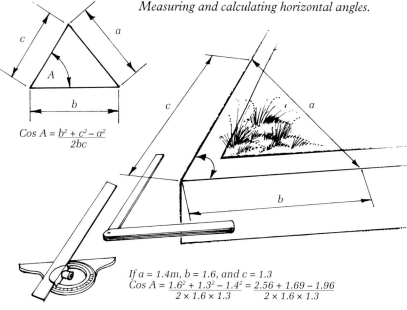

Measuring and calculating horizontal angles.

Cos A = $\dfrac{b^2 + c^2 - a^2}{2bc}$

If a = 1.4m, b = 1.6, and c = 1.3

Cos A = $\dfrac{1.6^2 + 1.3^2 - 1.4^2}{2 \times 1.6 \times 1.3} = \dfrac{2.56 + 1.69 - 1.96}{2 \times 1.6 \times 1.3}$

Cos A = $\dfrac{2.29}{4.16}$ = 0.5505 = 56 degrees 36 minutes

stringer, for example – may similarly be established, or may be measured more easily by placing a spirit-level horizontally on an adjustable square. Engineers' combination squares usually have an integral spirit-level and can measure this kind of angle directly.

Since linear measurements can be used to set out an angle on a full-size layout drawing or a scale drawing, using a pair of compasses, it may not be immediately necessary to know the numerical value of the angle. An angle can be brought back from the site in the form of an adjustable square set to the angle, or even a piece of paper, marked or folded to the angle and used as a template directly on the layout drawing. However, it is advisable to determine the numerical value of the angle, so that it can be noted for later use.

Angles in the horizontal plane can be measured directly with an adjustable square and read off with a protractor, using straight-edges, if necessary, to provide reference surfaces. Straight-edges are useful to 'average out' irregular surfaces of the corner being measured, and provide a precise point if the corner is radiused. An angle bounded by straight faces – walls perhaps – can also be measured using a prismatic compass, the kind used by walkers and mountaineers. Siting each face from the corner gives two bearings, the difference being the angle. Provided bearings are taken from close to the corner, local magnetic variation should not affect them. Angles can also be determined with great accuracy by measuring the dimensions of a triangle, which includes the angle, and applying the appropriate formula. The size of this triangle is a matter of convenience.

Surveying Curves

Many curves surveyed in or around buildings are likely to be arcs of a circle. If the concave side of a curved wall is accessible, its radius can be surveyed by trial and error, pivoting a line or straight-edge, until the centre point of the circle is located. The radius can then be measured with a steel tape. If a centre cannot be located, the curve is not part of a circle. If the ground surface is suitably hard, the end of the line or straight-edge can be held on the ground by an assistant and the centre point marked with chalk. On soft ground, a steel pin can driven in to act as a pivot. Alternatively, a pivot point can be provided higher up, so that the line clears any obstructions, by the kind of tripod stand or 'blacksmiths helper' commonly used in the workshop to support the end of a bar. This offers a stable reference point, is easily moved to find the correct position and is heavy enough to hold the line in tension. A string line with a loop or ring at the end can be dropped over a pivot pin made to fit the stand. If necessary, this method can be used without additional help. A similar approach can be used to measure curves in a vertical plane – an arch, for example. The centre point or points can be located by trial and error using a thin line, with the end held by an assistant against a piece of timber wedged temporarily in place.

If the centre point of a horizontal arc is likely to put you in the traffic, or is inaccessible – leaving you with access to the convex side – the curve is best measured by using chords. A chord is a straight line whose ends lie on the circumference of a circle. Concave arcs can be measured, using a straight-edge of known length and a steel rule or tape. Convex arcs require a straight-edge with an equal extension leg at each end. It is important to establish that the curve is actually part of a circle. This can be done by moving the straight-edge to different points along the curve and checking that dimension 'h' remains the same. If it does not – the curve is not part of a circle.

By either of these means, the centres and radii of curves can be established. If two or more separate curves are involved,

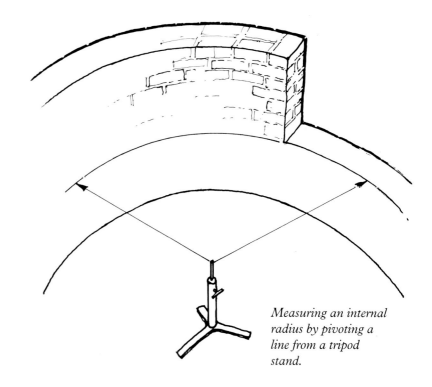

Measuring an internal radius by pivoting a line from a tripod stand.

Measuring a convex curve: h = a–b

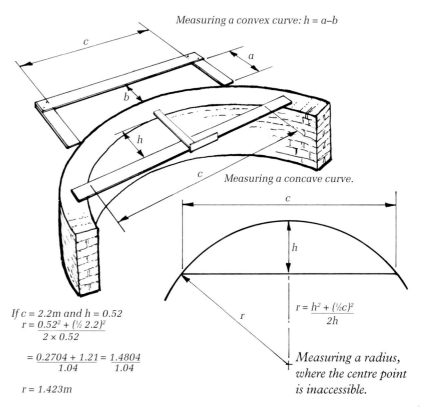

Measuring a concave curve.

If $c = 2.2m$ and $h = 0.52$

$$r = \frac{0.52^2 + (\frac{1}{2} 2.2)^2}{2 \times 0.52}$$

$$= \frac{0.2704 + 1.21}{1.04} = \frac{1.4804}{1.04}$$

$r = 1.423m$

$$r = \frac{h^2 + (\frac{1}{2}c)^2}{2h}$$

Measuring a radius, where the centre point is inaccessible.

Measuring off-sets on site.

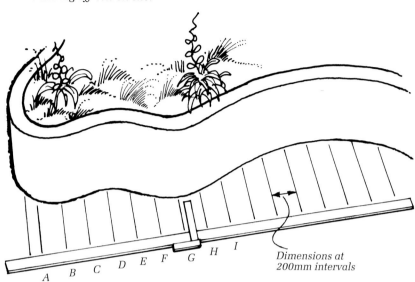

A B C D E F G H I

Dimensions at
200mm intervals

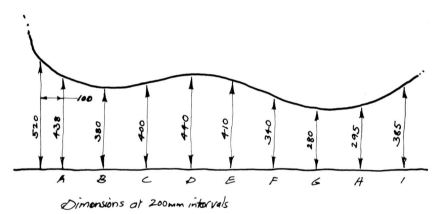

520 438 380 400 440 410 340 280 295 365

100

A B C D E F G H I

Dimensions at 200mm intervals

Survey Drawing

Surveying a free curve by taking off-set dimensions.

A long straight board or length of steel flat provides a better line to take dimensions at right angles, since it is easier to use a square against it. The line should be set up in some convenient position close to the curved wall with its ends approximately equidistant from the wall. Keeping the distances as short as possible makes measuring that bit easier. Working from one end, mark a series of equal divisions along the line – for example, at 200mm (8in) intervals. These are the points from which a series of dimensions must be taken, strictly at right angles, from the line to the wall. Where the wall runs away at an acute angle to the measurement, or where there is some odd bump or other feature, it is good practice to insert an extra measuring point or points, to increase the definition. In order to keep track, it can be easier to start with a regular spacing and, where necessary, insert additional measuring points afterwards. It also helps to identify the points by number or letter.

If a wall is so long or convoluted that it cannot be surveyed from one datum line, a second or third can be set up to take more measurements, further along. It is vital to record the relationship between the datum lines, and allow some overlap between the sets of measurements. It is one step from this to placing datum lines at right angles to each other – making a grid – and recording dimensions in each plane, making an 'x' and 'y' axis. These are known as co-ordinate dimensions. An example of this might be surveying the freely curved shape of a garden pond in order to make a safety grille. In this kind of application, parallel string lines can be laid out at right angles or, if it is a small pond a piece of welded steel reinforcement mesh can be laid over the pond to provide the grid geometry. In this case surveying blurs into template making, and simply chalk-marking the welded mesh may well provide enough information.

their centres must be related to each other by measurement, to enable them to be set out in the workshop or on the drawing board. Some curves may comprise two or more different radii blending into each other, and can be measured in the same way.

Other curves may not be parts of circles at all. A randomly curved wall or coping can be surveyed by taking regular offset dimensions from a datum line chalked on the ground, or from a rigid straight-edge.

Templates

There comes a point where conventional surveying becomes so complicated that it is better to make a template to fit curves or complex profiles. The means used will depend on the nature of the problem. To record, for example, the outline of an arch to fit a gate or screen, a template can made from any easily cut material like thin sheet metal, fibre board or even card. A timber frame can be made on site, wedged into place, and strips of sheet screwed where required, butted together round the edge. Each piece can be roughly shaped, then offered up to the wall and 'scribed in' using a pencil compass, one leg tracing the profile of the wall while the pencil marks the sheet material. While the line is being drawn, the compass must be orientated in the direction the template will be fitted. The sheet can then be trimmed with a knife, scissors, tin snips, jigsaw, angle grinder or file.

To record the curve of a coping or the string of a stair, a heavily notched flat bar, cut like the teeth of a comb, some 30 or 40mm (1¼ or 1½in) wide, can be cold bent to pick up a flat curve, or bent and twisted to fit the curve of a stair string or handrail. Only a pair of bending wrenches are needed, so the bar can be shaped and fitted to the stair string while standing on the stair. Once bent to shape, the projecting ends of the teeth can then be tack welded together to lock the bar in shape, providing a rigid template. Notched flat bar is available commercially and seems like a good idea in principle, but I cannot speak from experience.

Beyond this, and serving the same purpose, there remains the entirely pragmatic approach of bending and fitting a flat bar on site, to sit, for example, on the string of a curved stair. Against the effort of transporting all that equipment, this does have the advantage of providing a direct, visible fit, and can produce either a template or the bottom rail of a balustrade itself. For a curved balustrade or handrail, complex three-dimensional information can be recorded in a way that is directly applicable in the workshop. The process requires at the very least a leg vice or anvil on site, preferably both. With a large anvil swage and hammer, forks and wrenches, the bar can be bent and twisted. If a swage block and gas cylinders can also be taken to site, so much the better. A great deal of shaping can be achieved cold, but bending a bar to form a wreath round a tight stair well will almost certainly need heat.

Carrying bars repeatedly up and down stairs to try them in place is laborious, but does offer the satisfaction of a convincing result. It is a matter of convenience to establish how long a length can be shaped at a time, and how this should be joined to the next. The shape of this kind of curved flat bar makes complete sense on site, but when carried back to the workshop, it may be far harder to understand unless careful measurements have also been taken to relate it to the site. Dimensions or angles at particular reference points should be marked on the bar with indelible marker, to avoid any confusion.

Timber and hardboard template made in situ to record the outline of a church doorway. The point of the arch turned out to be some 75mm (3in) off centre.

The finished gate fits snugly into the rebate of the arch and carries stainless steel mesh to provide ventilation, but keep out the birds.

5 DESIGN AND REGULATIONS

THE DESIGN PROCESS

Design is an activity that brings together a diversity of functional and aesthetic requirements, judgements, feelings, engineering problems, craft skills and imagination, and in consequence is often not the logical, linear thought process we might like it to be. Different people work in different ways. A wide variety of creative and practical decisions have to be made, which eventually come together as a complete design proposal. However, the order in which the decisions are made can vary considerably. Some creative ideas seem to come through intuition and arrive fully formed; others are more of a struggle. So anything that can be done to give the design process a more organized pattern is worth trying. Alongside intuition, there is a range of means, methods and approaches that can help with the development of ideas and prevent the process grinding to a halt for lack of another thought.

Particularly in the early stages, it is important to keep an open mind and try not to become too devoted to one idea too soon. It might be absolutely the right one, or it might equally be obscuring your view of a better idea. It is crucial to look at alternatives, if only to test your first thoughts. The term 'site-specific' is implicit in the idea of architectural metalwork. The metalwork is part of the architecture. A good piece of architectural metalwork should complement the building to the extent that if it were to be removed, the building would be the lesser for it. Conversely the metalwork should gain from its relationship with the building. They should not just tolerate each other.

Architectural metalwork can offer a building a different level of detail, a focal point, a character, which contrasts with the solidity of timber, brick, stone and concrete. The linearity of forged metalwork, its ability to draw three-dimensional lines in space, its capacity to provide strength without visual mass or mass for dramatic effect, the contrast of thick and thin, of structure and decoration, are all part of the artist blacksmiths' palette. The defining characteristics of hot forging demonstrate the plasticity of metal through changes in section of the bar and the mark of the hammer. These qualities can bring a tactile level of detail to a large structure, speak of hand craftsmanship and offer a humanizing touch. In fact the metalwork may *be* the part you touch – the gate, the balustrade, the handrail. The metalwork often provides a point of contact between people and the building or site. Move the latch, open the gate, grip the handrail, climb the stairs and you are in another place.

OPPOSITE PAGE: Detail of gates by Alan Evans at Southampton Railway Station. (Photo: Chris Fairclough)

'Architectural metalwork can offer a building a different level of detail'. Buchanan Street Galleries screen, Glasgow. Large, plain wall surfaces enhanced by some powerful metalwork, spanning two floors of the multi-storey car park to the shopping centre. (Ironhorse Studios)

Being Critical

However you choose to develop the design, it is vital to make judgements critically and objectively, throughout the whole process. Does the proposal really look as good as it should? In fact, is it going to look as good as you think it will? Sometimes, leaving drawings for a day or two and coming back to look at them afresh, is time well spent. Converting the design into even the simplest form of model in paper, wire or card can resolve visual problems. Drawing on tracing paper, amongst other virtues, has the advantage that its transparency allows the image to be viewed from the back, offering a fresh view of the idea.

Design is a process of observation, speculation, experiment, modification and evaluation. The constant creative question should be: what if? What if I try this? What if I try that? Like choosing clothes, you only know whether it will fit if you try it. Implicit in all this – and fundamental to it – is learning to look, with an educated eye and enough concentration to take in a whole range of qualities and make a reasoned assessment of them. Blacksmiths are good at looking, for example, along a 2m bar to check and make it perfectly straight – a remarkable skill. Visual, design judgements require the same intensity of observation, but are based on aesthetic rather than objective criteria. Like knowing how to straighten a bar, the skill to make confident aesthetic judgements takes time to develop and needs practice to maintain. Looking critically at the work of other blacksmiths, artists and craftspeople – as a matter of habit – is a crucial part of developing aesthetic awareness and keeping it honed. Athletes need to train constantly to keep up their level of fitness and skill. It becomes a way of life. Artists and craftspeople are no different.

Concept and Design

As you begin to draw initial ideas, an important basic design strategy is to appreciate the distinction between a 'concept' and a 'design'. A concept identifies the broad outline of an idea, but is not a design in itself. A 'design' is the detailed proposal, from which a piece of work can be made. A concept is like the chapter heading in a book. The heading identifies a topic, while the chapter itself contains the detailed information. Offer a design concept to a room full of designers (or a chapter heading to a room full of writers) and they will all produce different finished results from the same basic notion. A concept for a piece of architectural metalwork might be a structural idea, like 'a gate without an external frame'. It may be a visual intention as vague as 'using diagonals', or it might question the convention of a hinged gate by asking 'what if it opened like the aperture of a camera lens?'. Simply stating an idea like this is a long way from producing a detailed design that actually works, but the fact that these statements and questions can be interpreted and developed in a variety of different ways is their great virtue, inviting the exploration of a range of answers. In this way, it is possible to look broadly at the implication and relevance of a concept before getting bogged down considering all the details.

Concept and design. These are just a number of concepts – configurations – for a table. Each one of them could be developed in a variety of ways. Not one of these is a design.

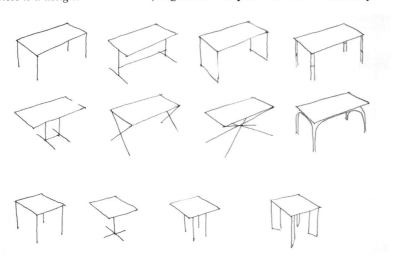

Design Sources

'Inspiration' is a word I tend to avoid. My *Concise Oxford Dictionary* defines it as 'a supposed creative force or influence on poets, artists, etc.' I am interested to read the word 'supposed', because in my experience 'creative force' usually requires hard work, rather than just waiting for some influence to arrive. Design ideas can derive from a broad diversity of sources and approaches. Sources can be looked for and provide that vital starting point, while approaches can provide the means of developing and manipulating ideas.

The place itself – the building, the street, the garden – is the most obvious source of ideas, and even if you leave with only the haziest feeling for the kind of metalwork to propose, this is still a valuable impression to nurture and develop. The period and character of the building or site may suggest qualities, details or motifs. Ask yourself questions. For example, should the design derive directly from the architecture? Should it pursue some other theme, to do with the function or history of the building, or the interests of the client? What qualities are appropriate? What should the metalwork be trying to say? Design ideas can come from visible sources like architecture, the landscape, nature, plants, animals and so on. They can come from the abstract symbolism of concepts such as security, friendship or power. They can derive from the history

of, or celebrate contemporary activities on, the site. They can be based on structural ideas, the rhythm of repeated units, the pattern of bars and connections, or some new discovery in the workshop – a joyful expression of what metal can do.

Some years ago, I was commissioned by a lady who was a retired research biochemist, to design a decorative handrail for the step by her front door. She had a beautiful garden, so when I asked if she had any particular motifs in mind, I thought she might suggest flowers of some kind. But 'Trypanosomes', she said. These, it turns out, are minute protozoan parasites found in the blood of mammals, and were her research subject for many years. I went away with a book of micro-photographs of these wriggly creatures and they became the theme for a small decorative panel.

ABOVE LEFT: *What is the metalwork trying to say? – 'KEEP OUT'. Formidable grilles in Amsterdam. Designer and maker not known.*

ABOVE: *What is the metalwork trying to say? – 'Come in'. A welcoming front door in Brussels, whose window grille has trickled down to become a handle. Designer and maker not known.*

LEFT: *Decorative handrail based on trypanosomes, by the author.*

ABOVE: *The Dwarf Fan-Palm, the only native European palm.*

ABOVE RIGHT: *Metalwork clearly derived from nature. Gates to the Casa Vicens in Barcelona, designed by Antoni Gaudi, in cast and forged iron.*

Asymmetry. An asymmetrical but plant-like garden gate by Brian Russell. (Photo: Brian Russell)

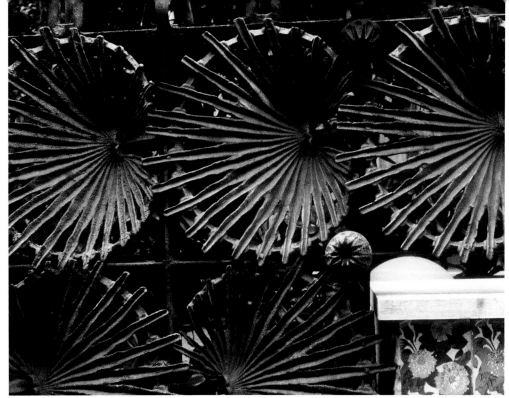

The point of this story is not simply that the most unlikely things can become design sources. It is also important to appreciate that it does not necessarily matter whether people recognize the source of an idea. The fact that it gave me a starting point and meant something to the client, are the crucial concerns. The viewer's appreciation of a design can be enhanced by an understanding of its origin or underlying symbolism, but it is not essential. In this case the client was delighted by the thought that only she and I would understand the origin.

STRATEGIES

Just as there are many sources of ideas, there are many ways of using them. The designers in my imaginary room are likely to produce different designs from the same source material by using it in different ways. Analysing historic and contemporary pieces of work, asking, 'What is it about?' can reveal some of these design approaches. Many art and design jargon words are worth understanding, because they offer specific ways of thinking about a piece of work. An entirely intuitive way of

designing relies on imagination, judgement and 'good taste', to provide answers. And if this works – use it. But having the terminology to identify and consider particular visual aspects is a step beyond intuition, because it can provide reasons why; why does this idea work so well? Or, even more importantly, what is wrong with that idea? Having a means at hand to analyse or explain the uneasy feeling that something is not quite right, is a valuable design tool that can lead to greater understanding and a better answer. The following terms are not intended as a comprehensive list, but attempt to describe some qualities that can exist in a piece of design, several of which may be embodied in the same work.

Asymmetry is the opposite of symmetry. It can look more disturbing or dynamic, and may be deliberately dramatic or visually balanced.

Balance. Like mechanical balance, where a large weight close to the fulcrum can be balanced by a smaller one further from it, visual balance describes an equilibrium, the sense that the various elements of the structure exist in a calm relationship.

Consistency describes a harmonious relationship that exists between all the components in a piece of work. Just as the twenty-six letters of a particular typeface are all different, yet clearly belong to each other, the details of a piece of design should all look as if they are part of the same family.

Contrast can be important to give a design some sense of variety – some dense areas, some lighter; some thick, some thin – rather than a bland, even, overall pattern. It is also a way of providing emphasis. Some very small or delicate elements can make the heavier ones appear bolder by contrast, and vice versa.

ABOVE LEFT: Consistency. Detail of a balustrade and handrail by Avril Wilson for Swindon Dance Theatre. Despite the variety of different forms used to terminate the uprights, they clearly belong to one family.

ABOVE RIGHT: Balance. An asymmetrical but beautifully balanced design. Gates by Alan Evans at Southampton Railway Station designed to complement a mosaic mural. (Photo: Chris Fairclough)

Contrast. An extraordinary gate in Barcelona, providing a rich, playful and varied pattern of open spaces, thin round bars, wide flat bars and formed plate. Designer and maker not known.

RIGHT: Gesture. A gate by Shelley Thomas exhibiting a wonderfully rebellious gesture, clearly determined to have nothing to do with its straight-laced pillars. (Photo: Bjanka Kadic)

Depth or thickness can be an overlooked dimension in architectural metalwork. Designing metalwork purely as a beautiful front elevation is to forget the visual possibilities of depth. The effect of an oblique view is to close up the spaces between the bars, to the extent that even a plain, vertical bar railing can shut off the view entirely, operating like a slatted window blind. If 25mm (1in) of depth can do that – what could you achieve with 75mm?

Depth. Railings at the rear of the Law Courts, Bell Yard, London. Opposite the two people on the right, the thickness – the depth – of the bars act like a slatted blind and make the railing completely opaque. Designed by the architect of the building G.E. Street, mid-nineteenth century.

(*See* the picture in Chapter 3 of a railing panel by Charles Normandale.) In an essentially flat structure, any feature that exploits or emphasizes the third dimension, will have an effect far greater than its size would suggest. The use of tables, raised collars and shadow bars in eighteenth-century ironwork, make this point. Interesting design possibilities can derive from exploiting the visual effects of depth and viewpoint. Like the advertising signs painted on the pitch at some sports matches, designed to read correctly only when seen from the position of the TV

camera, distinct forms outlined by the edge of a flat bar can become abstract patterns from other viewpoints.

Gesture is the sense of apparent movement; the stance, attitude or pose of a piece of work.

Negative and positive space. Negative space is the empty area between solid objects; the shape of the gaps between the metalwork. In design terms, the gaps have as much value and require the same consideration as the solid forms at either side. Many eighteenth-century iron balustrades used repeated, separate decorative balusters producing repeated but different decorative shapes in between. When you look at a chess board, are you seeing white squares on a black background, or black squares on a white background?

Proportion describes the relationship of one part to another within a structure; for example, the thickness of the bars in relation to their length, or the overall relation of say height to width. A historic, mathematical basis for good proportion is provided by the Golden Section (1:1.618), which has informed architecture since Ancient Greek times, and the related Fibonacci series 1, 1, 2, 3, 5, 8,

13, 21... where each number is the sum of the two that precede it. The great Swiss-French architect Le Corbusier used these to devise a modular architectural system in the late 1940s, which he applied to the design of subsequent buildings. These are interesting values, but why only one proportion should be considered 'good', I am far from clear. By way of comparison, the standard British and European ISO 'A' paper sizes are in the ratio of 1:1.414. (*See* the picture top left.)

Repetition, involving the use of repeated bars, motifs, structural or decorative elements is a familiar part of the artist blacksmith's repertoire. It also brings with it a number of other concerns like rhythm, texture and the use of negative and positive space.

Rhythm refers to the character of the repetition and the spacing of elements within a design.

Scale is not simply a measure of overall size. More importantly it refers to the visual effect of the size of components in relation to the whole. The size of bar that might look unremarkable as part of a pair

LEFT: Negative and positive space. The flower-bud shaped motif used as a split but positive form at the top of the gate, appears again in the middle as an outline; a negative space. Similarly the verticals of the gate start at the bottom as solid flat bars then become 'outlines'. An intriguing garden gate by Brian Russell. Measured across the posts the proportion of width to height corresponds closely to the golden section. (Photo: Brian Russell)

MIDDLE LEFT: Repetition. Detail of a gate fronting the Law Courts, The Strand, London. Note the strategy of the repeat, the motif between the central bars is flipped about a vertical axis alternately left and right as it ascends. Designed by the architect of the building G.E. Street, mid-nineteenth century.

Rhythm. Railing in Aldwych, London, showing a number of different rhythms in the spacing of the gilded cast iron panels, small oval motifs and open spaces. Designer and maker not known.

RIGHT: Stylizing. Two small art deco window grilles in a door in Amsterdam. The three tall upright forms in each grille are stylized to the point where they become almost abstract forms. They suggest flowers but are they thistles, tulips, buds or what?

FAR RIGHT: Scale. Detail of a gate by David Tucker (see Chapter 10). The slender round vertical bar is made to look thinner still by contrast with the heavy mass of the back stile – and vice versa. (Photo: David Tucker)

of large driveway gates, could look massive in a small garden gate and vice versa.

Stereotypes are powerful, well-recognized forms or details; for example, a square, a circle, a triangle or vertical, horizontal or parallel lines. Since these are such fundamental forms, they possess a self-evident rightness and our eyes are very sensitive to them. As a result a 'horizontal' line that is slightly askew can be very distracting.

Stylizing is the process of simplifying and

reducing a representational image to its basic elements. At the extreme, this might become an almost abstract form or symbol.

Symbolism is the use of forms to represent a particular idea, image or object. Some symbols may be a recognizable image, which carries a message, e.g. a dove symbolizing 'peace'; a stylized version of an object, e.g. a circle, might symbolize the sun or a human face; or a completely abstract cipher, such as £, $, π.

Symbolism. Car park railings at the National Youth Theatre of Great Britain, Holloway Road, London, by the author. The 'blown over' corners of the flat bars in the foreground are a repeated motif symbolizing the dog-eared corner of a script.

FAR LEFT: *Symmetry. Christchurch gates, by David Tucker. As a pair, the gates have a powerful and elegant symmetry, which echoes the gothic arches of the church. (Photo: David Tucker)*

LEFT: *One of four security grilles by the author, in the Crafts Gallery of Portsmouth City Museum and Art Gallery, seen in the distance as a silhouette.*

BELOW: *A detail of the same grille close to.*

Symmetry describes a form or structure mirrored at either side of a centreline. It is a powerful and familiar quality that brings a feeling of completeness, and is a fundamental characteristic of classical architecture.

Texture is exactly what it says. Probably most evident from a distance, it is the grain or gross pattern of the structure. Quite apart from keeping animals in or out, the short vertical dog bars at the bottom of traditional country house gates provide an area with a visually denser texture. (*See* the illustration on page 107, which shows a gate with three different textures.)

Viewpoint. Architectural metalwork is often seen both at a distance and at arm's length. It is important to consider the design from both viewpoints. At a distance, often only the essential pattern or silhouette can be seen. Standing next to the metalwork, the quality and detail of the structure and its surface texture become visible, and provide a reward to the viewer, who has approached more closely. Seeing an interesting structure in the distance can attract people. But if, having taken the trouble to walk closer, they find that it looks just the same but bigger, an opportunity has been lost. Different viewpoints make different demands.

Viewpoint is crucial in another sense. Because gates, grilles, fences and so on tend to be flattish, panel structures, and because of the way we visualize and draw them, the tendency is to design, as it were, from the front. If this indeed is how it will be seen, the approach is fine. However, if the gate is to be left open – so that only its edge will be seen – at the very least it needs to look interesting.

PROBLEM-SOLVING

Problem-solving can offer a way of finding design solutions, by side-stepping all those other factors that normally temper and modify decision-making. It relies on breaking down the overall design problem into a series of specific questions, which are considered in isolation, on the basis that if you can identify a problem, you can solve it. The objective is to focus on this single concern and to think of all the possible ways of providing an answer. Problem-solving can deal with very broad issues. For example, considering concepts for a gate, by asking how many ways could I block a gap in a wall? Or it can deal with small details, like asking how many ways can I imagine to join two steel bars together to make a T-joint? Draw every solution you can imagine, but make no judgements about the quality or appearance of the answers. Do not censor anything. Under these rules, it is just as valid to suggest using elastic bands, rope or wooden pegs, as forged mortise and tenon joints. I have set these kind of questions to various groups of people and we have all been impressed by how many possibilities are generated in some twenty minutes.

The point is that you give yourself permission to consider silly answers; to let your mind wander beyond the normal, grown-up, well-understood kind of solution we might all usually think of; and more particularly, divorcing this one particular problem from all the others. Creativity is not always sensible. It is very easy during the course of an ordinary design day, to have a number of wild, off-the-wall ideas and instantly dismiss them, because they did not immediately fit. The original, highly successful, front-wheel-drive Mini car, which began production in Britain in the 1960s, used blocks of rubber, rather than conventional springs to provide the suspension. A problem-solving kind of solution. Crazy, but it worked.

DRAWING

Drawing is the language of design. Different kinds of drawing serve different purposes, and are listed here in the order in which they might be employed in any notional project.

1 Site survey drawing, is initially a sketch with dimensions, from which a measured architectural drawing can be produced. (*See* Chapter 4.)

2 Sketch drawings record imagination. They allow you to get things out of your head and on to paper, so that you can see them clearly and decide whether they are any use.

3 Sketches to scale can be made on tracing paper, laid over the survey drawing or by drawing on photocopies of a scale elevation.

4 Measured engineering drawings of the metalwork are required to bring together all the information from the site survey and the structural details of the metalwork proposed. They are a way of resolving dimensional problems.

5 Presentation drawings are intended to give the client an impression of the character and appearance of the finished work.

6 Workshop layout drawings provide full size information, to enable the metalwork to be made and assembled. (*See* Chapter 3.)

In my experience, although most projects involve these things, the design process does not always take place in this neat order, and tends to skip backwards and forwards, different stages occurring in parallel with each other. The phases of work these headings represent are discussed in more detail below. I make no distinction between hand or computer-generated drawings, their function is just the same.

Site Survey Drawings

The survey information brought back from the site enables a scale drawing to be made (*see* Chapter 4), but this is not the only fixed concern to which the design must respond. The requirements of regulations and other considerations can be added to the drawing. These might include the regulation height of balustrading or the line and height of handrails, and factors like the necessary position of fixings, hinges or latches, the convenient unit lengths of railing panels, or the height and swing of a gate. The scale drawing now provides a kind of dimensional framework – a skeleton – which the metalwork must fit, whatever its final appearance.

Sketch Drawings

Freehand drawing is an indispensable way of looking both at broad concepts and details, and reviewing and considering a number of ideas and approaches. It is a way of discussing the project with yourself. This is the hardest and most creatively demanding part of any project. It is where the ideas are born.

Interpretation – the way we understand what we see – is important. Faced with something we have never seen before, seeing it fleetingly, or from an unusual angle, can sometimes confuse our perception. We may interpret the image incorrectly. We are also inclined to see what we want to see. If you are out scanning the landscape for your lost dog, then every bush, rock or tree stump begins to look like a dog. Similarly, when making drawings, you must look carefully in order not to delude yourself. Yet, conversely, the fact that a drawn image might be interpreted in a number of ways can provide a useful design tool, a way of generating ideas. An elevation sketch of a grille will show the width and shape of the bars, but will say almost nothing about the other dimension. It can be read in different ways. Are the bars round, square, or flat in section? Are the thin bars

in fact, flat bars on edge? Where the width of a bar changes from thick to thin, is the bar forged down, or is it a flat bar twisted? Do some bars pass in front of others, or fit through punched holes? And so on. Asking these kind of questions of a drawing, can produce new ideas.

In order to promote this deliberate ambiguity, particularly in the initial design stage, it can be better not to use a thin pen or pencil line to delineate each edge of a bar, but to draw all the bars or other elements with a brush or felt pen as a single line, in effect a silhouette. There are numbers of felt pens available, varying from very thin to very thick, which allow a line to be drawn with a consistent width, or to a particular scale. Using these is quicker and more precise in describing bars of different thicknesses. It also allows more accurate judgements to be made about the pattern of visual weight and balance in the design, before any decisions are made about joints and other details.

Viewpoint. I was suddenly caught by the sight of this strange object (left) bolted to a wall in my home town, and for a second could not recognize it: it turned out to be a familiar pub sign (right).

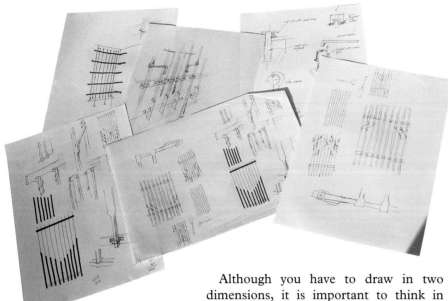

Security grille for the Oxfordshire County Museum, Woodstock. Typical sketch drawings.

Sketches to scale. Railing proposals traced freehand over an elevation drawing, to look at alternative details.

Although you have to draw in two dimensions, it is important to think in three – which is, after all, the way we see the world. Drawing in perspective – even badly – is infinitely better than not drawing at all, and drawing badly is the best reason for drawing more. Although this kind of sketch drawing is a means to an end, the better the quality of the drawing, the easier it is to make a judgement about the thing you are drawing. But it is not entirely as simple as that. If, as you draw, you have clearly visualized what you are drawing, the fact that your ability to transfer this to paper may be less than perfect, need not be a major problem. There is

something about the act of drawing that helps us to understand better what we are trying to depict. It is important to keep all sketches in a job file, not least because they represent solutions to problems that might apply elsewhere. Today's thought may be useful years later and should form part of a personal data bank. Do not rely on memory. Good ideas can be elusive things and may arrive at inconvenient moments. For this reason, it is a good habit to keep a sketchbook in your car.

Sketches to Scale

As design ideas begin to develop, by using tracing paper over the relevant elevation or by photocopying it, the metalwork can be drawn freehand to the correct size and proportion. This offers a quick way of evaluating ideas and the small scale of the survey elevation is a help at this point, encouraging more freedom in sketching ideas quickly. It can also be useful to sketch the scale outline of a person on the drawing, as an immediate reminder of the size of the metalwork. From a human eye level, there is a distinct perceptual difference to heights that are above or below. Go above it and things begin to feel big – so this reference is an important one.

Measured Engineering Drawings

The conventional engineering or architectural drawing process using plans, elevations and sections to scale – orthographic projection – is an invaluable tool for describing shapes and profiles, sizes, details of construction, and for working out such things as the movement of a hinge or bolt, the fit of one part to another, or the flat blank to produce a three-dimensional form. This is the standard means of communicating designs in the architectural and engineering industries and is a very prescribed and precise visual language, with its own rules and conventions. But it is far less good at providing an image that allows

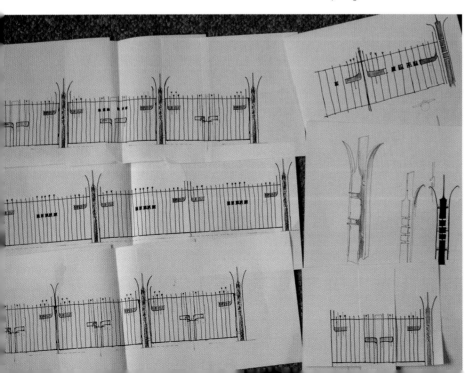

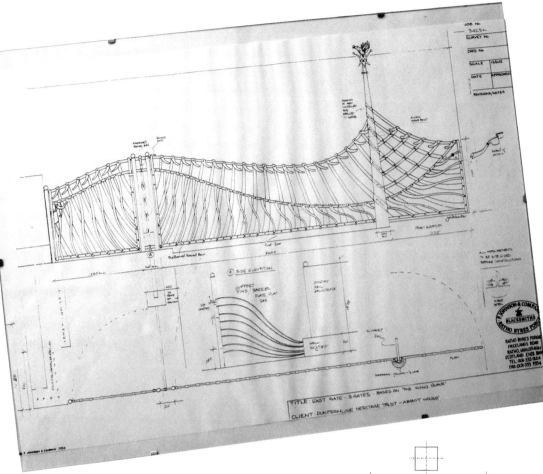

Engineering drawing. A vehicle gate and pedestrian gate for Abbot House, Dunfermline Heritage Centre, and a wheelchair access gate for the adjoining property. Designed by Phil Johnson and Jois Hunter, design drawing by Jois Hunter (see Chapter 10). (Photo: P. Johnson & Company)

you to make reliable visual judgements about what something will look like.

This is true at the very simplest level of, say, drawing two parallel lines to represent a particular thickness of bar. However accurate the drawing, the bar will not look like that in three dimensions. One elevation of, say, a 20mm (¾in) round, square or rectangular bar, will appear to be exactly the same on an engineering drawing. Viewed in real life, the round bar will look somewhat thinner, because of the light and shade on its curved surface; the square bar will look thicker when viewed from even a slightly oblique angle; and, depending on which edge of the bar is shown, a rectangular bar might look considerably thinner or thicker than the drawing suggests.

Some decisions can only be made with confidence by looking at the real thing.

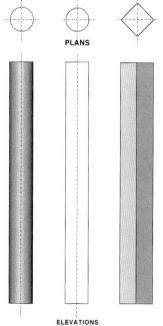

PLANS

ELEVATIONS

Some of the visual limitations of engineering drawing.

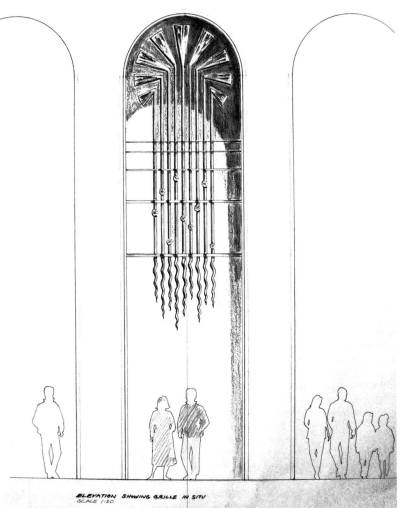

ELEVATION SHOWING GRILLE IN SITU
SCALE 1:20

An elevation drawing, with applied colour. Designed by Terry Clark and the author, and drawn by the author, as a demonstration piece for a design master-class at the ABANA Conference in Kentucky, USA. The grille is designed for the arched facade of a Planetarium building, and represents the sun shining down and the nine planets of the solar system.

ABOVE: An elevation drawing in pencil on textured paper. David Tucker's graphic presentation drawing for the church gate on page 57. (Photo: David Tucker)

Choosing particular thicknesses and sections, or combinations of bars, is far better achieved in the workshop, by looking on the bar rack. No matter how good are your powers of imagination and visualization, there is no substitute for taking pieces of the appropriate material, laying them out and comparing them. The same is true of making trial joints, details or even a sample panel.

Presentation Drawings

However much they may like your previous work, presentation drawings are usually what sells a project to the client. For this reason it is worth taking some trouble. A useful illusion of reality can be achieved by photocopying an elevation drawing and using watercolour, pencils or felt pens to put colour and shadow on the print. In making clear what is metal and what is space, and laying shadows across surfaces, this gives solidity and a sense of depth to the view. It can also serve to distinguish round from square bars and curved from flat surfaces. Colouring elevations was widely employed as a routine engineering drawing process in the nineteenth century, but remains a surprisingly effective technique.

It is not difficult to draw perspective views on a drawing board, once you understand the principles involved. It may take a little time (and so can computer modelling) but the fundamentals of the process are far simpler than might be expected. Consciously or not, most people use perspective when making sketch drawings.

Many books are available on this subject. Even drawing part of a design proposal in perspective can be helpful in explaining the idea, without going to the trouble of drawing the whole thing. Photographs of the building or site can be photocopied, scanned or taken digitally and used as a background, either tracing over to produce a drawn perspective view or by pasting on a drawing of the metalwork, physically or on computer. Tracing paper provides the durable, traditional medium and allows Xerox prints to be taken and worked on to add colour, texture and shadow, without risking the original drawing. A computer-modelling program can be used both to draw plans and elevations, and to convert them into perspective views, which can be oriented to show images as seen from different viewpoints.

MODEL-MAKING

Model-making is very similar to drawing, in that it provides both a useful design tool and a way of presenting a proposal to a client. It offers a means, for example, of investigating and demonstrating the way light passes through a structure and how this alters as the viewpoint changes. The more three-dimensional the structure, the more useful a model is likely to be, rather than a drawing. A great deal can be learnt from even the simplest assembly of plastic, wire or card. If you are dedicated to metal-working, scale models can be made by cold forging annealed copper or gilding metal using the same techniques as a full-

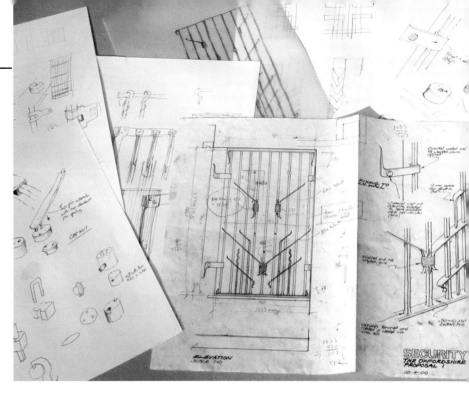

size bar, and soft-soldering parts together. Bars can be pieces of wire, or cut with a guillotine or snips from different thicknesses of sheet.

Alternatively there are ranges of extruded plastic sections and sheet available from shops that cater for model enthusiasts. These are made in a range of sizes and sections, solid, round, flat and square; tube, angle, channel and 'I' beam. Small plastic sections can be quickly filed or cut to a taper, bent and even twisted, while sheet can be cut to represent spread or shaped pieces. Joining by solvent welding is quick and easy. Pieces are held in place, or passed through holes and the liquid solvent applied to the joint with a small brush. It dries almost instantly.

Combinations of material are possible in a scale model. Paper, card, plastic, metal

Oxfordshire County Museum, design proposal developed from the sketches shown previously. Detail sketches and an elevation and part perspective drawing, by the author, the worse for wear after use in the workshop. Another print of the same drawing was tinted with watercolour for presentation purposes

Model by the author, at 1:10 scale, made in steel and plastic showing a typical railing panel for the National Youth Theatre building.

and wood can be glued to each other quite well enough to hold together for the purposes of making judgements about the design, or to use for presentation purposes. The whole assembly can be painted to unify different materials, using aerosol spray paint, the same graphite paste you might use for pieces of interior metalwork or paint from the model railway shop. Tins of metallic paints are available to simulate copper, bronze, brass and stainless steel. Stainless steel – both mirror or satin finished – can also be modelled using metallic card available from shops supplying art materials. The only downside of all this is the anxiety of transporting a fragile model, to present it to the client.

REGULATIONS

Like it or not, the design of architectural metalwork has to take account of regulations. So it is important to appreciate how these operate. Doubtless there are relevant regulations, recommendations and standards in every country. In England and Wales these are *Approved Documents*, which derive from *Building Regulations*; and *British Standards*. Scotland has its own building regulations.

Building Regulations (currently *The Building Regulations 2000*) are a statutory instrument – a law – which imposes particular requirements on people undertaking building work in England and Wales. The onus is on the person doing the work to demonstrate that they are complying with the regulations, which are stated in the form of broad, somewhat convoluted, but basically common-sense requirements. For example, requirement *K2 Protection from falling, collision and impact* requires that:

> (a) Any stairs, floors and balconies and any roof to which people have access, and (b) any light well, basement area or similar sunken area connected to the building, shall be provided with barriers where it is

necessary to protect people in or about the building from falling.

Building Regulations: Approved Documents are publications intended to provide 'practical guidance' on the application of particular regulations. So requirement K2 is expanded to a detailed consideration of the concerns and solutions that meet the needs covered by the requirement above. However, the approved document itself states that:

> there is no obligation to adopt any particular solution contained in an Approved Document if you prefer to meet the relevant requirement in some other way.

British Standards provide a framework of agreed and recognized specifications, but are not legal requirements in themselves. There are straightforward standards for paint colours, or the composition of steel; and there are also standards that lay down 'codes of practice', for example, 'The design, construction and maintenance of straight stairs and winders'. *British Standards* are often quoted and embodied in approved documents.

The existence of these regulations raises the question how important are they, and to what extent do they apply to architectural metalwork? The answer is not simple, and varies quite considerably with the nature of the building and role of the metalwork. *Approved Documents K* and *M* contain the information most often needed. They require careful reading, since guidance can apply differently to public buildings and to private houses, to new buildings, to extensions and to historic buildings. Exactly what applies in a particular case might best be left to the architect to determine, if one is involved. Under the *Disability Discrimination Act* what *Approved Document M* calls 'building control bodies' will expect to see an 'access statement', which is likely to be prepared by the architect and should clarify some of these concerns. *Building Regulations* apply to buildings. So metalwork in a street, park, garden or other open place may strictly fall outside the regulations. On the other hand, *Building Regulations* are concerned with 'access to a building', so any handrail, balustrade, guard or barrier within the site, which gives access to a building, will be subject to the regulations.

More force has been given recently to some existing guidance by the *Disability Discrimination Act 1995*. This states rather tortuously that as from 1 October 2004, 'all those who provide services to the public' are required 'to take reasonable steps to remove, alter or provide a reasonable means of avoiding a physical feature of their premises, which makes it unreasonably difficult or impossible for disabled people to make use of their services'. The spirit of this is that any building that can normally be accessed by the public should be provided with reasonable measures to allow safe access for disabled people. This includes access 'from the entrance point at the boundary of the site, and from any car parking that is provided on the site, to the building'. This guidance is embodied in *Approved Document M*, which in some instances now supersedes details in *Approved Document K*.

Although *Approved Documents* emphasize that the details are intended as 'guidance' and note that 'there may well be alternative ways of achieving compliance with the requirements', some guidance is in fact very prescriptive. For example, *Approved Document K* contains the well-known rule that in a balustrade, the construction should be such that 'a 100mm (4in) sphere cannot pass through any opening in the guarding'. Because of the nature of our craft, it is no comfort to know that – as an alternative – you could use solid brickwork or a sheet of plywood. So the effect for artist blacksmiths is that 'guidance' is essentially a requirement.

It should also be noted that since regulations have been added layer on layer, they are open to interpretation. In trying to make sense of hundreds of pages of material, it seems to me that there are relatively few regulations with which, as an artist blacksmith, you absolutely must comply. I quote these regulations in the appropriate chapters. This leaves other elements in *Building Regulations* and particularly in *British Standards*, which fall into the interesting but not essential category. I have also listed these in the relevant chapters. At the end of the day, these broader standards exist and it is as well to know they are there, even if you rarely need to refer to them. In the absence of any other reference, it could be useful to be able to state that the work conforms to a particular standard.

Building Regulations: Approved Document K – Protection from falling, collision and impact and *Approved Document M – Access to and use of buildings* are not very expensive and should be on the shelf of anyone involved in making architectural metalwork. Unlikely as they may sound, these two titles contain most of the regulations that might be required.

Reference libraries usually have copies of *Building Regulations* and books are also available, which are interpretations or explanations of them. A good reference library will also have Internet access to *British Standards*. You can consult an index of *British Standards* from your own computer, but an expensive licence is necessary to access more material and find out what a particular standard actually contains. As publications they are expensive. However, larger libraries are licensed and you can view and read each standard, but are not allowed to download copies. You are allowed to print one page from a particular standard, but there is nothing to prevent you making as many handwritten notes as you wish.

6 HANDRAILS

Compared with other types of architectural metalwork, handrails are usually modest structures. But because of the safety concerns they involve, and the situations in which they are required, they can embody many of the complexities required by more elaborate pieces of metalwork. Their geometry is closely related to stair balustrades, but since there are many situations where handrails are free-standing or fixed to walls, they are considered separately here.

Some handrails are simple, straight rails, but others may need to link several flights, or take into account changes of angle and curved or uneven walls, requiring careful surveying and installation. Setting out in the workshop requires some accuracy and may involve elaborate jig making if, for example, a 'drum' has to be fabricated to reproduce the curve of a wall. A number of regulations apply to the siting and design of handrails. For these reasons they require every bit as much imaginative design as metalwork, which is more obviously demanding and decorative. In an architectural space, the visual effect of a handrail can be out of all proportion to its size. Borrowing Paul Klee's concept of taking a line for a walk, the rail provides a sense of movement and direction, which reduces the zig-zag of the stairs to a simple ribbon, describing changes of level.

Handrails are intended to assist people ascending or descending ramps or stairs, or in corridors to provide help for elderly or disabled people. They may also be required at the top of horizontal parapets at the edge of landings, where guarding is necessary. Handrails in themselves, whether fitted to walls or supported by free-standing uprights, are not intended to guard a drop. For my purposes here, guarding a drop is the defining function of a balustrade. This definition may appear to be somewhat blurred, since occasionally a free-standing handrail can have some decorative metalwork below it, but so long as this is not guarding a drop, it is still a handrail.

DESIGN CONSIDERATIONS

The handrail structure may consist of a rail and brackets for wall fixing or a rail fitted to free-standing uprights. In either case the handrail can be directly fixed to its supports or may comprise a 'core rail', over which is fitted a 'capping rail' to provide

Handrail and balustrade by Alan Evans in Holy Trinity Church, Brompton, London. The handrail consists of a heavy, round-edged steel T-section supported on heavy forged brackets. (Photo: Alan Evans)

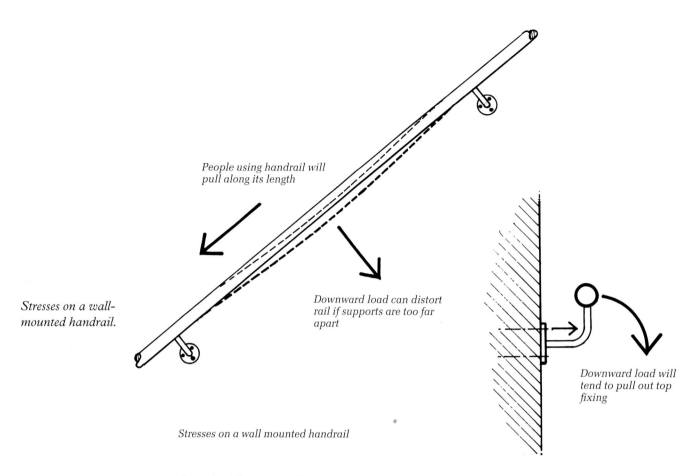

People using handrail will
pull along its length

Stresses on a wall-
mounted handrail.

Downward load can distort
rail if supports are too far
apart

Stresses on a wall mounted handrail

Downward load will
tend to pull out top
fixing

the grip. The core rail is usually a flat bar section, often rebated into the capping rail, and joined where necessary by half-lap joints and countersunk screws. The cap rail is often secured to it by countersunk screws, driven from underneath. Some bronze or brass capping rails are attached to the core rail using special long-head, countersunk bronze or brass screws driven from above, through the cap rail itself, and are filed off and polished to provide an invisible fixing. Countersunk flush rivets, in a metal matching the cap rail, can be used to similar effect.

Self-evidently, a handrail is there to be handled and touched. It is therefore essential that the design avoids projecting details that might trap an unwary hand or snag clothing, and the surface eliminates burrs, sharp edges, projecting pins and so

on. It is important to allow sufficient clearance between the handrail and the wall, consistent with not adversely reducing the width of the stair, ramp or corridor. The handrail is a safety device and, in normal use, has to carry considerable loads and may be subject to sudden heavy stresses, if used to restrain a fall. People ascending a stair will tend to pull down on the rail, while those descending will push down. These dynamic loads must be considered both in the design of the rail itself and in the provision and means of fixing.

Recent disability rights legislation, the spirit of which is to 'provide a more inclusive approach', provides recommendations for the design and detailing of handrails on the basis that making access easier for people with disabilities should help everyone. *Building Regulations: Approved Document*

M makes the point that:

> People who have physical difficulty in negotiating changes of level need the help of a handrail that can be gripped easily, is comfortable to touch and, preferably, provides good forearm support.

For access to, and for use within, buildings other than dwellings, it also details two approved profiles for handrail sections, one circular the other elliptical, both derived from research information. Neither of these bears much resemblance to standard, flattish 'half round' rolled steel or extruded brass handrail sections. Interestingly, research published by the National Research Council of Canada in 1988 also recommended a circular section handrail, although of a slightly smaller diameter of 38mm (1½in) for adults and 29–32mm (1⅛–1¼in) for children.

To provide a handling surface, particularly in public buildings, handrails are often made from materials like brass, bronze, aluminium, stainless steel, timber or plastic. In domestic interior situations, forged mild steel with a lacquered or waxed finish can be very effective. Wear produces a smooth patina, which is better both to use and to look at than a worn painted surface. It is worth noting that in particularly exposed positions or in more extreme climates than Britain, an outdoor handrail can become too hot or cold to be used comfortably. This problem might be overcome by using a capping rail made from an insulating material like timber or plastic, or if solar heating is the main

Handrails in Newcastle upon Tyne, by Brian Russell. The handrails are circular in section and supported on ingeniously interlaced, forge-welded uprights. (Photo: Brian Russell)

Making

Straight handrails may be made directly to the dimensions established on site, without the need for a layout drawing, or they can be can be drawn out full size and assembled on a flat surface. Curved handrails may need to be laid out on a drum, fabricated from the site survey dimensions or made to match a template bar bent on site. Even with otherwise straight handrails, there is often a need to make smooth bends and transitions between the straight sections. A handrail made from round section material, as recommended above, can seem very attractive, since it is easier to bend, when compared with the difficulty of edge-bending plain flat bar or flat handrail section. The problem is to prevent the bar twisting as it is bent on the flat. A few bends in steel can be achieved at the anvil by traditional hot processes, working to a chalk line marked on a plate or, if the bends are not too tight, by progressively edge-bending the metal cold, using a rail bender, fly-press or hydraulic press.

Numbers of matching bends may require the fabrication of formers and bending jigs, both to edge-bend the flat bar and to bend it the easy way. Since it is

Wonderfully elegant, gently tapered, octagonal handrail by Alan Evans, in a private house. Due to the confined space of the stair, the photograph does not do this justice. The handrail is cantilevered from the fixing and terminates in thin air, top and bottom, beyond the edge of the picture. (Photo: Alan Evans)

ABOVE RIGHT: Hot bending a flat stainless steel bar handrail for Guildford Cathedral, over a former in my workshop.

problem, by using reflective materials such as polished stainless steel or aluminium.

Approved Document M makes recommendations that handrails should extend for a minimum horizontal distance beyond the top and bottom of ramps and the top and bottom nosings of stairs. The purpose of this is to offer stability and give a tactile warning of a change in level. It also suggests that handrails – including those fitted to walls – should be designed to terminate in such a way that clothing cannot easily be caught by the free end of the rail. The word 'continuous' is used throughout the document, both to mean that the handrail should not have gaps in it, and to suggest that, where possible, handrails should continue across landings, to link to the next flight. For the artist blacksmith 'how will it look?' is a major design concern. In this instance 'how will it feel?' is equally important. Against this background, imagining the use of the handrail in pitch darkness is instructive.

The same handrail being pulled to a curve in the other plane. The wide bending former was necessary to accommodate the entire flat bend and was similarly used to bend a second handrail as a mirror image of the first.

desirable to maintain an unmarked surface, in order to minimize the finishing, bending is better done by leverage rather than impact. Where it is necessary to hit the metal, a heavy rawhide mallet is indispensable. If the bending jigs are carefully designed, the straight handrail can be set up to a mark, clamped in place, heated with a torch and pulled round the curve. When edge-bending, it is important that the jig has a flat fence or back plate behind its curved edge, so that the bar can be dressed down with a mallet to prevent it kinking. This also provides a surface to which the bar can be progressively clamped as bending proceeds. Soft materials like brass need to be worked carefully to avoid overheating, which can cause the metal to tear under pressure, but at the right heat it will stretch very well. Brass can mark easily and, where possible, clamps should be padded with timber.

Whether straight or curved, if lengths of wall-mounted handrail require more than two fixing brackets, packing plates may be needed behind the brackets to make up for irregularities in the wall surface. Some general concerns in setting out and assembling handrails and balustrades are dealt with in Chapter 3.

Neat handrails 'tumbling' down the steps, by David Tucker. Since they are in the bar of a restaurant, it was considered unlikely that they would be used by children. (Photo: David Tucker)

HANDRAIL REGULATIONS

Summarized from *Building Regulations: Approved Documents K* and *M.*

NOTE See drawing 'Location of handrails' for position of dimensions **A**, **B**, **C**, **D**.

Situation	Handrail requirement	Height to top of handrail from ramp, pitchline or landing floor (A, B, C)	Maximum extension from top and bottom of ramp or stair nosing (D)
Access to and into a dwelling K Stairs	Continuous on one side, if three or more risers.	850–1,000 **(A)**	300 **(D)**
Inside dwellings K Stairs	Continuous on both sides if three or more risers and clear width over 900. Otherwise on one side.	900–1,000 **(A)**	-
Access to and into buildings other than dwellings K Ramps and stairs	Continuous on both sides if 1,000 clear width, or on one side if less.	900–1,000 on ramps **(A)** Consider additional handrails at 600 for children **(C)** (900–1,100 on landings **(B)**	300 **(D)**
Inside buildings other than dwellings K Stairs	Continuous on both sides if 1,000 clear width, or on one side if less.	900–1,000 on ramp or stair **(A)** (900–1,100 on landings **(B)**	300 **(D)**
Common stairs in blocks of flats	Continuous on both sides if two or more risers	900 on ramp or stairs **(A)** 1,000 on landings **(B)**	300 **(D)**

All dimensions in millimetres (approximate conversions: 600mm = 23⅝in; 850mm = 33½in; 900mm = 35½in; 1,000mm = 39in; 1,100mm = 43in).
*Additional handrails should be provided to divide stairs or ramps into channels not less than 1m wide and not more than 1.8m wide, where the overall unobstructed width is more than 1.8m (*see* 'Dividing Flights' drawing, below right).

Location of handrails (Documents K and M).

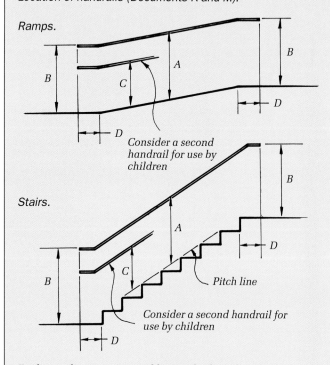

Ramps.

Consider a second handrail for use by children

Stairs.

Consider a second handrail for use by children

Pitch line

For key to dimensions see table 'Handrail regulations'

Handrail design (Document M).

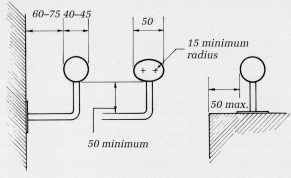

60–75 40–45

50

15 minimum radius

50 minimum

50 max.

Dividing flights.

If more than 1.8m wide, the flight should be divided

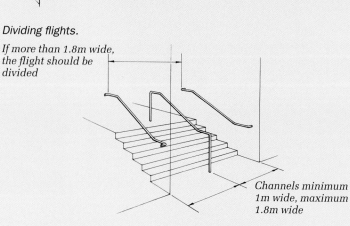

Channels minimum 1m wide, maximum 1.8m wide

SPIRAL STAIR CALCULATION

One special problem is the handrail for a spiral stair. The geometry of a spiral seems daunting until it is appreciated that the stair sits inside a theoretical cylinder, so that the line of the handrail or string becomes the hypotenuse of a right-angled triangle, when the cylinder is unrolled and opened out flat. On this basis, the length of the handrail can be calculated and, perhaps more importantly, the diameter to which it must be bent on the flat – its developed diameter – can be determined. The handrail must be rolled to this diameter before being pulled up into a spiral. The crucial information is the vertical height and the *effective diameter of the stair*, being the diameter of the line on plan, which passes through the centreline of the handrail. It must similarly be remembered that the developed diameter, once established, is the centreline diameter of the required curve. This method of calculation also provides the basis for setting out the balustrading on a spiral stair. (*See* Chapter 7.)

Regulation
Building Regulations 2000:Approved Document K. Protection from falling, collision and impact. Building Regulations 2000: Approved Document M. Access to and use of buildings. BS 8300: 2001 Design of buildings and their approaches to meet the needs of disabled people – code of practice.

Spiral staircase.

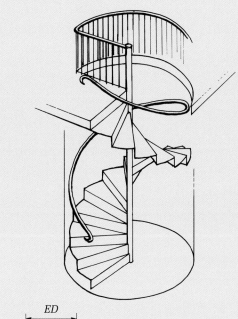

Spiral staircase elevation and plan.

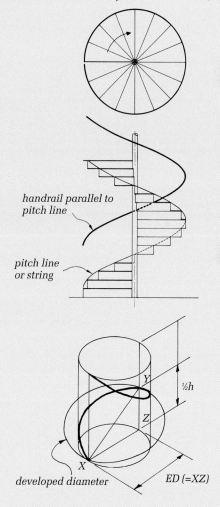

handrail parallel to pitch line

pitch line or string

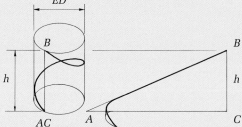

Spiral stair calculations.

Cylinder opened out to form right-angle triangle.
Note that h = height at which spiral stair has rotated a full 360 degrees.

Calculating handrail length
If Effective Diameter ED = 2.2m and total height BC (h) = 2.8m then:
Circumference of circle 2.2m diameter = $\pi \times 2.2 = 6.91\text{m} = AC$
Considering triangle ABC
$AB = \sqrt{AC^2 + BC^2} = \sqrt{6.91^2 + 2.8^2} = \sqrt{47.748 + 7.84} = \sqrt{55.588}$
$AB = 7.455$ = Length of handrail = 7.455m

Calculating handrail angle
$\text{Tan angle A} = \dfrac{BC}{AC} = \dfrac{2.8}{6.91} = 0.4052$
angle A = 22 degrees 3 minutes

developed diameter   ED (=XZ)

Calculating handrail development
Considering triangle XYZ
$XY = \sqrt{XZ^2 + YZ^2} = \sqrt{2.2^2 + 1.4^2} = \sqrt{4.84 + 1.96} = \sqrt{6.8}$
$XY = 2.607\text{m}$
Developed diameter = 2.607m

7 BALUSTRADES

My *Concise Oxford Dictionary* defines 'balustrade' as 'a railing supported by balusters, especially forming an ornamental parapet to a balcony, bridge or terrace'. A 'baluster' is defined as 'one of a series of often ornamental short posts or pillars supporting a rail or coping'. It then adds – reprovingly – 'often confused with banister', which it defines as 'the uprights and handrail at the side of a staircase'. Well I admit to the confusion. I always thought a banister was a timber balustrade. So, somewhat reassured by *English Architecture: an Illustrated Glossary*, which tells me that a banister is 'a vulgar term for baluster', I am using the word 'balustrade' here to mean the uprights, the infill and handrail guarding a balcony, terrace, edge of a floor, landing or stair.

Balustrades of all kinds are primarily intended to guard a drop, unlike railings or fences, which divide areas of land. They are necessary both inside or outside a building, to provide a safe edging, where there is a sudden change in level. Stair balustrades combine the two functions of guarding a drop and providing a handrail. The handrail is usually constructed as the top element of the guarding, although more as a matter of convenience than in response to regulations. The regulation heights can often be matched, but since those for guarding are a minimum, so long as a handrail is fitted at the required height, a balustrade itself may be taller.

Since balustrading is required where there is a change in level, a balustrade is almost by definition going to be seen from dramatic viewpoints. Stairs are often a major architectural feature both inside and outside buildings, providing access and expressing changes in level and direction. They can bring drama to the interior of even a modest building, since the stair well allows the full height of the inside space to be appreciated, and offers glimpses of the different levels within the building. Their design in grand country houses left a legacy of staircases as almost theatrical features, still evident in the entrance halls of public buildings today. Forged metal balustrading can visually articulate and emphasize the lines of stair and landings, and provide a finer level of scale and texture against the flat surfaces of the building interior.

OPPOSITE PAGE: Straight and circular balustrades by Charles Normandale in a house in Dorset. (Photo: Charles Normandale)

Balustrading work in progress for the same commission, by Charles Normandale. The right-hand one of two mirrored, S-shaped staircases leading from the entrance hall, shown before the handrail is attached. The complex curves of the stair were surveyed by bending a dummy handrail bar in situ. The spiral design flows through the whole flight with no apparent joints. (Photo: Charles Normandale)

Stair types and terminology.

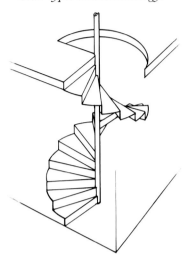

ABOVE: *Spiral/geometrical stair. A spiral or helical stair is one of a broad category of geometrical stairs, often with an open well, in which all the treads are winders. These include elliptical, circular, winding or curved stairs.*

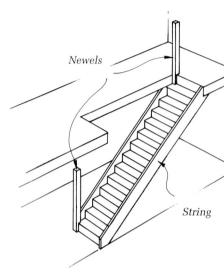

Straight, closed string stair.

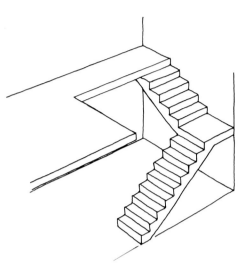

Quarter turn, open or cut string stair.

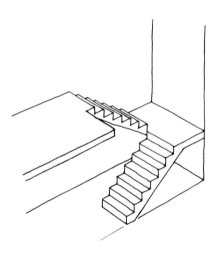

Half-turn stair.

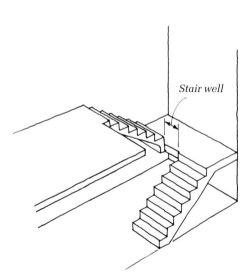

Half-turn stair with open well.

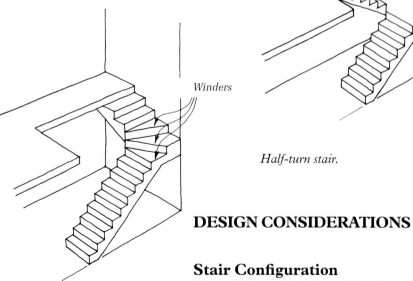

Quarter-turn stair with winders.

DESIGN CONSIDERATIONS

Stair Configuration

The problems of making stair balustrading depend, in the first instance, on the configuration and complexity of the stair.

Surveying, setting out and making straight flights of balustrading between newel posts is a relatively straightforward operation, because they are flat panels. Indeed, much balustrading consists of flat panels, but complications occur when flat panels turn a corner, or the whole stair is curved in

some way. As stairs turn, the structure of the balustrade becomes fully three-dimensional, and surveying, laying out and making become far more demanding (*see* Chapter 4). The wreath, as the balustrade turns and changes angle in the tight space of a stair well, calls for careful measurement and jig making. The better the representation of the stair that can be achieved in the workshop – the better it can be replicated – the easier it is to visualize and construct these transitions from one flight to another. If space allows, setting out and constructing balustrades vertically, in the attitude they will assume when installed, may be preferable to considering them as a series of flat panels. With spiral or curved stairs this may be the only way (*see* Chapter 3).

Structure

A fundamental choice in the design of a balustrade is whether to treat it as a series of panels – notionally top and bottom rails with infill – bridging between uprights or standards, or as an apparently continuous structure. In the grand, country house ironwork of the eighteenth century, every upright of a balustrade – every baluster – was often leaded or grouted directly into the masonry. This provides a visual simplicity and an appearance of continuity, and on stairs avoids the awkward triangular space where a bottom rail bridges between the nosings of adjacent steps. It also means that every upright shares part of the load. However, it does call for considerably more work on site, and some temporary bracing for the bottom – unrestrained – ends of all the

A free-formed stair balustrade, just fitting under the workshop roof, allowing it to be assembled vertically. Robert Kranenborg and Andy Quirk. (Photo: Andy Quirk & Robert Kranenborg)

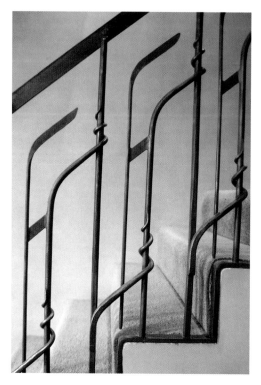

RIGHT: Detail of the lower flight of a quarter-turn stair balustrade, by the author, using a flat bottom rail, shaped to follow the profile of the concrete steps, and providing an edging for the fitted carpet.

FAR RIGHT: The upper flight and landing of the same balustrade. Since there is no well between the edge of the landing and the stair, the stair balustrade becomes a screen extending upwards to become the landing balustrade. In consequence, the handrail that forms the top of the lower balustrade has to be carried on brackets.

uprights during the handling required while finishing and transporting to the site. A variation of this is to use a bottom rail, which sits directly on the floor and follows the profile of each step, so that the balusters are tied at top and bottom, and fixings may be placed anywhere along it. On stairs this calls for precise surveying and fitting, but provides the kind of continuous appearance already described. If stairs and landings are carpeted, a flat bottom rail sitting on the floor will provide an edging for the carpet, whose thickness will mask the edge of the rail when viewed from above. For reasons of simplicity, balustrades are perhaps more often designed as panels of metalwork supported by standards, or by the newel posts on timber stairs. The length of each panel and the position of joints is a matter of convenience, but in the case of stairs, it might typically be one flight and one wreath – the angled transition to the next flight or landing. To a greater extent than

with other kinds of architectural metalwork, it seems to me that stair balustrades call for a particular care in their design, and in the intimacy and scale of their detailing, because they are so close. As you climb the stair with a hand on the rail, the metalwork is right there, a few inches away at eye level.

Perhaps the single most constraining factor in balustrade design is the *Building Regulations: Approved Document K* requirement that to 'prevent children being held fast by the guarding', the construction should be such that a 100mm (4in) sphere cannot pass through any openings and that children will not readily be able to climb it. It goes on to suggest that horizontal rails in the guarding should be avoided. The 100mm-sphere requirement also applies to the gap between the treads in an open-tread staircase. However, this guidance is only intended to apply to stairs 'where buildings are likely to be used by children under 5 years of age'. Which begs the question of what 'likely' really means. However, it seems to me that like most regulations, they only hurt if you try and fight them. I am sure I am not alone in happily sketching ideas on a drawing board, then feeling unreasonably constrained by the need to squeeze up a gap, to prevent that sphere passing through. But then I have come to realize that I would feel just as irritated if it was a 120mm or 150mm sphere.

Since balustrades guard a drop, installing them can put the smith in exactly the kind of hazardous position the balustrade is designed to prevent. Careful planning and design is therefore necessary at the outset to decide how installation will be achieved, and where fixings should be placed, both for structural strength and safe access during installation. Similarly, how panels can be carried to their particular site and held in place while they are secured is an important concern in determining the size and weight of each component. In a clear open space mechanical options may be available, but at the top of a high, narrow staircase, several pairs of hands may be the only answer.

Strength and Rigidity

The value of a balustrade as a safety barrier depends on its ability to withstand the sideways – essentially outward – dynamic load of people leaning, falling or pushing against it, and also, in the case of a stair balustrade, of users pulling or pushing down the line of the handrail. The uprights or standards transmit the sideways load to their fixings, and panels between standards must be reassuringly rigid. Happily, blacksmiths have a tendency to over-engineer metalwork, but it is still worth making the point that the minimum *Building Regulation* horizontal loadings that a balustrade should be able to resist at its top edge (given by British Standard 6399 Pt 1) vary considerably with the type of building and the expected

FAR LEFT: *A small detail – a wreath – of a very long stair balustrade for a house in Chelsea, London, by Jim Horrobin. Intriguingly, the design does not repeat throughout the length of six flights. (Photo: Jim Horrobin)*

LEFT *The timber former or 'drum' marked with the layout drawing for this particular wreath. (Photo: Jim Horrobin)*

BALUSTRADE REQUIREMENTS (Guards and Barriers)

Summarized from *Building Regulations, 2000: Approved Documents M and BS 6399 – 1:1996.*

Type of Building	Minimum required height to top of barrier					Typical BS 6339 horizontal uniform load***
	Stairs	Ramps	Landings	Internal edges of floors	External balconies	
Single family dwellings	900*	900*	900	900	1100	0.36kN/m²
Residential, institutional, educational, office and public buildings	900**	900**	1100	1100	1100	0.74kN/m²
Retail	900**	900**	1100	1100	1100	0.74kN/m²

NOTE Except on stairs in a building that is not likely to be used by children under 5 years, the guarding to a flight should prevent children being held fast by the guarding. The construction should be such that:
• a 100mm sphere cannot pass through any openings in the guarding, including openings in the risers;
• children will not readily be able to climb the guarding.

All dimensions in millimetres (approximate conversions: 900mm = 35½in; 1,100mm = 43in)
*Guarding is required in dwellings where there is a drop of more than 600mm.
**Guarding is required when there are two or more risers (or equivalent).
***These figures are examples. For a given situation, consult BS 6399-1.

RIGHT: How do you deliver metalwork to the site? Balustrading at the top of the tower, Tutbury Castle, Staffordshire. (Photo: David Tucker)

FAR RIGHT: Neat and simple balustrading at the top of the tower, by David Tucker. (Photo: David Tucker)

One end of a large balustrade for a balcony, incorporating built-in seats at either end, by Shelley Thomas. Note the large, unapologetic joints in the top rail, where the panels connect; a good example of the philosophy that if you cannot hide it, make a feature of it. (Photo: Shelley Thomas)

usage. For example, balustrading in areas where people may congregate, such as restaurants or bars, must withstand more than four times the loading required for a domestic stair or balcony. Busier areas, where overcrowding may occur, like the wide public footways adjacent to sunken areas in shopping malls, call for a loading over eight times the domestic requirement.

Fixings should be designed to withstand these loads, to provide the necessary strength and rigidity, as well as carrying the dead weight of the metalwork, if this is side fixed. Since all the loading is concentrated on relatively few fixing points, it is vital that these are more than sufficient to carry the stress, and that the building material is sound in these places. If the site survey reveals dubious brickwork or timber supporting the work, this may provide a good argument for fixing every upright in the structure, to spread the load and allow some redundancy, should any of the fixings

be doubtful. As a general principle, architectural metalwork is installed by offering it into place and drilling through, or marking through, and drilling fixing holes in the timber, brickwork or masonry. It is, in effect, self-jigging. But in practice, drilled holes can wander and surfaces being drilled may not be flat or true, so some form of adjustment is important.

Within buildings, straight balustrades are often relatively short and gain rigidity from wreaths or bends at either end, or they can be braced to adjacent walls. Curved balustrades are inherently more stable. However, where long straight runs of balustrading are required, rigidity can become a problem (*see* Chapter 8). Side fixing is likely to be better than floor fixing in this respect, since the screws or bolts can be placed further apart to provide greater stability, but this in itself may not be enough. A traditional remedy common to railings is to buttress the uprights at intervals with backstays. At the simplest,

ABOVE: Railings guarding a drop, which by my definition are classified as a balustrade. The freedom of the foliage contrasts beautifully with the simplicity and formality of the railings. (Photo: Steve Lunn)

The railings themselves are leaded-in to the top of the coping, while the backstays are similarly fixed to the stonework. Work by Steve Lunn. (Photo: Steve Lunn)

these are angled straight or curved bars securely fixed to brace the upright by providing a triangulated column. The requirement to provide 'outrigger' frames of this kind at intervals provides an opportunity for dramatic or decorative design, since it brings metalwork out of the flat plane of the balustrade. The repetition of these units can add visual interest to the uniformity of long lengths of balustrading. In some instances they might also be able to provide other functions such as carrying signs or acting as lighting columns.

Adjustment and Fixing

Surveying, making and fitting balustrading to stairs and landings is probably the most exacting kind of architectural metalwork a blacksmith can be called upon to produce, since it is restrained in all three dimensions. Unlike the woodworker, who can scribe in, and saw or plane a component on site to make it fit, the metalworker must essentially anticipate the problems and build some tolerance or adjustment into the work itself. Any device that can be employed to allow adjustment is worth considering at the design stage. Even with the most precise surveying and making, packing pieces or washers are likely to be needed at fixing points, to take up irregularities in the wall, step or floor surfaces. The geometry of different situations will present different problems and call for a variety of different answers. Means of adjustment may be needed up and down, sideways or along the length of the structure. It is important to be aware of the effect of tolerances building up, as balustrade panels and standards are butted together, which might, for instance, make a run of horizontal balustrading just too long to fit between walls at either end. As a general principle, it may be better to make panels fractionally too short than to make them too long, and adjust them by fitting spacers in-between or at the end fixings.

Side fixing – securing the metalwork to the vertical side of a stair, landing or balcony – is attractive, in that the balustrading does not intrude over the width of the stair or floor, and the fixing points do not have to conform to the geometry of the steps. This configuration may also allow metalwork to be fitted over the face of an opening, rather than being confined between walls. It does, however, require that the structure be temporarily supported during installation, until the dead weight of the metalwork is taken by the fixings. One answer is to lay a number of short steel or timber beams across landings or stairs, with one end weighted down and the other projecting, to carry the balustrade. Balustrading on a balcony or landing may similarly be hung from projecting bars, clamped to the top rails of weighted steel trestles, positioned to overhang the edge of the floor.

Fixing standards or uprights to the top face of step or floor has the advantage that a run of balustrading can be assembled and will sit in position, where it can be correctly aligned, before fixing holes are drilled or marked. However, since the holes cannot be too close to an edge, particularly in concrete or stone stairs, this configuration consumes some of the width of the stair. Screw fixing through a plate or flange may need oversize holes for lateral

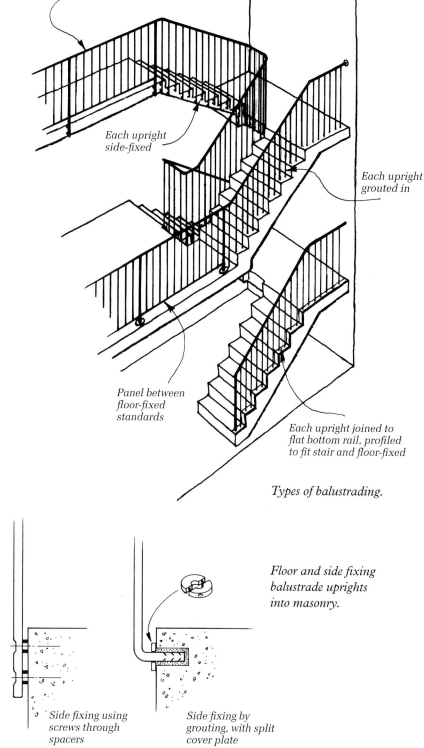

Panel between side-fixed standards

Each upright side-fixed

Each upright grouted in

Panel between floor-fixed standards

Each upright joined to flat bottom rail, profiled to fit stair and floor-fixed

Types of balustrading.

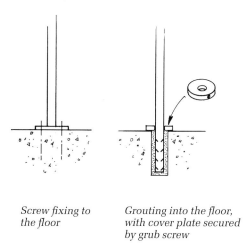

Screw fixing to the floor

Grouting into the floor, with cover plate secured by grub screw

Side fixing using screws through spacers

Side fixing by grouting, with split cover plate

Floor and side fixing balustrade uprights into masonry.

adjustment and packing pieces underneath for vertical adjustment. Grouting-in the standards allows some tolerance in positioning, since the holes need to be oversize to take the grout. Each standard can also be adjusted vertically, using packing in the hole, before pouring in the grouting material. Particularly in buildings, fixing this way is likely to need some form of cover plate to hide the grout, and disguise the fact that the standard may be off-centre in the hole. Cover plates can be slid over the tails of the uprights as they are placed in their holes, and held up temporarily with tape, while the grout is poured in. Plates can be secured by a grub screw or screws, or bonded in place with silicone sealant, after the grouting has set. Split plates provide an alternative where access is restricted. If holes can be accurately aligned, and the grouting material chosen to relate to the concrete, brick or stonework, leaving it exposed may be acceptable, particularly in outdoor situations. Leading-in is a good traditional alternative, and has the advantage that caulking the lead can, to some extent, visually compensate for the standard being off-centre, and allow it to be haunched up to shed rainwater. Out of doors, care must be taken with any grouted fixing to bring the material up above the mouth of the hole to avoid water penetration into the joint. A traditional remedy is to paint over the grouting to match the metalwork, but its effectiveness depends on regular maintenance (*see* Chapter 12).

Some stone or concrete slab stairs, and some timber stairs, may be constructed in such a way that holes can be drilled right through the step or string, allowing the threaded end of an upright to be passed through the hole to be secured on the other side with a nut and washer. It is usually preferable, with the light construction of domestic timber stairs, to fix to the string rather than the steps. When deciding how to fix balustrades on landings, care must similarly be taken to ensure that the timber is genuinely structural and not simply a trimmer, fascia or cladding piece, which is, for example, only nailed to timber struts wedged between the flanges of a steel 'I' beam. Drilling a small trial hole to check the thickness of the timber can provide a good indication.

Balustrading guarding the edge of a stair in a restaurant. Shelley Thomas. (Photo: Shelley Thomas)

Particularly on stairs where the person ascending has a very close view of the fixings, a neat joint between the metalwork and the step is important. Using crosshead, countersunk wood screws or squarehead coach screws into timber, or plugged into masonry, seems to me to be visually acceptable. But hexagon bolts or nuts used to secure expansion or resin anchor fixings always looks to me more like engineering than blacksmithing and are incompatible with the need to provide a high level of detailing because the viewer is so close (*see* Chapter 12).

SPIRAL STAIRS

Some of the mathematics related to spiral stairs are dealt with in connection with handrails, in Chapter 6. The example below illustrates how this can be used to determine the number of uprights required to provide a balustrade, which complies with regulations.

Referring to the spiral stair drawings on page 73 and using those dimensions, the effective diameter of 2.2m (86½in) gives a circumference of 6.91m (272in). Since there are sixteen stairs, dividing this by sixteen gives 432mm (17in) for the outside length, on the curve, of each step. In order to satisfy the requirement that a 100mm (4in) ball cannot pass between the bars, and assuming plain 10mm (⅜in) diameter uprights, each step will need four uprights. Dividing this into 432 gives a centre to centre spacing of 108mm (4¼in). These distances can be directly set out on the steps, but also need setting out on the handrail, which passes above each step at an angle. Four uprights on each of sixteen steps, gives a total of 64. This figure can be divided into the calculated total handrail length of 7.455m (293in), to give 116.5mm (4½in), which will be the centre-to-centre spacing to be punch-marked on the handrail, before it is rolled to its flat curve. After rolling, and assuming that each

upright passes through a hole in the handrail, these holes will need to be drilled at the correct angle, which can be established by referring back to the triangle ABC and calculating angle A, which gives 22 degrees 3 minutes.

Like determining the length of a spiral handrail, the dimensions for the string of a spiral stair can be calculated by considering it as a parallel strip of the chosen depth, the top edge of which becomes the hypotenuse of a right-angled triangle, when the theoretical cylinder is opened out flat, as illustrated in Chapter 6. In this way, its length and angle can be determined. Spiral stairs almost certainly need to be assembled vertically, as do other curved forms of stair. This allows the plan to be set out on the ground and extended vertically with plumb-lines to meet horizontal dimensions determined by the heights of the risers.

DRILLING HOLES AT AN ANGLE

The need to drill holes at particular angles through a flat core or bottom rail, to take the tail of an upright, or fit tenons, screws or rivets, is a perennial problem in making stair balustrades. Taking the trouble to make a drilling jig can save a lot of time and frustration. The jig shown is made by drilling a hole though the end of a piece of square bar, then cutting it off at the correct angle and welding it to a piece of flat bar to provide a base-plate, which is thicker than, but of the same width as, the rail to be drilled. After welding, the hole in the jig is carefully drilled further, through its baseplate. The drilled hole in the jig is larger than the finished hole required, to allow machined steel bushes to be inserted. These are made on a lathe, one drilled with say a small pilot hole, the other with the finished drill size. These are fitted to the jig and ground off flush underneath at the appropriate angle and can be locked in place with a grub screw if necessary. If a lot

An angle drilling jig.

CONSTRUCTING A SPIRAL STAIRCASE IN PHIL JOHNSON'S WORKSHOP

Forging a pair of helical staircases for Barclay Church, Edinburgh, in Phil Johnson's workshop. These provide a new access to an existing gallery, from either side of the church. The upper part of each stair has to accommodate a complex series of steps and angles as it passes through the raked floor of the gallery.

ABOVE: *The string for the upper part of the stair and landing, held on temporary supports over a plan drawing, laid out on the workshop floor. A lower stair is visible in the background. (Photo: P. Johnson & Company)*

ABOVE: *The upper-stair string, with uprights for the balustrade, and the core rail being fitted. The other lower stair is in the background, on its own temporary supports. (Photo: P. Johnson & Company)*

ABOVE: *Hot bending the inner string for the lower stair, over a former. Note the dashed lines on the former to mark the line of the spiral. (Photo: P. Johnson & Company)*

RIGHT: *Fitting the forged infill of the balustrade to the upper string. Both lower stairs are visible in the background, above the timber rail. (Photo: P. Johnson & Company)*

ABOVE: The finished upper stair, showing the balustrade and handrail formed in relation to the raked gallery floor. (Photo: Lloyd Smith)

LEFT: The finished lower section of the stair installed in a timber well in the church. (Photo: Lloyd Smith)

of holes are needed, it is worth machining the bushes in carbon steel and hardening them to avoid wear. Even using carbon steel without hardening increases their useful life. An accurate centreline can be scribed on the side of the jig to register with marks scribed on the rail to be drilled, when the jig is clamped in place. Since the jig locates the drill and prevents it kicking sideways, the end of the drill can be ground to whatever is the necessary cutting angle to drill the hole. The drill may even be given a flat end, with two sharp edges like a two-flute milling cutter, so that its edge bites first. Bushes may seem like an unnecessary refinement, but they do take care of the wear problem and allow holes of different diameters to be drilled, for example, for tapping and clearance holes and to fit a round bar.

Regulations
(See the table of handrail regulations in Chapter 6.)
Building Regulations 2000: Approved Document K. Protection from falling, collision and impact.
Building Regulations 2000: Approved Document M. Access to and use of buildings.
BS 8300: 2001 Design of buildings and their approaches to meet the needs of disabled people – Code of Practice
BS 6399: 1996 Loading for buildings. Part 1 Code of practice for dead and imposed loads. Buried in this is a table showing the minimum horizontal loads that a parapet, barrier or balustrade is expected to be able to resist.
BS 6180: 1999 Barriers in and about buildings. Code of practice.

8 RAILINGS AND FENCES

Railings and fences sound far less glamorous than balustrades, but since they are all barriers, they may look very similar. For the purposes of this book, I am defining railings and fences as barriers that provide a boundary or divide areas of land, while balustrades guard a drop. This distinction is important. Since balustrades are often situated in or about a building, they are subject to *Building Regulations* in Britain, which, amongst other things, call for barriers guarding a drop to be constructed at specified minimum heights and with bars spaced to prevent children being 'held fast', as they quaintly put it. Where they are remote from buildings, railings and fences are technically not subject to *Building Regulations*, which allows more freedom in their design. However, if at some point a fence does guard a drop, regard should be paid to *Building Regulations*.

There is no dictionary difference between a railing and a fence, although it seems to me that the word 'railing' has something of an urban ring to it, fronting grandly terraced houses and surrounding parks and gardens in city squares. A 'fence' sounds somehow more rural; a barrier round a field. Whether railing or fence, historically ironwork has fulfilled both purposes, keeping people out and sheep in. Ironically having tried to make this distinction, the most common type of iron livestock fencing to be seen all over Britain, probably since the eighteenth century, is commonly referred to as 'estate railing'.

DESIGN CONSIDERATIONS

Balustrades in or around buildings are either designed to fit the specific angle of a stair or the horizontal top of a wall, a landing or floor. Fences and railings may similarly be required to fit to the horizontal surfaces of a wall or coping, but may also need to accommodate the varying angles of land surfaces. A rigid rectangular panel railing or fencing system can only accommodate itself to sloping ground by stepping the panels where they meet the posts,

OPPOSITE PAGE: Gate and railings by Alan Evans, at the Public Record Office Kew, London. The substantial and imposing metalwork provides a fitting entrance to the institution, which houses the nation's military and civil archives. The tall 'post' structure derives its form from images of ships' masts and notched wooden 'tally sticks', which were used for keeping accounts. (Photo: Alan Evans)

Estate railings by Terry Clark. These have a galvanized finish and some extended posts to carry two strands of wire. Note the curve of the railings and the small wedge securing the rail through the post in the foreground. (Photo: Terry Clark)

Alternative approaches to fitting railings on sloping ground.

Stepped down a slope

Surveyed and made individually to fit the slope, or 'self-adjusting railings'.

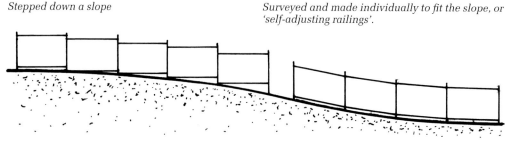

Panel and post railings

Estate railings
Continuous bar construction conforming to the slope

BJB self-adjusting railing construction.

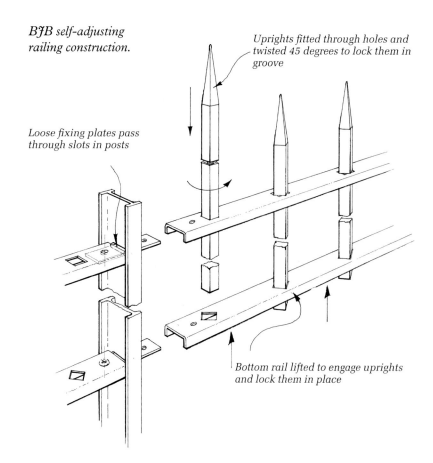

Uprights fitted through holes and twisted 45 degrees to lock them in groove

Loose fixing plates pass through slots in posts

Bottom rail lifted to engage uprights and lock them in place

or by making special panels to match the ground angle. But, if flexibility is built into the joints of the panel itself, a rectangle can be distorted into a parallelogram, to conform to the ground angle and, if the bars of the panel are light enough, they can also bend a little to provide a curve on plan.

Estate railings do just this. They are constructed from long lengths of flat bar horizontal rails, with a top rail of round bar, or occasionally of square bar, set 'on the arris', all passing though holes and slots punched in flat bar posts. These posts normally have wide, double-pronged feet, which are simply driven into soft ground. The construction is such that the rails slide freely through their holes and are connected at a joiner post, which has double-width slots for the flat bars, allowing them to overlap side by side, engaging notches at the bottom edge of each rail and securing them with wedges at their top edge. The top round bars are similarly connected at the joiner post, butting together though a tubular socket, to be secured by screws or pins. Once erected, the railing snakes smoothly over the contours of the landscape with no obvious joints. Heavier posts are only needed at corners and gateways. Due to their 'dry' construction, components can be delivered to the middle of a field, as a compact bundle of rails and posts, to be assembled on site. This feature doubtless originated in the days of horse and wagon transport, but offers a lesson in economical transport today.

Similar in its ability to accommodate sloping ground, but of a more conventional upright, 'railing' appearance, was a 'self-adjusting railing' system made in Britain by the Wolverhampton firm of Bayliss Jones and Bayliss, now gone. This was produced in large quantities during the late-Victorian period and was still listed in their 1938 catalogue. It used simple pointed or spear-headed, square bar uprights passing though channel section rails, top and bottom, which are screwed to loose brackets passing though slots in 'I' section posts. Square holes are punched through the top rail, aligned with its axis, while the corresponding holes in the bottom rail are set on the arris, at 45 degrees. To assemble these panels, a top rail is fitted between two posts and all the uprights are passed down through it, leaving perhaps 150mm (6in) projecting. At this point the square upright has notches across its corners, so that it can be twisted 45° in the square hole, locking it to the top rail and allowing the lower ends of all the uprights to enter the holes in the bottom rail, which is lifted into place and screwed to the posts at either end. Once the uprights are located in this position, they can no longer be withdrawn but they will allow some vertical movement, so that the panel can become a parallelogram, hinging on the loose fixings through the posts. This type of railing was also designed to be delivered as bundles of components for assembly on site.

I mention these two designs, because it seems to me they offer an important lesson in providing a simple, adjustable barrier, using concepts that side-step the need for meticulous surveying and a conventionally rigid structure. Neither of them is the most exciting railing you ever saw – although estate railings do have a certain rural charm and elegance – but the design thinking behind them provides food for thought. The conventional black-smithing approach tends to assume a need for heavy, forged components, assembled in accurate, flat and rigid panels, supported by substantial posts. In a sense, the dead weight of the material in each panel calls for more structure to support it; so, like a bridge, a good part of the metalwork serves to support the rest of it. Lightness is not normally considered a major virtue in forged architectural metalwork, but there is an appealing structural economy in both these systems, which against a background of rising steel prices might suggest a new kind of design challenge.

Light and delicate 'dancing' railings at Swindon Dance Theatre, by Avril Wilson. These qualify as a railing rather than a balustrade by the clever expedient of including a flower bed within the overall design, just below the entrance level. On a sloping site, this reduced the immediate drop to below the dimension which would have called for the balustrade regulation to be applied, requiring bars to be spaced to prevent a 100mm sphere passing through. Fixed by Richard Quinnell Ltd.

ABOVE: *Post and panel railings by the author, fronting the National Youth Theatre of Great Britain building, Holloway Road, London. The large inverted U-shape posts echo the round arched facade of the building.*

ABOVE RIGHT: *An apparently continuous, zig-zag railing, with an intriguing moiré effect, in Newarke pedestrian subway, Leicester. Designed and made by Alan Evans, to complement a mosaic mural by Sue Ridge, the railing serves to provide a screen, preventing an attacker from lurking out of sight of people emerging from the subway. (Photo: Radovan Specak)*

Pattern and Function

These historic systems also illustrate the fundamental design choice of considering an apparently continuous railing without obvious joints or a pattern of panels and posts. Visually, the first provides the effect of a continuous ribbon, while the second can exploit the rhythm of repeating units. More than most other kinds of architectural metalwork, railings and fences can be very large features, operating at a landscape scale of size, where their design may be seen at a distance, essentially as a pattern or texture. The implication of this is that it is crucial for the design to be considered in its totality – as a string of repeating units. Designing a beautiful panel and assuming it will work in repeat, may miss the point that just as the panels repeat, so do their posts and joints, all of which contribute to the overall appearance. The design of the individual panel should be judged by its visual effect in context.

It is also an important design concern to establish what purpose the railings are intended to serve, in their particular situation. They may be there physically to prevent people gaining access or to be purely decorative. Estate railings can easily be climbed by people, but provide an effective barrier against livestock. Some railings – those, for example, with plain vertical uprights, traditionally used around urban public parks and gardens – are very hard to climb and form a physical barrier. Others, by virtue of their height or design are more symbolic, and may serve to indicate a boundary rather than to prevent people entering. Some public parks use two semi-circular loops of thin steel bar, no more than 600mm (24in) high, simply pushed into the turf at the corners of paths to deter people from taking a short cut and wearing out the grass. Not exactly a fence or railing, but a small metal message saying 'keep off', and an example of just how minimal an effective barrier can be.

Like the balustrading inside a building, fences and railings outside can also provide a level of detail and a decorative value that contrasts with the solidity of the building or the enormity of the landscape. They are there to mark a boundary but in doing so they can say something about the place, enhance the landscape, make an impression or just provide a decorative flourish.

Rigidity

The length of a railing or fence panel – or a balustrade – is both a visual and an engineering concern. From a structural point of view it is a decision based on the vertical rigidity of the panel. Is it likely to sag? Continuous fences, of the 'estate railing' type are made in long lengths, typically 4.5m (15ft) but are constructed with supporting posts at 900mm (3ft) intervals. Continuous railings, where every upright is leaded or grouted into the foundation, are totally supported. So in these cases, sagging is not an issue.

However, conventional post and panel railings may indeed sag and are often given some intermediate support or supports, underneath the bottom rail. The need for

this is a matter of proportion – the ratio between the height and length of the panel. Balustrade, railing and fence panels tend to be considerably longer than their height. Considered as a piece of structural engineering, a railing panel is a truss; a deep beam suspended at both ends from supports. But the ubiquitous, plain railing with vertical bars passing through flat top and bottom horizontal rails is not a good truss and, as a conventional form of construction, owes more to convenience than to structural efficiency. Within limits it works well enough, although even if every upright is tenoned, and riveted or welded, it will sag if made a little too long, because the rails will bend. The orientation of the flat top and bottom rails would suggest that the

A fun departure from spear railing finials, which just shows the trouble you need to go to, to keep London folk out of the rhododendrons. A railing by Shelley Thomas. The uprights are all grouted into a groove in the coping. (Photo: Shelley Thomas)

panel is primarily designed to take a sideways load, yet most of the time the main stress on the railing is its own weight. (Lay a panel flat, support the two ends, and it will resist sagging better than when upright.) If this were a bridge truss, it would consist of top and bottom horizontals linked by a number of verticals and

LEFT: Not a conventional railing. An exuberant railing feature in a new housing development by Steve Lunn. (Photo: Steve Lunn)

diagonals, creating a series of triangles. The bars forming each triangle are either in tension or compression, and are not subject to bending like the railing panel. The implication is that any diagonal introduced into the design will dramatically reduce the tendency of a panel to sag. A straight diagonal bar or two, like those in a farm gate, could, for a given height, conceivably double the practical length of a railing panel. Railings do, of course, also need to be able to resist sideways loads. The combination of the traditional flat top and bottom rail with round or square uprights, plus diagonal bracing bars would come closer to meeting these structural demands.

Presumably for reasons of aesthetics rather than engineering, structural diagonal bars have never been a common feature of historic forged metalwork, and are seldom found in contemporary blacksmithing. Decorative elements within the design of a panel are often employed which, through their cumulative effect, provide diagonal bracing, and these can make a crucial difference to the panel as a structure. The patterns of scrolls in traditional ironwork are often cited as an example. But for some reason, overt diagonals are rare. It is as if,

even early in the development of architectural metalwork, it was thought that ironwork for buildings demanded a horizontal and vertical emphasis, whose drama would be spoilt by diagonals. As a result we rely to a great extent on the fit of mortise and tenon, riveted or welded joints.

As well as for reasons of strength, the length of a railing panel for a particular situation is also determined by a convenient division of the total length to be covered, how the panel looks in that proportion, a practical length to be transported and other factors of this kind. In an open-ended situation, there may be some leeway in the total length of a run of railings. But where they are confined at each end, between walls, for example, some form of adjustment is necessary to avoid an accumulation of tolerances building up to a point where they will not fit. The most obvious way is to allow for some packing at all, or some, of the joints between panels, or even to allow for adjustment simply at the ends of the run where fixings enter the wall. Using simple expedients, like oversized or slotted holes, can add up to a small but significant range of adjustment.

Loads on railing panels.
A. Railing panel held rigid between posts;
B. The panel should not sag;
C. The panel should not bend sideways;
D. A panel can be allowed to twist since the posts will hold it straight as in A;
E. The panel considered as a truss; diagonal bracing prevents sagging in a panel twice the original length.

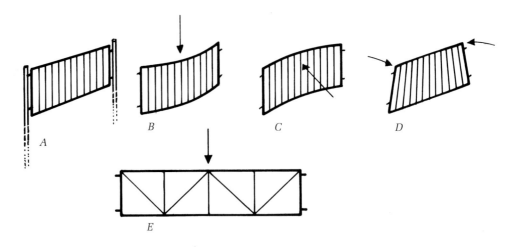

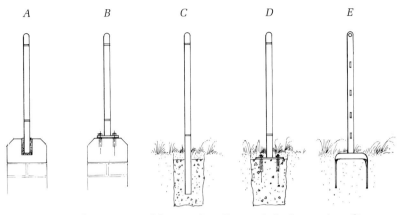

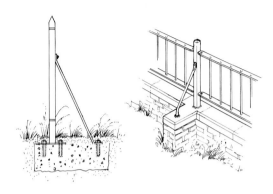

Fixing posts: A. post grouted into coping; B. post bolted to coping; C. post set in concrete; D. post bolted to concrete foundation block; E. 'estate railing' post – twisted and pointed flat bar prongs pushed into ground.

Backstays. LEFT: Typical post with backstay. RIGHT: Wall-mounted railing with backstay fixed into a short buttress.

Backstays

Since railings and fences are often employed in long, straight runs, they are very dependent on the solidity of their supporting posts. The strength of the whole railing is only as good as the foundation provided and the lateral stability of the fixings. This suggests that railing panels themselves do not necessarily need to resist twisting. So long as they can support rather more than their own weight without sagging, and do not deflect sideways when pushed by people or animals, the fact that as loose panels they may be flexible hardly matters if the posts are rigid. Once fixed, the posts prevent the panels twisting. To ensure the stability of posts, backstays are often required at intervals along a straight run of railing. These may be no more than an angled bar, bracing the post to a foundation, creating a rigid triangular frame. Ornamental curved bars have been used traditionally, or the backstay may be elaborated into a structure such as narrow decorative screen or a lighting column. Seventeenth- and eighteenth-century railings were often fitted on low walls, which were built with small brick or masonry buttresses to provide anchoring points for backstays. This kind of design detail always seems to me to be preferable to

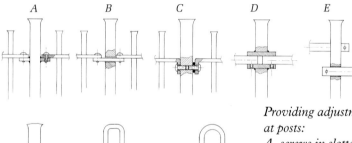

allowing the backstay to vanish into the grass, where it is doubtless bedded securely in stone or concrete, but has the look of an afterthought.

Installation

Fences or railings are usually fixed by 'self jigging', using the panel to determine the position of the next post. A string line is laid out in open ground, or a line marked on the wall or coping, and the first post and panel are set up along the line, propped in position and the next post bolted to, or located against, the panel so that its fixing holes or position can be marked, ready for drilling. With straight

Providing adjustment at posts: A. screws in slotted holes; B. loose fixing plate through post; C. packing washer in joint; D. round rails locate through a sleeve, secured by grub screws; E. round rails, stepping at post and secured by stainless steel pins; F. round rail through hole punched in heavy bar post, secured by grub screws; G. U-shaped post with round rail secured by pins; H. U-shaped post with round rail secured by screwed end caps.

Railings in Fareham, Hampshire; an item in a range of street furniture by Charles Normandale. Note the expressive wrap-over joint at the top of the post, secured by a bronze strap. The railings were forged in wrought iron, as part of an ambitious millennium project in the town to celebrate the life of Henry Cort, who developed new methods for producing and rolling wrought iron there, two hundred years earlier. (Photo: Charles Normandale)

A neat and striking car park railing at the Grace Barrand Design Centre, Surrey, by Terry Clark. (Photo: Terry Clark)

lengths of railing, placing a post or marker at either end of the run can allow the line to be sighted directly, as each post is positioned. A new panel is attached to the previous one and the process repeated. The design of the post and its fixing depends on the situation. Posts can be provided with base-plates or flanges, allowing them to be bolted into concrete or masonry, or they can terminate as a plain bar foot and be directly grouted in place. It may be thought that for this kind of fixing the end of the post should 'ragged', by punching, cutting, spreading or twisting the metal to provide a better key into the grout material. But since the dead weight of the structure holds it down, it would need a considerable force to pull the post upwards, so unless the railing is very light, it is unlikely that this kind of detail serves any very useful purpose.

On open ground, posts can be set into concrete, digging holes at each position, packing up the panels to take the weight and pouring in concrete, in much the same way that timber fences are installed. Little if any adjustment needs to be built into the design of railings fitted in this way. Each post can be bolted tight to the previous panel, and the post adjusted up to level, before pouring the concrete. However, this advantage is somewhat offset by the need to allow time for the concrete to cure, which is likely to require another visit to the site, a day or two later, to remove temporary packing or bracing. Posts with base-plates that are bolted into place may well require packing pieces under the plates to adjust their heights. If these are subsequently buried under earth or masonry, the appearance hardly matters.

But if they are going to be visible, it is important to ensure that, as far as possible, the surface they are fitted to has been laid to an accurate level. If there is a discrepancy – and there usually is – determining the difference between the highest and the lowest point will provide a measurement that it may be possible to share out amongst a number of posts. In this way a small disparity in height might be accommodated by having oversize holes fixing the panels to the posts. Where this is not enough, and packing pieces or washers are needed under the posts, the resulting gap should be pointed with mortar or grouted up with a dry mortar mix, both for rigidity and appearance.

In some situations, it may be preferable to lay out the post positions along a line and fix them before attaching the panels. This demands a high level of accuracy, both in making the metalwork and placing the posts. Making the panels on an assembly jig in the workshop and using a spacing jig to set out the posts on site is essential. The spacing jig is crucial, being in effect a dummy panel. It seems to me that the one

advantage of adopting this kind of method is to avoid the heavy lifting and temporary packing that are usually required when using the next panel to position the next post. The heavier the panel, the more worthwhile it may be.

Regulations
BS 1722 Fences, includes twelve separate parts, of which only a few are relevant.
BS 1722-8: 1997 Mild steel (low carbon steel) continuous bar fences and hurdles. This details the kind of traditional flat bar railing, often described as 'estate' or 'country house' railing, designed to keep in livestock.
BS 1722-9: 2000 Mild steel (low carbon steel) fences with round or square verticals and flat horizontals. This covers the design of fences with plain individual uprights and with round bar, bow topped uprights, looped in pairs. Tables give recommended bar sizes for a wide range of panel widths and heights, intermediate supports, post sizes and so on.
BS 1722-12: 1999 Steel palisade fences. Covers the design of security fencing made from rolled or formed steel strip uprights.

Railings by Alan Evans at Quaggy Park, Lewisham, London. What seem at first sight to be straightforward post and panel railings, turn out to be hung dramatically from their split posts. (Photo: Alan Evans)

9 SCREENS AND GRILLES

Screens and grilles are usually fitted to openings in buildings to provide some level of privacy or security. A screen suggests a structure with an essentially visual purpose, a decorative way of restricting a view; while the word grille implies a physical barrier, required for reasons of safety or security. Screens may be fitted outside buildings for largely decorative reasons, or may be used inside to divide one area from another, to allow a view through or to provide daylight. Like foliage in a garden, they can give a feeling of privacy while still offering a view and the sense of a larger space. Grilles are fitted to windows, to glazed doors and ventilation openings, over voids in buildings and to guard a drop. At each extreme it is possible to label the metalwork as a screen or grille by its specific function, but there is a middle ground where the terms may be interchangeable and where, in practice, they are both likely to involve security and decoration in differing proportions.

In many parts of Europe, doubtless because of the warmer climates, there is a historic tradition of external window grilles, both for public buildings and for dwellings. You can sleep peacefully at night in your house in Spain, Italy or southern France with the windows wide open and not worry about intruders. Although window grilles are not unfamiliar in Britain and can be seen on Victorian city buildings, they have never been adopted to any great extent domestically and are very rarely seen on contemporary houses. There does seem to be an odd contradiction in one thriving industry supplying domestic alarm systems and security locks

OPPOSITE PAGE:
Vernacular ironwork, a strikingly simple grille over a door in Mende, Lozère, France.

Strikingly powerful entrance grille by Alan Evans, above the door of Cheltenham Museum and Art Gallery, Cheltenham, Gloucestershire; designed in response to the arts and crafts movement content of the museum and the facade by Sir Hugh Casson. (Photo: Alan Evans)

for windows and doors, while another is busy fitting large, vulnerable windows. The British seem to have an aversion to securing their houses with window grilles, perhaps because we value what little light we get. Thinking about this, the only window grilles I have ever made for a house were decorative but intended for security, fitted internally, and designed so that when the owner was in residence they could be easily removed. Much of their use on public or commercial buildings in Britain seems to be motivated by reasons of security, and even there, grilles are inclined to be fitted only at the back of the premises, where visual concerns are largely ignored.

DESIGN CONSIDERATIONS

Security

The challenge of designing a security grille for a window, is to make it secure without giving the client the feeling they are living in a prison. For strength and rigidity, vertical and horizontal bars do need to support each other at fairly close intervals, but are probably better arranged in anything but a regular grid pattern. It is important to consider whether the grille is expected to simply deter an intruder, or whether it is intended to physically prevent access. Even if an external grille has exposed fixings, so long as these are not wing nuts, it is at the very least going to slow down an intruder. On the same basis, slender bars well supported by frequent intersections can provide a worthwhile barrier, without shutting out too much light or appearing too intimidating from inside. Security grilles can be fitted inside or outside a window and in either case may be directly grouted or bolted into the window reveal; or they can be fixed to the internal or external face of the wall. For external grilles, more security is provided (crudely)

by burring over threads or by using special nuts or bolts (*see* Chapter 12) or, for internal grilles, by placing fixings well back from the window opening, where they cannot be reached from outside if the window glass has been broken.

Perhaps the most effective answer, where this is possible, is to grout fixings directly into the window reveals. Like insurance, considering the requirements of a truly burglar-proof grille has ultimately to be a balance between risk and expense. The risk is a function of the weakest link. There is little point in designing a heavy, all riveted, stainless steel grille if the whole thing can be levered off the wall with a crowbar, but equally fixing with expensive security bolts is a wasted exercise if the bars of the grille can be stretched apart with a car jack. Plain, parallel bars need to be tied at frequent intervals. Almost by definition, a window grille has the great structural advantage that it can be fixed at the top and bottom as well as both sides, which can make even a fairly basic piece of grille work a very difficult barrier to breach.

Visual Concerns

It is worth remembering that, of all kinds of architectural metalwork, grilles are the

Hyper Realism by Brian Russell. An impressively forged and painted steel grille and stainless steel nameplate, replacing an unused gate in the garden wall of a private house. (Photo: Brian Russell)

most likely to completely fill their allotted architectural space, like a picture in a frame. While the ribbon-like format of a railing, fence or balustrade tends to lead to a design approach of repeated elements, the singularity of a grille – and indeed a gate – suggests the need for a more self-contained design statement.

From the outside of a building, an internal window grille may hardly be visible; the framing of the windows and reflections from the glass are likely to obscure it. From inside a building, both internal and external grilles usually appear as a dark silhouette against the light. The design significance of this is that, while an external grille will be seen and appreciated as part of the architecture of the building, a grille inside the window belongs to the room. It becomes

an interior design element. Like it or not, if a grille is silhouetted against the daylight, it means that a great deal of its surface detail and subtlety will be lost; so the design will be seen, and should perhaps be considered primarily, as a pattern of flat profiles, like the leading in a stained-glass window. The effect of artificial light inside the room illuminating the grille and revealing more detail is a bonus. If the glazing is divided into small panes, the window frames too will be silhouetted, so it may well be appropriate to follow the geometry of the glazing, using it as a grid over which to plan the design of the metalwork.

Screens in European cathedrals were traditionally designed to divide the chancel from the nave and mark the boundary of smaller dedicated chapels, offering

Screens and gates in the crypt of Rochester Cathedral, elegantly simple in appearance but complex in structure. Part of a scheme by Charles Normandale, forged in steel and bronze, with timber framing and glazed throughout. (Photo: Charles Normandale)

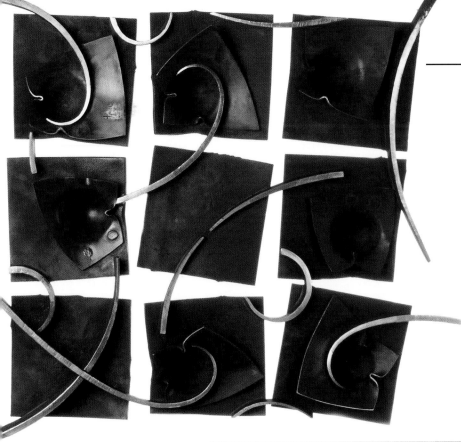

ABOVE: *A beautifully detailed, decorative interior grille by Gunvor Anhøj. Forged, hot cut and pressed, with a rusted and waxed finish; a creative exploration of a technique. (Photo: Gunvor Anhøj)*

RIGHT: *The fish are still alive in this screen by Elspeth Bennie, which provides an overthrow sign for a close off the Royal Mile, in Edinburgh, where the fish market used to be. The design has a touch of whimsy and its delicate construction contrasts effectively with the heavy masonry of the architecture.*

some privacy and separation, while preserving the sense of one whole space. Despite the transparency of many cathedral screens, the eye is caught by the detail and intricacy of the metalwork and a feeling of enclosure is created by what often amounts to a few lines in the air. This is what ironwork can do so well.

Sacred or secular, screens in buildings serve to separate functions within a space, define where you may go and where you may not, provide richness, decoration and texture, while allowing a view through. Glimpsing other parts of the building through the spaces in a beautiful piece of metalwork is somehow an

ABOVE: Part of a simple and neat garden feature by Paul Margetts, comprising two screens and a matching gate. This is a screen arresting the eye but encouraging a view through. (Photo: Paul Margetts)

*TOP LEFT: A screen? Some pieces of work defy categorizing. This could be called a balustrade, barrier, indoor fence or even a railing, but its function is to screen diners from a walkway in the Bar Estilo in Birmingham. A characteristically gestural and tactile work by Shelley Thomas. Steel with a lacquered and waxed finish.
(Photo: Shelley Thomas)*

*BOTTOM LEFT: One of several almost minimal, but highly effective window grilles on a newly refurbished office building in Cardiff, by Andrew Rowe. Since the offices contain a great deal of documentation, the design is based on the idea of lever arch files and ring binders. It uses 25mm and 30mm diameter round bars, zinc sprayed and finished with micaceous iron oxide paint.
(Photo: Andy Rowe)*

entirely different experience from just looking.

External screens can fulfil another role, becoming almost literally 'jewellery for buildings', providing embellishment, a visual focus or architectural feature as part of the facade of a building, serving perhaps to highlight the entrance. Although the notion of public art is widespread in Britain, these kind of grilles are a rare example of a piece of architectural metalwork that has effectively no utilitarian purpose and is almost entirely aesthetic in its objectives.

The illustrations above show a range of design approaches and applications for a diversity of screens and grilles.

Fitting a grille to be grouted in:
A. inserting tails in the holes on one side;
B. pushing tails home until those on the other side clear the reveal;
C. centralizing the grille in the opening.

Methods of fixing window grilles.

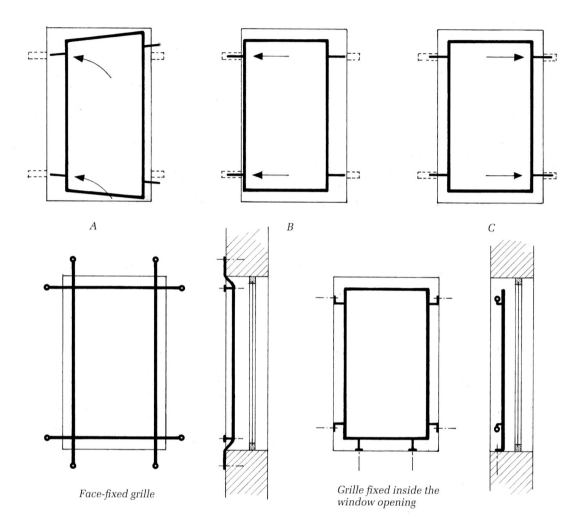

A

B

C

Face-fixed grille

Grille fixed inside the window opening

Fixing

As mentioned above, the options for fixing grilles in windows or other openings are either to grout tails into the reveals or to bolt to the reveals on the inside or outside face of the wall; these considerations apply to any grille. Inside a building, transporting the metalwork to its site and lifting it into place can present problems (*see* Chapter 12). If the grille is to be face fixed, it will need to be offered up and held against the window opening, either propped on trestles or hung from a portable crane or pulley block, while fixings are drilled or

marked. Face fixing means that the vertical load – the weight of the metalwork – becomes a shearing load on the fixings. As long as the masonry is sound and there are enough fixings, this is fine. Alternatively, much of the load can be transferred directly to the sill of the window if the grille is designed fit into the depth of the reveal and sit on the sill. The fixing brackets or tails can still be brought out on to the face if required, but they only need to hold the grille in its vertical position, causing far less stress on the fixings. Screw or bolt fixing the grille inside the reveal means that the grille can be designed to sit directly on its lower fixings, simplifying the problem of holding it in place, while holes are marked or drilled.

Grouting the metalwork into the reveals may similarly call for some mechanical lifting if the grille is too heavy to manipulate by hand. The grille must again be offered into place against the face of the window opening, while the tail positions are carefully transferred on to the reveals with a square or spirit-level. If there are not many tails, it may be easier to plot the positions by measurement or make a fixing template to locate them. The holes can then be drilled and cut to shape with a chisel, if necessary, one side being twice the depth of the other. This allows the grille to be eased into position, one set of tails engaging in their holes at an angle, until the tails on the other side clear the window reveal, allowing them to be lined up and the grille pushed into place. The metalwork can then be centralized in its space, wedged level and grouted in.

Security grille in the Oxfordshire Museum, Woodstock, by the author. Forged from 20mm square mild steel bar, with a continuous frame to meet the specifications of the Museums, Libraries and Archives Council. The grille is secured to the wall with resin anchor studs and special bronze nuts, but its weight is carried by the window sill.

Regulations

Surprisingly, for a building component whose performance in use is critically important, there seem to be no *British Standards* relating to security grilles. In a particular situation, where the purpose of a window grille is primarily for security, some insurance companies may well require that specific design criteria be met before insuring particularly valuable goods, such as antiques or works of art. But I have not been able to find any general insurance recommendations for the design of security grilles. The only specifications I know of in Britain – and, as it happens, have worked to – are published by the Museums, Libraries and Archives Council, a government body. These comprise some general specifications for 'Decorative Wrought Iron Grilles', 'Internal Window Bars' and 'Internal Window Grilles' and can be downloaded from their website at www.mla.gov.uk/information. These are basic, common-sense specifications for the minimum size of bars, spacing bars with no gaps greater than 100mm (4in), not using bolts or screws in the construction, and a recommendation that bars and grilles should be grouted into window reveals, if at all possible.

If a grille provides guarding where there is a drop, the *Building Regulations* will apply. For example, it must not be possible to pass a 100mm (4in) diameter sphere through any gap in the structure. But if a grille is required in a window or other opening above a drop, whether the regulations apply will depend on the height of the lower edge of the opening. *Building Regulations* call for guarding up to a minimum height of 900mm (35½in) or 1,100mm (39in) depending on the situation. If the sill is above this regulation height, guarding is already provided by the wall below the window. It follows that if the sill is lower, the guarding regulation only needs to apply up to that height.

10 GATES

If television advertisements are to be believed and certain German car engineers really do spend time developing a car door that closes with an authoritative 'clunk', then similar concerns must reside in the gate. Even if they do not, the fact remains that we gain significant impressions of quality in this way. Feeling the inertia of the gate and hearing the latch dropping solidly home, provides a fleeting but significant experience.

There is a great deal of symbolic importance invested in the idea of a gate. Push the latch, open the gate and you are somewhere else. The gate is the threshold to another world, either real or imaginary. The pearly gates are a familiar image or, as Joel Chandler Harris says, in *Uncle Remus* – in plain English – 'How many poor sinners will be caught out late, and find no latch to the golden gate?'.

The great country house gates at the beginning of the eighteenth century were not designed and made simply to keep the sheep in and the peasants out. They fulfilled a far more powerful symbolic function, expressed by the hymn 'The rich man in his castle, the poor man at his gate'. The fact that gates were very often considerably taller than the railings at either side, suggests that their ceremonial importance outweighed simple concerns for security. These gates carried a message. They were there as a visible sign of the status, authority, wealth, education and good taste of the owner. They might be wonderfully decorative but, nevertheless, put even a very discerning peasant firmly in his place.

Perhaps less overtly, gates convey a similar message today. They are still sometimes taller than the adjacent walls or railings, and a pair of gates may also be taller at the centre – where the two leaves meet – than they are at the hinges. This is a feature that defies the logic of both structure and security – nobody would attempt to climb a gate in the middle anyway – but, crucially, it does provide significant visual drama. Much as they might want to suggest impregnability, gates are seldom impossible to climb and are, in any case, often unlocked or are unlockable. Their primary purpose is not so much security as a statement of ownership. They are the threshold that divides public space from private space. On the face of it, a gate is just a movable piece of railing or fence, but, invariably, it is more elaborate and more

OPPOSITE PAGE: Detail of gates at Worcester Cathedral, by Paul Margetts. (Photo: Paul Margetts)

Gates for a private house by Bill Cordaroy. A contemporary design interpreting traditional themes, such as the raised profile at the centre and an echo of 'dog bars' in the pattern of wide flat bars at the bottom. (Photo: Bill Cordaroy)

'There is no reason why a gate cannot be welcoming, friendly, or amusing'. A gate and fence for a private house by Shelley Thomas. (Photo: Shelley Thomas)

decorative. It is there to flag the entrance and attract attention by creating a focal point in the architecture of the wall, fence or hedge.

The message need not only be one of power and authority. The design may reflect the concerns and interests of the owner, or make reference to the function or architecture of the building. Arriving as a visitor, the gate is our first point of contact, so the impression it creates is important. There is no reason why a gate cannot be welcoming, friendly or amusing – say 'hello' rather than 'keep out'. For all these reasons, gates provide blacksmiths with a significant aesthetic design challenge, alongside the structural and engineering demands of pivoting a piece of metalwork.

DESIGN CONSIDERATIONS

The purpose of a gate and the reasons for commissioning it, raise a number of questions. Is it, for example, required for largely decorative reasons? Or for security? Should it be a single gate or a pair? Does it need physically to prevent children or animals from climbing over or squeezing through the bars? How tall should it be? Which way should it open? Should it open both ways? How often is it opened? Does it need to be locked? Is it likely to be left open for much of the time? And so on. These questions need an answer, because they relate to genuine concerns the client may have, but they need thinking through. Is the dog really let loose in the front garden? How big is the dog anyway? The same questions apply to the children.

Clients often warm to the idea of security and like to think that their vehicle gates will be locked, but frequently leave them wide open. This is not a criticism but an observation, which points to the need for discussion to resolve these kind of issues. If, for example, gates are normally left open, they will probably need a drop bolt or latch to hold them there, and it may well be better to design them to look interesting in that position, if that is how they will mostly be seen.

Surveying the site is particularly important, because it is possible to overlook factors that physically limit the swing of the gate. A fall in the ground across or though a gateway can give rise to a number of problems. It may not be possible to allow the gate to swing, as it were, uphill, unless it has a considerable clearance underneath, which could of course conflict with the need to stop the dog escaping. Gates usually open inwards, swinging into the property to which they belong. If an outward opening gate would foul a path, pavement or roadway, there is really no alternative. But in other situations there may be advantages in opening gates outwards, or allowing them to swing both ways. Opening outwards might be the answer to the problem of the sloping driveway, while on level ground the facility to swing a gate both ways can help vehicle access, particularly if the approach through the gateway is at an angle.

There was a prevailing tradition in Britain in the eighteenth century, for gates to have short intermediate, vertical bars at the bottom called 'dog-bars'. These would indeed prevent the odd Jack Russell from making a break for liberty, but also had the visual effect of creating a pattern of bars that is more rhythmically dense at the bottom. As a design strategy, this kind of emphasis has continued, and in some gates today, the spacing of elements is tighter at the bottom than the top. Whether dogs are the reason or not, this does provide the

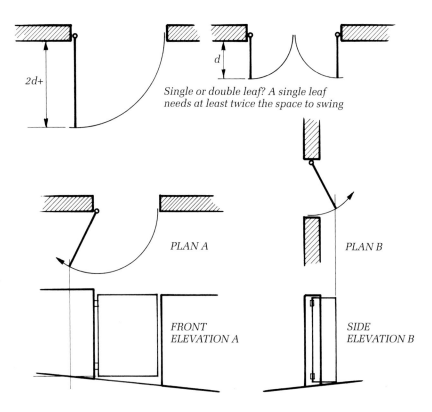

Single or double leaf? A single leaf needs at least twice the space to swing

Crucial concerns. Consider both the plan and elevation of the gate: A. the ground slopes across the opening; B. it slopes through the opening. In both cases the gate will jam at the point shown.

Consider the swing of the gate. Will it foul mouldings or copings above the gate? At the position shown, the gate frame will hit the stone coping. A gate profiled to fit deep in an arch will hardly open at all – think about it.

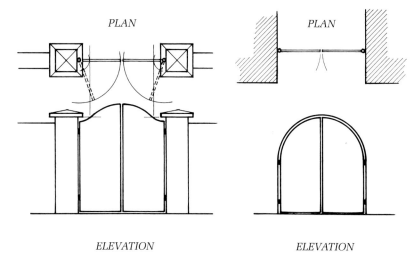

ABOVE: The Halifax
Gates at Winchester
College, by Charles
Normandale. A slender
and elegant pair of gates,
some 4m high, tall enough
for each leaf to need three
hinges. The right-hand
leaf contains another
pedestrian gate. Note the
transition at the top, where
verticals converge and
change from a round to a
pointed arch form. (Photo:
Charles Normandale)

ABOVE RIGHT: 'A picture
in a frame', Red House
Hare gate, a workshop
picture. A gate using
pictorial imagery, by Chris
Topp. (Photo: Chris Topp)

gate with a visually solid base, building upwards to a more open structure. Possibly for similar reasons, there is a European tradition of gates having not dog-bars, but an opaque band of plate at the bottom, sometimes only some 300mm (12in) high or occasionally extending almost half way up the gate to the level of the lock rail. Irrespective of its other functions, this adds to the rigidity of the structure.

A basic decision in the design of a gate is whether to adopt a frame and infill structure, or to construct the gate panel in some other way. Visually, a frame running round the edge of a gate can give it a self-contained appearance, a certain formality. If the frame is conspicuously heavier than the infill, it can also create something of the effect of a picture in a frame. The frame and the infill are perceived as separate elements. In contrast, if the gate is designed without an obvious frame, if the infill and the structure are one and the same, there is no clear visual distinction between what is structural and what is decorative. Without a distinct edge, the structure can appear lighter, more informal, perhaps more dramatic.

Structure

The traditional structure of a gate is a rectangular frame with some form of decorative infill, which braces the frame. The frame comprises two vertical bars, called 'stiles', linked by a top rail and a heel bar at the bottom, both tenoned through the stiles and riveted over at both ends. The back stile is usually square in section – the heaviest bar in the gate – and carries the hinges, the heel of the heel bar fits to it, while the thinner, flat bar front stile carries the latch. Intriguingly, this usage of the word 'stile' is not employed in any other context in the English language, and derives from the Dutch word *stijl* meaning a post. Depending on the size of the gate, its infill is often divided into a series of horizontal bands by flat bars, through which pass uprights or between which are panels of decorative scroll work. How ever, even centuries ago, not all gates were constructed in this way. Today a wide variety of structural concepts are employed, but all with the same objective of providing a rigid panel.

Like so many other pieces of architectural metalwork, gates are essentially

panels and, on the face of it, fitting hinges at one edge is only a small departure from a balustrade or railing panel. However, the design implications of hanging a gate impose special problems on the design of the structure, because the loads on it are asymmetrical. A gate is usually only held by hinges at two points on one edge, so what must prevent it sagging and twisting is its own rigidity. In contrast, a railing panel is usually held by at least two fixing points at both ends, bracing it to the posts and preventing it twisting. As a result, the structure of a gate needs to be stiffer than a panel for a balustrade or railing.

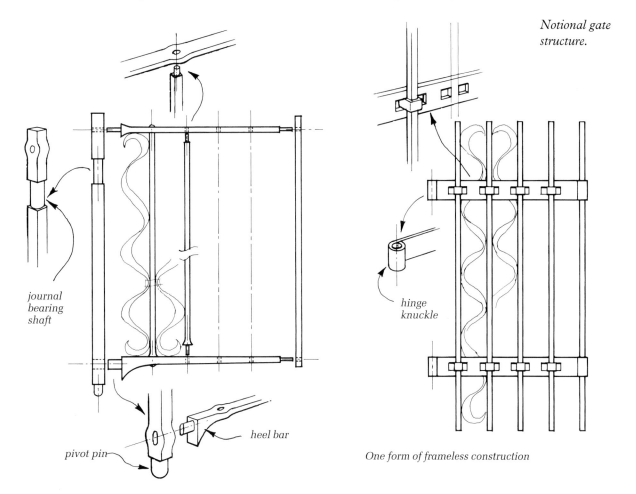

Notional gate structure.

journal
bearing
shaft

hinge
knuckle

One form of frameless construction

heel bar

pivot pin

Traditional mortise and tenon frame with infill construction

Framed or frameless? Back stile, front stile and heel bar, but no top rail. A wonderfully intricate piece of forging by Brian Russell.

Rigidity or stiffness need some consideration. A gate panel could distort in a number of ways under a load. Very often the heaviest load on a gate is its own weight, to which should be added the weight of the occasional swinging child or, on a larger gate, the weight of an adult intruder trying to climb over. (On the assumption that the intruder will climb the hinge side of the gate, the strain caused by his weight is likely to be very similar to the weight of a child swinging on the latch side.) These loads act vertically downwards, and may have two effects. If the frame is not well-braced and if the joints are not sufficiently strong, they can bend causing the gate to sag, distorting from a rectangle to a parallelogram. Or, under a heavy load, the back stile could bend between the hinges, distorting the whole frame. Very large gates are sometimes designed with three hinges on the back stile to prevent this happening.

If it is insufficiently rigid, the frame can also twist. This may be an effect produced by a swinging child but can also be apparent as the latch engages. In theory, a latch should be fitted to the front stile, operating on a line centred between the two hinges; in which case the impact of the latch hitting its stop is symmetrical and will not twist the gate. In practice, latches are, not surprisingly, placed where they are at a convenient height for a human being to operate; so, irrespective of the height of the gate, the latch tends to remain at the same level. As a result, if a gate is fairly heavy and its latch is substantially off the centreline, when the gate is slammed shut the latch will engage, but inertia causes the rest of the gate to carry on, making it kick or spring. This twisting may be entirely elastic – so it will spring back to its original flat profile – but the effect is not reassuring. If the structure is reasonably rigid, these off-centre, twisting loads will have no noticeable effect, but if the frame is unduly flexible, the whole gate can vibrate, suggesting flimsiness.

Scale

The lack of rigidity of a gate can be an effect of scale. Developing the design for a large gate from the experience of successfully making a smaller one has its pitfalls.

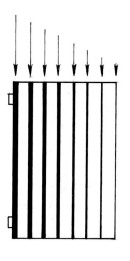

Stresses on a gate.

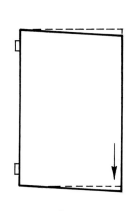

A gate can drop...

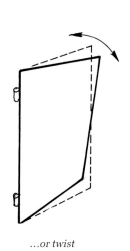

...or twist

Each succesive 'slice' of the gate must carry more weight

BELOW: A large gate, with wall-mounted hinges, in Portman Square, London, by Terry Clark. Forged with a frame, the top of which completes a circle in the semi-circular arch, the structure is a simple grid whose formality is offset by festoons of stainless steel plant forms. (Photo: Terry Clark)

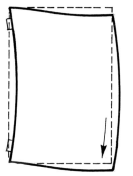

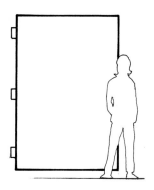

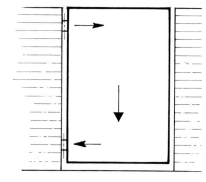

A very large, heavy gate may need a third hinge to prevent the back stile bending

The weight of a gate acts to pull on the top hinge and push on the bottom hinge

Simply scaling up every dimension of the design is not an answer. If the entire gate is doubled in size, its weight is not twice but eight times the original. A 50mm (2in) cube is twice the dimensions of a 25mm (1in) cube, but contains eight times the amount of material. Weight is a function of a linear dimension cubed. Alongside this, the strength of materials in tension or compression relates to their cross-sectional area – the thicker the bar, the stronger – which is a function of a linear dimension squared. A piece of 50mm square bar has four times the tensile strength of a piece of 25mm square bar. So, as a structure grows larger, its strength increases with the square of the size, but its weight increases with the cube. The effect is that the weight is increasing faster than the strength, until eventually the weight dominates completely, and the structure becomes too heavy to hold itself together. This is ultimately the limiting factor in determining, for example, the size to which a tree can grow or, at the other end of the scale, explains why ants are a great deal stronger in relation to their size than we are.

These effects of scale apply to any structure, but are more apparent in the design of gates because the asymmetrical stresses on the post or back stile are sufficiently high for them to become apparent. Directly enlarging a gate in this way is not in fact a very practical proposition, because the spaces between the bars would also be increased, so the dog would get out for sure. It is nevertheless important to appreciate that the relationship between small and large structures is not as direct as it might seem. The lesson is that large pieces of metal behave differently from small ones. However, this is not the whole story. The rigidity of a gate depends on an efficient structure, as well as the strength of its materials. Bending strength has a major part to play and this is as much an effect of the shape of the section as the strength of the metal. A steel rule will easily flex in one plane but is rigid in the other. Choosing the right section can be a more effective way of providing strength where it is needed, rather than simply increasing the size of a bar and incurring a weight penalty. For example, a

given length of 50mm (2in) square bar contains almost exactly the same amount of steel as a 178 × 102mm (7 × 4in) 'I' beam, but the beam – set properly on its edge – will span a far longer distance before sagging under its own weight. This is not an argument for replacing the 50mm back stile of the gate with a piece of 'I' beam, but is an illustration of the efficiency of a particular metal section, used for a particular engineering purpose.

Structural Efficiency

In Britain the anatomy of an iron gate has, at least since the eighteenth century, consisted of an arrangement of vertical and horizontal bars. The rigidity of the structure relies on the solidity of numbers of mortise and tenon joints and, to some degree, the bracing effect of panels of decorative scroll work. Where the decorative infill was absent or insufficient to brace the structure, substantial heels were often upset on the ends of the cross-rails, to provide a larger shoulder to the tenon and create a more rigid joint. The use of mortise and tenon joints derives from ancient woodwork practice, which also routinely used diagonal bracing in timber building construction to maintain the rigidity of a frame. But while the tenon joint has persisted in forged metalwork, the diagonal brace is unusual enough to merit comment.

The familiar timber ledge and brace cottage door and the farm gate have used diagonals to create rigid panels, at the very least since medieval times. The diagonal bracing of a farm gate allows its width to be three or even four times its height. In other words it is a very efficient way of using materials. The gate is triangulated in much the same structural engineering fashion as a roof frame or truss. Some timber gates even extend the back stile upwards, well above the top rail, so that the diagonal tension member is at a less acute angle, and provides more support.

Diagonal bracing in action. Like improvising jazz, once in a while putting something together instinctively can really sing. A gate by Robert Kranenborg, assembled very quickly from salvaged metal, to enclose the site where he is making a steel narrow boat, at Rowhurst Forge, Leatherhead.

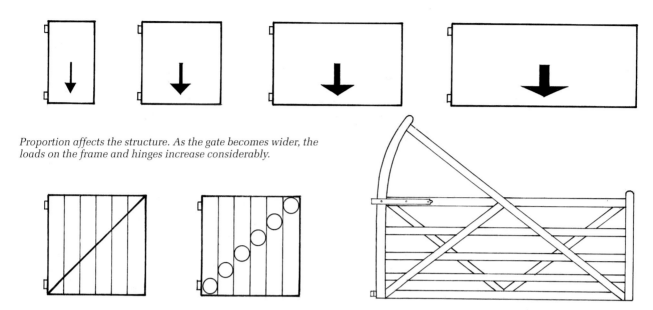

Proportion affects the structure. As the gate becomes wider, the loads on the frame and hinges increase considerably.

Diagonal bracing offers a simple way of increasing rigidity. The single diagonal bar may be replaced by decorative elements.

Timber farm gates gain rigidity by the use of diagonal bracing, sometimes linked to an extended back stile

Strangely this simple engineering device of triangulating the structure by using diagonals is very rare in forged architectural metalwork, although it is common in fabricated tubular steel or flat bar farm gates today. Iron and steel are materials with a high tensile strength, yet are seldom used in this way by blacksmiths. The great advantage of this approach is a reduction in weight. In European smithing and German work in particular, there has long been an aesthetic that derives from the idea of expressive and visible construction, the ingenious joint being the major decorative element of the design. So, perhaps not surprisingly, there are some contemporary examples of gates by European smiths that use diagonal bracing, but it is seldom seen in Britain.

Pursuing the idea of structural efficiency, it is also worth examining the use of particular sections in the construction of a gate panel, and considering whether they are being used to their full effect. The back stile, for example, is almost invariably made from square bar, presumably so

that circular sections can be forged near the top and at the bottom to provide pivots, and to allow mortises to be punched through for the cross-rails. But if the loads on the back stile are considered, it is apparent that they are not equal in all directions – which the square section would suggest – but act primarily in one direction. The stresses on the back stile caused by the weight of the gate, pull down and along in the plane of the gate, whether it is shut or open. If the back stile is going to bend, it will bend in that direction. In which case, it would be better to make it rectangular, with the long axis in the plane of the gate panel. Similar considerations apply to the use of flat bar cross-rails, with their long axis horizontal, making them better able to resist a sideways load than a vertical one. Yet the major load is the weight of the gate acting downwards. These examples all have perfectly good explanations as a convenient means of putting a gate together. Cross-rails made from flat bars used flat, allow holes to be punched and uprights

Proportion and bracing.

threaded through them. But it is important to appreciate the point that constructional convenience is not necessarily the same as good structural design.

Proportion

The relationship of the width of a gate to its height is a crucial decision to take and has an effect on the kind of structure and method of hinging that might be considered. The wider the gate in relation to its height – or more precisely in relation to the distance between the two hinges – the heavier the loading on the hinges. There are three stress components to be considered: the weight of the gate acting downwards, the resulting outward pull on the top hinge and inward load on the bottom hinge. If the gate is narrow in relation to the distance between its hinges – say the proportion of a domestic door – the vertical load of its weight is the main concern, because its centre of gravity is close to the line of the hinges. But if the hinges remain the same distance apart and the gate becomes wider – reaching farm-gate proportions – its centre of gravity is well away from the hinge line, so as its weight

acts downwards, the gate behaves like a lever, pulling heavily outwards against the top hinge and pushing in at the bottom.

In many instances, the site will determine the proportions of a gate, but there is an appreciable range within which there can be a choice; where a single gate or a pair of gates might be equally viable. In the end this can only be resolved by considering the balance of a number of factors like the cost, the space available to accommodate the gate or gates when they are open, and the kind of appearance that might be appropriate. A single leaf could be cheaper, so long as it is not too wide and difficult to engineer, but two leaves might look grander. A structure that is just taller than your eye level tends to look more impressive and imposing than one that is only an inch or two below. The perception of 'large' or 'small' has a great deal to do with our viewpoint. This height is therefore very critical and the decision to make the top of a gate just a little above or below eye level will have a far greater visual impact than the difference in dimensions might suggest.

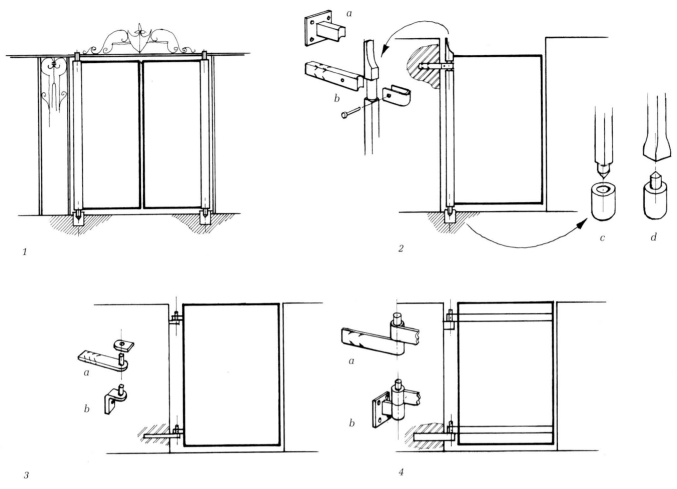

1 *Back stile pivoting on pins, top and bottom.*
2 *Top journal bearing and bottom pivot:*
  (a) Plummer block for screw fixing.
  (b) Plummer block and strap, for grouting in.
  (c) Pivot pin on back stile in ground socket.
  (d) Socket in back stile fits ground pin.

3 *Pintle hinges:*
  (a) Hinges for grouting in.
  (b) Hinges for screw fixing.
4 *Pintle hinges with straps:*
  (a) Hinges for grouting in.
  (b) Hinges for screw fixing.

Gate hinges. NB
Elevations not to scale.

Hinging

Large country-house gates in the eighteenth century were usually pivoted on pins that extended from the top and bottom of the back stile, forged on its ends like large tenons. Whether set between masonry piers or iron pilasters, these gates were invariably fitted beneath an overthrow – a sometimes very elaborate panel or cresting – which added grandeur to the entrance and often featured a coat of arms or family initials. The bottom bar of the overthrow, which linked the piers or pilasters, provided a transom immediately above the gate into which the upper pivot pin could be housed. The bottom pin fitted into an iron socket let into the paving at ground level. So long as the back stile is sufficiently rigid, this provides a very elegant system, with the mechanical advantage of placing the bearings at the greatest possible distance apart. In the eighteenth century the top pivot was often left open to the elements, doubtless to be regularly greased by a dutiful gardener. Lubrication is important to the survival of a simple

ABOVE: *Top and bottom pivoted gate by P. Johnson & Company. This is the gate shown during assembly in Chapter 3. (Photo: P. Johnson & Company)*

ABOVE CENTRE: *A pair of gates by Terry Clark, forged in steel and copper, with a top journal bearing and bottom pivot, for a private house in Reigate, Surrey. A boldly asymmetrical design, which brings together a number of rural images and echoes of waterfalls and granite from the client's other property in the Lake District. (Photo: Terry Clark)*

ABOVE: *A pair of gates with a top journal bearing and bottom pivot, by Andy Quirk and Robert Kranenborg. An elegant example of the power of symmetry, in a design constructed from a series of continuous looping bars. (Photo: Andy Quirk & Robert Kranenborg)*

metal to metal bearing, which if allowed to dry out will corrode and wear.

This top and bottom system is still used today. But a far more common variation, particularly for heavier gates, employs a similar bottom pivot, forged on the end of the back stile and seating into a socket let into the ground slab. The upper bearing is provided by swaging, cutting or machining into the back stile to produce a cylindrical shaft, which pivots in a bearing provided by a fixed plummer block and strap, a journal bearing. The block is either made as the end of a heavy rectangular bar, grouted into the masonry, or is bolted in place. The strap is secured to the sides of the plummer block with screws, and since the weight of the gate acts to pull outwards on the top bearing, these screws take most of the load as a shearing stress. There are refinements to this system. A split self-lubricating brass or bronze bush can be

inserted into the top bearing, the bottom socket bearing can similarly be fitted with a bronze bush or even a precision thrust race, and grease nipples can be fitted to both top and bottom bearings. Even if the bottom bearing is provided with a grease nipple, there is no guarantee that it will be used. The traditional arrangement of the bottom pivot pin seating into a socket at ground level is open to the problem of rain water entering the socket and causing rust. If the budget allows, there is a design advantage in reversing this arrangement, forging the socket on the bottom end of the back stile and fitting the pin to the ground slab. It is important to appreciate that in a gate of this kind, the top journal takes all the outward load, but no downward load at all, while the bottom hinge pin and socket take the entire weight of the gate, together with an inward thrust, pushing towards the post side of the socket when the gate is closed.

Pivot hinges at the top and bottom of a gate do not have to be part of the back stile. The gate can be designed to pivot

Centre-pivoted gate in stainless steel, by Matthew Fedden, for Portishead School. (Photo: Matthew Fedden)

about any vertical line across its width. This is likely to be more appropriate for pedestrian gates, since even in its open position the gate obstructs the full width of the opening. This may, of course, be used to advantage in preventing vehicles driving through a wide opening, while allowing the maximum access for people. Pivoting a gate in this way liberates the design from the need for an external frame and infill, and if it is centre pivoted, the concept becomes more one of a spine and ribs. A centre-pivoted gate may also be set on a single large, floor-mounted pivot pin or shaft, without the need for a top bearing above the gate. This calls for a substantial vertical shaft with shoulders machined to receive upper and lower angular contact or thrust bearings, on to which the centre tube of the gate is seated. Ensuring that the pivot shaft is truly vertical is important, to prevent the gate rotating under its own weight.

Pin Hinges

Pin or pintle hinges transfer the weight of the gate into the wall or post, rather than into the ground slab, and in consequence tend to be used for lighter gates. They usually consist of brackets grouted into the masonry, or bolted to the post or wall, supporting vertical hinge pins engaging in holes in short brackets projecting from the

back stile of the gate. Drop forged pintle hinges and eyes are available commercially for bolting directly to a gate frame and post, and are frequently used for both timber and steel agricultural gates. Often both pins are fixed facing upwards and the gate is simply lowered into place over them. It is literally hung. Since there is a risk that the gate could be lifted off and stolen, some additional security is desirable, such as circlips or grub screws locating in grooves machined in the pins, lock-nuts on their ends, splitting and splaying the end of one hinge pin, or simply burring it over. Alternatively, the upper hinge can be bolted in place in an inverted position. In this case, the lower hinge carries the weight and the inward thrust, while the upper one takes the outward load. If both hinge pins face upwards, depending on how the hinge brackets are set, the weight may be taken by either the bottom or top hinge, or if the shoulders of both hinges are in contact, the weight will be shared between them. Which hinge carries the weight can be adjusted by fitting brass washers, until the thrust is carried where required.

Pintle hinges may be fitted to the gate as separate units, or they can be integral with its structure. Flat bar cross-rails, with the long axis vertical and spanning the width of the gate, can become strap hinges terminating

Centre-pivoted gate for Abbot House, Dunfermline Heritage Centre, Fife, Scotland by P. Johnson & Company. Design by Phil Johnson and Jois Hunter. (Photo: P. Johnson & Company)

A frameless garden gate, by the author, for a private house in Cambridge. Hung on pin hinges in a wall sited at 45 degrees to the house, the gate has 50 × 6mm flat bar uprights set on edge, so that when viewed obliquely they obscure the view through.

with eyes or knuckles, which engage with pins and knuckles grouted into the masonry or bolted in place. Hinges made in this way can take a substantial weight, not least because the flat bar is set the right way round to carry the load. They also have a reassuringly solid appearance.

Hinge Geometry

Whatever the system, it is crucial that when the gate is assembled the top, bottom and (if fitted) the middle bearings or hinges are all set on the same centreline, which is parallel with the gate frame. Journal and socket bearings depend on the back stile being accurately straight, so that the centreline of the stile itself provides the datum. The precision resides in that single bar. Pin and eye hinges must be fitted to the gate so that the eyes are in line, and parallel with the back stile of the gate A simple way to ensure this is to carefully select or straighten a piece of round bar of the same diameter as the hinge pins, and use this as a jig, greasing its ends and passing it through both hinges to line them up. This should be kept in place until they are welded, riveted or otherwise fitted. If they are not truly in line, the hinges will jam. At best this will cause friction at some point

in their rotation. Worse still, it may cause a distinct twisting movement of the hinges, which can 'work' the fixings in the wall or post, damaging or loosening them. At worst, the gate may not fully open at all. If the pivots or hinges are not fitted parallel with the back stile, the gate will not balance and may be trying to swing up or down as it opens.

There is a particular kind of self-closing hinge arrangement for small gates, which uses the principle of putting the gate off balance. This hangs the entire weight of the gate on a conventional but loose top hinge pin. Where the bottom hinge would be, the back stile carries a bracket that projects a little way to either side of the gate, notched at each end to engage with two matching pins carried on a bracket secured to the gatepost. These are, in effect, two pivot pins set some 75mm (3in) apart. At rest, the inward thrust of the bottom of the gate seats both notches against their pins. As the gate is opened – in either direction – it pivots against one pin. Since this is offset from the centre line of the top hinge, it kicks out the bottom of the gate causing it to swing 'up hill'. Let go the gate and it falls back into its closed position, no springs, just gravity.

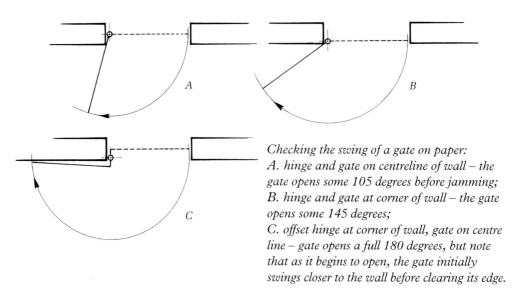

Checking the swing of a gate on paper:
A. hinge and gate on centreline of wall – the gate opens some 105 degrees before jamming;
B. hinge and gate at corner of wall – the gate opens some 145 degrees;
C. offset hinge at corner of wall, gate on centre line – gate opens a full 180 degrees, but note that as it begins to open, the gate initially swings closer to the wall before clearing its edge.

The other important aspect of the movement of a gate relates to the position and design of the hinge. The throw of the hinge – the distance to which it opens – can make a major difference to the final position of the gate when it is fully open. Equally, where the hinge is positioned in the gateway will affect the open position of the gate. Considering the path of the gate as it swings seems to be a very simple matter, but problems can occur unless this is analysed carefully. Sloping ground, a projecting cap stone, a corbelled brick course or arch, can foul the gate as it opens, unless this has been considered in the design. It is vital to examine the gateway both in plan and elevation. There is no substitute for drawing the gate in its opening at the largest convenient scale, tracing over the outline of the gate on tracing paper, sticking in a pin on the hinge centre and rotating the tracing of the gate; or copy, paste and rotate the gate on a computer screen. Being able to test the effect of shifting the centre of rotation reveals the advantages and disadvantages of particular hinge details and positions. In this way it can become apparent that placing the hinge a very short distance one way or the other can make the difference between a gate being able to open 90 degrees or 180 degrees, or wedging at some intermediate angle against the pillar or post.

Latches, Bolts, Locks and Stops

An important detail of a gate, from the point of view of the user, is the latch, handle or bolt – the part you actually touch. Finding the latch, discovering how to operate it, the feel of the latch handle, and the movement of the gate as it opens and shuts, are all part of what the marketing men might call the 'gate experience'. It is not always obvious where the latch is, or whether you should push, pull, twist or slide the handle. A good gate deserves a good latch, and a good latch should at

least go some way towards indicating visibly how it operates.

Most catches either pivot or slide, but the way they are operated – how the movement is conveyed mechanically from the handle to the catch itself – may vary

A self-closing hinge system on a gate at Binsted, Hampshire.

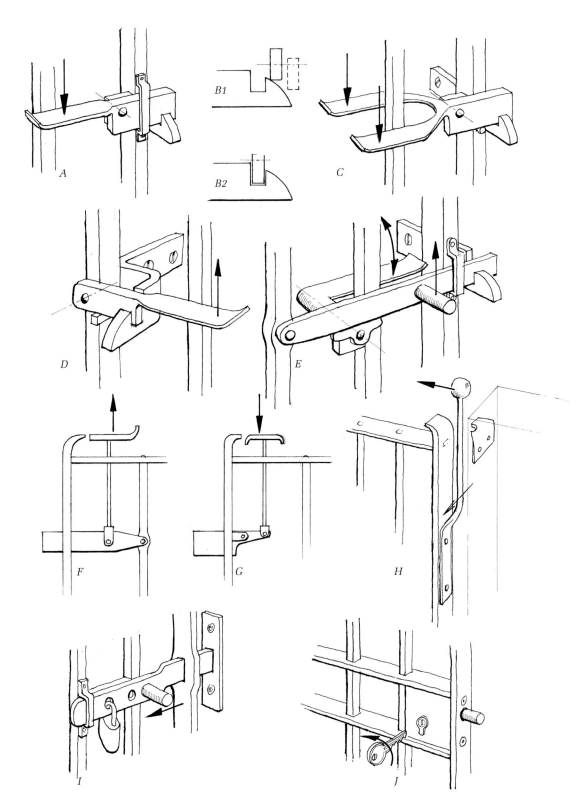

Gate latches. The arrows indicate the movement required to open the latch:
A. pivot latch;
B1. elevation showing how the latch blade is lifted by the angled face of the striker plate;
B2. latch blade fully located;
C. double-handled pivot latch;
D. pivot latch;
E. pivot latch operated by rotating a lever;
F. pivot latch operated by a pull handle;
G. pivot latch operated by a push handle;
H. spring bar latch;
I. sliding bolt with padlock provision;
J. commercial deadlock gate latch.

considerably. A typical pivoting catch for a garden gate can be designed very simply so that the blade end lifts when the handle is pushed down or when it is lifted up, depending on the position of the pivot pin relative to the blade. Or the blade may be made to lift by the rotation of a knob or lever handle, operating a lever or cam underneath it The pivoting movement of the latch blade readily lends itself to a self-closing action, without the need for springs. As the gate swings closed, the blade of the catch can be made to ride up the inclined edge of the striking plate, attached to the post or pier, to drop down under its own weight and seat securely in its notch. The design of the latch and handle is a challenging exercise, providing the opportunity for some neat, user-friendly detailing. It is important to remember that the catch must be both seen and operable from both sides of the gate, which in some cases may require a double handle, one on each face of the gate.

A plain sliding bolt is less convenient than a pivoting latch, but somewhat easier to design for securing with a padlock. Sliding bolts must normally be opened or closed by hand, and can only be self-closing if they are spring-loaded. An angled face on its end wedges the bolt back against the spring as it contacts the striking plate, and when the gate locates in its closed position, the bolt is pushed forward to engage with its hole. Most commercially available, mechanical locks work on this principle, but the bolt can also be operated and deadlocked with a key. The kind of mortise deadlock or cylinder lock used on domestic timber doors can be fitted to an internal forged steel gate or door, but is not usually adequate for external use. This kind of mortise lock normally has both a spring catch operated by a handle and a key-operated deadlock bolt. Since most of these locks are designed to work with plastic or aluminium alloy knobs or lever handles, if forged steel lever handles are

proposed then care must be taken to ensure that the return springs are powerful enough to rotate them back to their normal horizontal position.

Exposure to the weather demands that a security lock mechanism has a good level of corrosion protection, and the geometry of a gate means that the throw of the bolt may need to be greater than that required for a timber door. Where the bolt of a domestic door lock might move some 16mm ($\frac{5}{8}$in), the bolt of a purpose made gate lock can throw some 40mm ($1\frac{1}{2}$in). The kind of fitting required by a steel gate is also likely to be different from that of a timber door. Mortise locks for timber doors are normally housed into the thickness of the timber, requiring a large slot, which would be unsuitably large to punch or cut through the frame of a gate. Gate locks are usually fitted to the inside face of the frame, with the bolt throwing through a hole in the front stile, so the bolt needs to have sufficient length to match the frame thickness when fully retracted. Some locks have their own casing and can to be left exposed, while others need to be housed in a lock box, constructed as part of the gate.

In addition to handles, locks and latches, there are a number of other items that a gate may require. It is important that the travel of the gate is limited, rather than simply swinging free and hitting the wall or post, conceivably damaging its hinges. If the gate is only intended to open in one direction, a stop can be incorporated into the striker plate of the latch, to prevent it swinging on through, or a separate slam plate or bar can be fitted to the wall or post. Double gates require a slam bar fitted down at least part of the front stile of one gate, to intercept and stop the movement of the other gate in the closed position. The first gate is secured by a drop bolt, housing into a socket in the ground. The second gate stops against it and the latch or bolt secures it to the first. It

Intriguing gates by Oliver Russell for the Craft Study Centre at the Surrey Institute of Art and Design, Farnham, Surrey. The curved profiles used in the gates are a bold contrast to the severely right-angled geometry of the building. Note the forged twist in the flat bar uprights, and the fact that although there is symmetry in the design of the gates, the leaves open asymmetrically.

should be appreciated that even if the latch or bolt is locked in the middle of the gate, if the drop bolt can still be lifted, the gates can be sprung open. A drop bolt needs to be designed so that it can both be locked in its down position, and retained in its retracted position while the gate is moved. Like the latch and handle, the bolt is another challenge for the designer, and there are many different answers to this problem. For example, a cross-pin or looped bend in the shank of the bolt can be arranged to engage with its bracket, which can be provided with a hole for padlocking, to prevent the bolt being operated. On a pair of gates, the drop bolt may be designed to engage in its floor socket and twist so that its handle sits between the edges of the gates when closed, trapped by a pin on the back of the gate preventing it being lifted.

Gates – particularly vehicle gates – may also need to be secured in the open position, to prevent them accidentally moving or swinging dangerously in the wind as a vehicle passes. Simple hooks and eyes may be all that is necessary, or ground sockets can be installed and drop bolts fitted to both gates to hold them open. Latches can be fitted to a wall or on the ground and arranged to hook a catch plate on the gate, or catch under the bottom of the gate, to hold it open. Latches fitted on the ground can be designed to be foot operated. Various kinds of spring or gas-strut operated closers are available, which will automatically close a pedestrian gate after it has been opened.

A wide range of electromechanical and hydraulic gate openers are available, capable of opening, closing and locking gates from small sizes up to well over a tonne weight. These may have visible actuators – rams or levers – bolted to the back of the gate or more discrete, buried rotary mechanisms, which in effect substitute for the bottom socket bearing of the gate, engaging with and twisting the pivot pin. I have been advised by someone with a lengthy experience of these systems, that rotary openers can be destructive to gates made like a conventional, hand-operated gate, with traditional mortise and tenon construction. The torsional stress applied to the back stile to move the gate can shear off tenons. Traditional construction was never designed to transfer twisting loads through the back stile to the heavy structure of the gate. Rotary opening systems are probably better used for gates with

joints welded all round. The ram and lever systems apply the load to a cross-member of the gate, at some distance from the back stile, pushing or pulling, rather than twisting.

It is possible to retrofit these systems to existing gates but the buried, rotary systems must essentially be part of a complete design and installation. In both cases, the power units require an electricity supply and, unless carefully sited or concealed, can sometimes appear very prominent. These can be controlled by a diversity of radio or infrared systems, which may be tripped simply by the approach of a vehicle, by a remote control from the vehicle, by a push button unit or by remote control via a voice or video link. The complexity and sophistication of this kind of equipment means that it is best fitted by a specialist company.

FIXING

To work effectively, all gates – or pairs of gates – have to be fixed to meet the same basic criteria of hanging true and vertical in both planes, swinging smoothly and engaging accurately with their catches or drop bolts and stops. But the process of achieving this will vary, depending on the scale of the gate and the way it is hinged.

Prefabrication

If the gate is part of a new build, the hinges, or a supporting frame carrying the hinges, can be built in to the structure. Posts carrying hinges or hinges on piers can be built into masonry or brickwork by the builder, using a supplied template. For a pair of gates hung on pin hinges, this may be a simple rectangular frame with sockets to locate the pins. For a pair of gates with upper journal bearings and socket bearings on the ground, the tails of the upper plummer blocks can be built in using a steel template frame spanning the opening, set up truly level at the correct

CASE STUDY

Fixing Jim Horrobin's Winston Churchill Memorial screen in the Crypt of St Paul's Cathedral, London, 17 November 2004. The screen consists of six gates: the large centre pair being some 3.5m (11ft 6in) high and 3m (9ft 10in) wide, and each pair of side gates some 2m (6ft 3in) high and wide. All the gates had to be moved a considerable distance through an underground car park and into the crypt, in their finished, lacquered condition, then lifted and lowered into their bottom pivot sockets, and held in position against the upper journal while the hinge strap was secured. To achieve this, a special trolley and lifting system was designed.

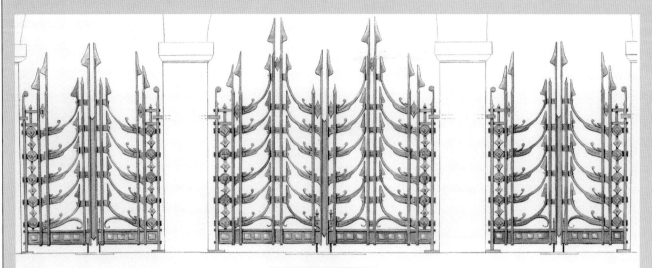

Elevation drawing, by Gabrielle Ridler, tinted with watercolour. (Photo: Jim Horrobin)

ST. PAUL'S CATHEDRAL
THE CHURCHILL MEMORIAL SCREEN
DWG NO 1   SCALE 1-20
JAMES HORROBIN 2003
DRAWN: G. RIDLER

ABOVE: *The 'Trojan Horse', an ingenious transport and lifting device, designed and made by John and Dom Hesp. The 'Horse' enabled each gate to be lifted on two scissor jacks and rotated into a vertical position on a spindle, moving in the slot between the two steel tube uprights, which act as slides for the jacks.*

RIGHT: *Two side gates on their transport trolleys, waiting to be fitted. Supporting frames are attached using tapped holes in the gates, later required for fixing decorative elements.*

CASE STUDY

A gate on its trolley has been docked with the Trojan Horse, and secured to the Horse before the trolley is removed. The picture shows the Horse beginning to lift the gate.

Once rotated vertical, the gate is wheeled into place, and can be precisely located by using the jacks.

Once the gate is in place and secured on its hinges, the horse can be removed.

Both side gates fixed in position and decorative details being screwed in place.

The centre and side gates nearing completion.

height and provided with dummy hinge pins to locate the plummer blocks. If a gate or gates fit in a covered opening, an entire steel portal frame – sides, top and bottom – can be constructed, the gate hung in the workshop and the frame subsequently incorporated into the building construction. In a similar way, the two posts for a gate or pair of gates can be welded to a horizontal steel rectangular hollow section or 'I' beam to produce a U-shaped frame, and the gates hung in the workshop. This frame is set on concrete pads, below the finished ground level, and bolted down, concreted in and the path or roadway finished over the top of the horizontal steel member. So long as site access makes this possible, the advantage of this method is that the gates can be accurately hung and their swing tested in the workshop, along with catches and other fittings, before the whole assembly is shipped to site and installed as one unit.

A single gate may be fitted to its hinge post in the workshop, with both the top bearing plummer block and bottom socket bearing, or top and bottom pin hinges, bolted or welded to the post. This post can then be installed on site, together with the catch post, bolted or concreted in place and set vertical in both planes, so the gate can be rehung with no further need for adjustment to the hinges. The catch plate and stop need to be designed with some vertical adjustment, using slotted holes, for example, to position them to suit the gate.

Bolt Fixing

In many cases, this kind of prefabrication is not possible, so the gate must be used as its own jig to set out the hinge positions on site. The principle is the same for most gates, but the details vary with the kind of hinge and fixing. The general procedure is to fit the hinges to the gate and hold them temporarily in place with string, tape or clamps, while the gate is manoeuvred into

position and set on timber packing pieces. Once in place, it must be carefully checked to ensure it is straight in the opening and vertical in both planes, before it is wedged or clamped tight. Holes are then drilled and bolts placed. Once secure, the packing can be removed and the swing of the gate checked before the catch and stop plate is drilled and fitted. This procedure is essentially the same for a pair of gates, ensuring, in particular, that the gap between them is correct and that at the most critical area, where the edges meet, they are not twisted relative to each other.

An elegantly detailed gate for a private house by David Tucker. Hung on pin hinges, the gate uses traditional concepts such as collared joints and dog bars but is entirely contemporary in design. (Photo: David Tucker)

In practice, adjustment must be built into the system because walls or piers are seldom smooth, flat or vertical. Where hinges are fixed with bolts, setting up the gate with at least one hinge fixing plate in contact with the wall and the edge of the gate plumbed vertical with a spirit-level will reveal any discrepancies. Packing pieces may be needed behind one or both hinge plates, and can be wedged in place before the fixing holes are drilled, to help stabilize the gate in position. If it is anticipated that the wall is out of true, a number of pre-painted steel shims can be prepared, in different thicknesses, drilled to match the holes in the fixing plates. Once the fixing holes are drilled, the appropriate shims can be tucked neatly in position behind the fixing plates and the bolts fitted. If the wall is twisted under the fixing plate, a shim may need to be cut and only part of it used to pack out the gap.

Ideally, once set in position, trued up and with any necessary packing in place, it should be possible to drill and fit all the fixings without having to remove and replace the gate. The implication of this is that the fixing holes are in positions that are accessible and have enough tolerance on their diameters to allow the appropriate drill to be inserted without vibrating the metalwork and possibly disturbing the whole set-up. The bigger the gate, the more desirable this may be. A small gate can be lifted easily in and out of position, but a larger one may be difficult enough to adjust into position just once. Using this method requires slim expanding fittings, such as through bolts or resin anchor studs and nuts, which may not always be mechanically suitable or visually desirable. The exposed end of screw thread provided by a stud fixing looks more like engineering than blacksmithing. Hiding this usually requires the making of special cap nuts, and demands that the end of the thread be cut to a precise length after fixing, to accommodate the nut.

The alternative is to use bolts screwed into expansion or resin anchor sockets. This allows less obtrusive, countersunk hexagon sockets or specially forged heads to be used, but the holes required for the sockets are larger than the clearance holes in the metalwork, so this must be moved to drill them. A drill can be accurately centred through the hole in the fixing plate by using a short piece of plastic or hard rubber tube as a bush. All the holes can be drilled with a pilot size to the full depth, before moving the gate just sufficiently to gain access with the larger drill needed to place the sockets. Which of these two options to use is a design decision to be made early in the project.

Large and heavy gates are usually hung on a top journal bearing and a bottom socket bearing on the end of the back stile, seated on a foundation block below finished ground level. In this case, adjustment of the attitude of the gate is normally made by moving the bottom bearing

Exchange Street Gateway, Dundee. A large pair of gates with unmistakably maritime associations, by P. Johnson & Company. (Photo: P. Johnson & Company)

socket. The top journal bearing is first bolted in place or may have already been positioned by building in. The gate is set in place on its bottom socket and the top bearing bolted up loosely. Its weight must be stabilized by a hoist and on props, packing pieces and wedges, as appropriate. The gate can then be adjusted using the hoist, crowbar or jack, until it is correctly positioned and truly vertical in both planes, before fully tightening the top bearing bolts. The gate is now positioned but the bottom bearing is not fixed. There are a number of options for securing it. If time can be allowed for it to set, concrete can be poured around the socket, on top of the foundation block, up to the appropriate finished level. The socket may be provided with a plate or flange drilled with a number of holes, through which fixing holes may be drilled directly into the foundation block to secure it. Alternatively, the socket may be set on to a piece of 'I' beam, channel or plate, previously bedded and secured in place for the purpose. Fixing holes can be drilled into this, tapped and screws fitted to secure the socket, or the socket can be welded to it *in situ*. Since this area must be brought up to a finished level, concrete is likely to be poured around the socket, so this and zinc-rich paint over the welds will prevent them corroding.

A more engineered arrangement is provided by a system used for gate dampers or automatic openers, which consists of an open-topped shallow steel box or tray, bolted to the foundation block before the gate is installed. Into this sits a smaller steel tray, to which the bottom socket has been welded. The sides of this box are drilled and tapped and fitted with a number of jacking screws, which bear against the outer box. These screws allow the position of the inner box and bearing to be adjusted very precisely, and locked in place. For dampers or openers, a cover plate is screwed in place to seal the box,

but if this system is used simply to provide adjustment, the box can again be buried in concrete once it had done its job.

Grout Fixing

Hinges can be grouted in place with molten lead, or with cement or resin-based materials. The holes are placed by measurement, or by temporarily positioning the gate to locate the hinge positions. The virtue of grouting is that it is infinitely adjustable and no packing pieces are required. A gate with a top journal bearing and ground socket can be fitted by locating the socket position first. If the socket is machined with a spigot projecting at the bottom, so the weight is taken by a flange sitting on the ground slab, the spigot can be resin grouted into a hole that is only 3 or 4mm (⅛in) larger in diameter than the spigot. Sufficient resin is injected in the hole so that when the socket is pushed into place a little resin is displaced around its edges and can be scraped away. Once this has hardened, the gate is set in the socket, with the top hinge strap and block bolted in place and its tail inserted into the hole drilled or cut in the masonry. The gate is then trued up and wedged in position, vertical in both planes, before the tail of the top hinge is grouted in place, as described in Chapter 12.

Gates with pintle hinges are set up in the same way with the hinges temporarily secured to the gate, allowing their tails to be inserted in cut or drilled holes. The gate is adjusted on packing pieces and wedged into place, true and vertical in both planes. The holes need to be sufficiently large to allow some small adjustment of the hinges, but not so large that a great thickness of grouting material is required. Cement-based or lead grouting can then be introduced, as described in Chapter 12, and is allowed to set or is caulked before the packing is removed. For small gates, the kind of resin used for securing threaded anchor studs may also used in much the same way. If packing pieces are carefully prepared when the gate is set up with the hinge tails in their holes, the gate can be withdrawn without disturbing the packing, resin injected into the holes in the masonry and the gate pushed back into place and wedged while the resin sets. Surplus resin will be displaced from the holes and must be cleaned off with a trowel or a scrap of sheet metal before the resin is too hard.

Regulations

Building Regulations 2000. Approved Document K. Protection from falling, collision and impact, does make some reference to gates, more from the point of view of protecting people from impact with a gate as it swings, rather than relating to the design of the gate itself. These concerns include: providing a clear view through a door or gate, in a zone from 900 to 1,500mm (35–59in) above ground level, where it is on a main circulation route and particularly if it can swings both ways; the need for power-operated gates to have safety features to prevent them hitting or trapping people; and an identifiable emergency stop switch and provision for manual opening, should the power fail.

The regulations regarding the spacing of bars for guarding purposes – that a 100mm sphere should not be able to pass through – do not strictly apply to gates so long as the gate is not guarding a drop. *(See* the table on balustrade requirements in Chapter 7.) However, unless there are other overriding considerations, and since the purpose of the regulation is to prevent children becoming stuck, using this spacing may nevertheless make sense in some situations.

BS 1722-8: 1997 Mild steel (low carbon steel) continuous bar fences and hurdles. Details traditional flat bar, 'estate' or 'country house' railing, designed to keep in livestock, and includes recommended design details for matching gates.

BS 1722-9: 2000 Mild steel (low carbon steel) fences with round or square verticals and flat horizontals. This covers the design of fences with plain individual uprights and with bow topped uprights, looped in pairs, and for gates of matching design. Tables give recommended bar sizes for a wide range of gate widths and heights, frame materials, square tube post sizes and so on.

BS 1722-12: 1999 Steel palisade fences. This includes a section on the design of matching gates.

BS 3470: 1975 Field gates and posts. This includes requirements for steel field and cattle yard gates.

BS5709: 2001 Gaps, gates and styles. Deals with the design requirements of gates on footpaths and bridle-ways, and includes disability access information.

Gates and overthrow at Worcester Cathedral by Paul Margetts. Contemporary metalwork with a Gothic flavour. (Photo: Paul Margetts)

11 MATERIALS AND FINISHES

Despite its scientific basis, terminology applying to metals is, to say the least, confusing. Terms that had a precise definition have, through historic usage, become confusing labels. This might be simply interesting if it were not that it muddies the water when forged metalwork is specified or restored. 'Iron' is a chemical element – a pure metal. Wrought iron is an almost chemically pure iron, physically mixed with slag. 'Wrought' is the archaic English word meaning 'worked'. The metal needed working – hammering – as part of its manufacture. Years ago, the metalwork made by a blacksmith could be properly called 'wrought ironwork'. But do not confuse the name of the material with the products made from it. The blacksmith today is far more likely to be hot-forging mild steel.

'Steel' is defined as an alloy of iron and carbon, usually with small percentages of other metallic elements. 'Mild steel' contains up to 0.25 per cent carbon, a very small percentage that could justify calling it – colloquially – 'iron'. By way of comparison, 22 carat gold – the purest commercially available jewellery alloy – contains 8 per cent of other metals and is still called 'gold'. High carbon steels contain up to 1.5 per cent carbon. Beyond that, at around 2 per cent carbon content, the metal can no longer be hot forged – it crumbles. At this point, and up to some 4 per cent carbon, the metal is no longer called 'steel' but becomes 'cast iron'. Not 'cast steel', which term applies to a steel that has been melted and cast.

At one level all this is historically explicable. Wrought iron was wrought as part of the manufacturing process and was worked by the smith who used it. Cast iron is melted and poured into moulds to make castings. But it leaves a confusion between the specification of a material, and a term describing a process or product. The fact is that wrought iron, cast iron and mild steel are different materials with different properties.

IRON

Wrought Iron

Wrought iron was the traditional material of the blacksmith, a nearly chemically pure iron, which was hammered, welded and rolled as part of its manufacturing process. As a result, the iron is physically mixed with up to 4 per cent glassy, silicate slag, with a linear, fibrous structure, not unlike the grain in wood. In the late nineteenth century, mild steel began replacing wrought iron as a general purpose, structural metal and in 1974 the last commercial wrought iron producer in Britain closed down.

Some supplies are still available as re-rolled, salvaged metal. Wrought iron is good to forge, it is softer than mild steel, readily lends itself to fire welding and, indeed, should be forged at a welding temperature to maintain the integrity of the metal. It is claimed to be more resistant to rusting than mild steel. However, it is considerably more expensive and can vary in quality. There is no existing *British Standard* specification for wrought iron.

Pure Iron

Pure iron is essentially just that – a high-purity iron containing just traces of carbon, manganese and other elements. Unlike wrought iron, it is a homogeneous

OPPOSITE PAGE: Detail of a screen by Gunvor Anhøj showing the richness of a rusted and waxed surface. (Photo: Gunvor Anhøj)

material. It is malleable, forges well and is claimed to be less prone to rusting than mild steel, but it is considerably more expensive. At one time it was produced by the America Rolling Mill Company and became known as 'Armco Iron'. As sheet material it is a desirable metal for repoussé work, since it will stand up to considerable deformation when cold worked.

STEEL

Steels are required to meet a wide variety of specific purposes and service conditions. For this reason they are manufactured to particular formulations, classified in Britain by *British Standard* designations. Most countries have their own system of this kind, which is essential to ensure that the metal will perform in a reliable and predictable way.

Corrosion around a poorly leaded joint securing this bootscraper, has burst the stonework of the step.

Mild Steel

Mild steel is now the most commonly available structural iron alloy, widely employed for structural engineering purposes and hot forged by blacksmiths. In this context 'mild' means 'soft'. The British specification describes an alloy of iron containing some 0.20 per cent carbon, 1.5 per cent manganese, far lesser percentages of sulphur and phosphorus, and just traces of other elements. Since it is in such widespread use for all kinds of fabrication purposes, mild steel is rolled in a large range of sections and sizes, including round, flat and square bars, tube, angle, channel and 'I' beam. Since its carbon content is so low, mild steel may be heated and quenched in plain water, as necessary, to assist working, without causing the metal to harden. It will not tolerate forging temperatures as high at those used for wrought iron, but can be forged and welded in a similar fashion.

It should be noted that there is no visible difference between bars of wrought iron, pure iron or mild steel. After heating in a forge, they all exhibit a dark grey, iron oxide surface or, cleaned with a file, they are the same silvery colour. They can be identified by their working properties, their context or the effects of corrosion on their surfaces, but as finished forgings they are indistinguishable. At an exhibition in London a few years ago, an institution that should have known better exhibited a number of pieces of contemporary African, craft metalwork. If the metal had been finished to give a bright surface, the piece of work was labelled 'steel', if it had a black oxide surface it was labelled 'iron'. This correlation is entirely spurious.

Carbon Steel

'Carbon steel' seems an unnecessary term, since steel is already defined as an alloy of iron and carbon, but it serves to describe alloys that are plain carbon steels and do not contain significant percentages of other elements. They are loosely categorized as: low-carbon steels, which contain up to 0.3 per cent carbon and include the mild steel mentioned above; medium-carbon steels, which range from 0.3 per cent to 0.6 per cent carbon; and high-carbon steels, containing from 0.6 per cent to something over 1.2 per cent carbon.

Medium- and high-carbon steels will become hard when rapidly quenched from a red heat, to the extent that they can crack or shatter when struck. As the carbon content increases, so does the strength and hardness, but the ductility decreases and the metal becomes very brittle when hardened. This hardness can be controlled by 'tempering' – reheating the steel to a precise temperature – leaving it with the required balance of hardness and toughness. In this way, the blacksmith can forge the metal to shape, then harden and temper the tool, choosing steels of a particular carbon content for particular purposes. All steels in the medium or high carbon category feel harder to forge than mild steel. The whole process of hardening and tempering is called heat treatment. Typically, a hammer head might be steel with a carbon content of 0.75 per cent, while a file could contain as much as 1.25 per cent.

Alloy Steels

Alloy steels contain – in addition to carbon – percentages of other metals, such as nickel, chromium, vanadium, manganese, molybdenum and tungsten, in various combinations. These produce steels with particular service properties, such as strength, springiness or resistance to wear, and include a wide range of alloys, tailored for particular purposes. Spanners, for example, are often drop forged industrially from chrome vanadium steel, while the teeth of earth-moving equipment are made from wear-resistant, high-manganese steel. Alloy elements also provide desirable working properties, enabling steels to respond to particular manufacturing processes, such as

machining, forging or heat treatment. Alloy steels are now widely used for making tools, machine parts and mechanical engineering components, to a large extent replacing plain carbon steels.

Weathering Steels

Weathering steels, often known by the trade name Cor-Ten, are low-carbon, structural steels containing small percentages of copper, nickel and chromium. They were developed for civil-engineering work; for example, enabling bridges to be built without the need for expensive anti-corrosion finishing and maintenance. The rust layer – fully developed after a year or two – is adherent and protects the underlying metal. To achieve an even dark brown rust coating, the completed metalwork must be prepared by shot blasting. Particularly during the initial rusting, some rust is washed off the surface and rain drip can cause staining to nearby concrete or masonry surfaces. Since these steels are marketed for heavy structural purposes, they are only available as plate, angle, channel and 'I' beam sections. Compatible bolt fixings are also available. Weathering steel can be forged, but bar material must be cut from plate.

Stainless Steels

Stainless steels are a particular range of alloy steels containing chromium and nickel. To qualify for the description, a stainless steel must contain a minimum of 11 per cent chromium. In practice, stainless steels used for architectural purposes also contain percentages of nickel, to increase corrosion resistance and improve mechanical properties. A typical stainless steel of this kind might contain 18 per cent chromium, 9 per cent nickel and 0.06 per cent carbon. These high-chromium, high-nickel steels have a particular metallurgical structure, known as 'austenitic'. They exhibit high corrosion-resistance, are malleable, respond well to hot forging – although they feel much harder to forge than mild steel – weld very well, and can be drilled and machined. However, stainless steels are expensive, being in the order of seven or eight times the price of mild steel.

FINISHES FOR IRON AND STEEL

Corrosion

The rusting of iron and steel occurs through the action of both oxygen and water. With only one of these present, corrosion does not occur, as demonstrated by

Bare mild steel, rusting gently in the Arizona sunshine. The back of a 'Stop' sign at Desert Mountain, an expensive housing development outside Phoenix.

the classic school experiment of immersing bright, clean iron nails in a glass jar full of boiled water. Boiling the water removes dissolved air. So long as the lid is tightly on the jar, the nails remain rust-free. The much vaunted Delhi Pillar – a bare iron column – has stood for 1,500 years without rusting away. The dry and unpolluted climate in which it stands, doubtless has as much to do with its present condition as the metal from which it is made. The rate of corrosion of iron is directly dependent on the length of time the surface is wetted. In an essentially dry climate, even occasional heavy rainfall evaporates quickly, particularly from a vertical surface. In Phoenix, Arizona some mild-steel structures are simply left unpainted and take on a pleasant orange-brown appearance. Do the same in Britain and you can kiss it all goodbye in a few years.

Unfortunately, the corrosion products of iron are physically larger than the metal they replace. A molecule of hydrated iron oxide – rust – is bigger than a molecule of iron. This means that surface rust grows too large to stay in place, flaking off to expose more metal to corrosion. In crevices the expansion of rust can jack apart substantial sections of metal, causing mechanical damage. Similarly, exposed iron components grouted into concrete, brick or stone can rust, expand and crack the masonry. The design of metalwork – the creation of water traps – can encourage corrosion. Small gaps or crevices can accumulate airborne dust, which will hold moisture in close contact with the metal. Familiar corrosion areas in historic ironwork are under collars, in places where bars are fitted side-by-side – a rail and shadow rail, for example – and in leaves where water can collect.

The corrosion reaction between iron, oxygen and water is chemical but also has an electrical component, creating small currents that flow between the corroding area and areas where no corrosion is occurring; this is called 'galvanic action'. In this context, the water, as an electrical conductor, should be thought of as an 'electrolyte'. Sulphur dioxide pollution in industrial areas or chlorides in marine environments are not only more chemically active than water, but act as accelerators by increasing the electrical conductivity of the water, creating a more efficient electrolyte.

Galvanic corrosion is a particular concern when dissimilar metals are involved.

If two different metals are in close contact with each other in an electrolyte, a current will be generated. The electric potential – the voltage – produced by particular metals can be measured against a standard reference and metals arranged in the order of their voltage, as a 'galvanic series'. Those high in the series are less likely to corrode and are referred to as 'noble', while those lower down are called 'base'. If a more noble metal is in contact with a base metal in the presence of an electrolyte, the base metal will corrode more readily, the corrosion being driven, theoretically, by the difference in electric potential. Mill scale, incidentally, is more noble than mild steel and lies next to copper in the galvanic series, so scale will actively encourage bare steel to rust. Conversely, a metal such as zinc will protect the steel, galvanic action serving to corrode the zinc preferentially. For this reason, sacrificial zinc anodes are fitted to steel boats in order to reduce corrosion of the hull.

On the face of it, the galvanic series offers a neat and scientific means of predicting corrosion – the further apart the two metals are in the series, the greater the risk of corrosion. However, the series is a hierarchy of voltages, not current. It is the current flow that determines the rate of corrosion. So, in practice, galvanic corrosion effects are mitigated first, by the tendency for some metals – stainless steels, for example – to 'polarize', causing a considerable drop in their galvanic effect; and second, by the relative areas of each metal exposed to the electrolyte. A (base) iron rivet set in the middle of a more noble, copper panel, will become the focus of corrosion and consequently rust away very quickly. However, the effect of a copper rivet in a steel panel is to spread very slight corrosion over a large area of the steel.

To summarize, aluminium, cadmium and zinc will galvanically discourage the rusting of iron and steel, while copper and its alloys, lead and stainless steels will tend

to promote it. It is important to remember that galvanic corrosion requires bare metal contact, in the presence of water and oxygen. So any insulation, such as paint finishes, plastic washers, sleeves, gaskets or even grease, will considerably reduce these effects, in the context of architectural metalwork.

The shadow bar at the top of this gate frame has been bent upwards by the expansion of rust in the joint. The torn rivets can just be seen.

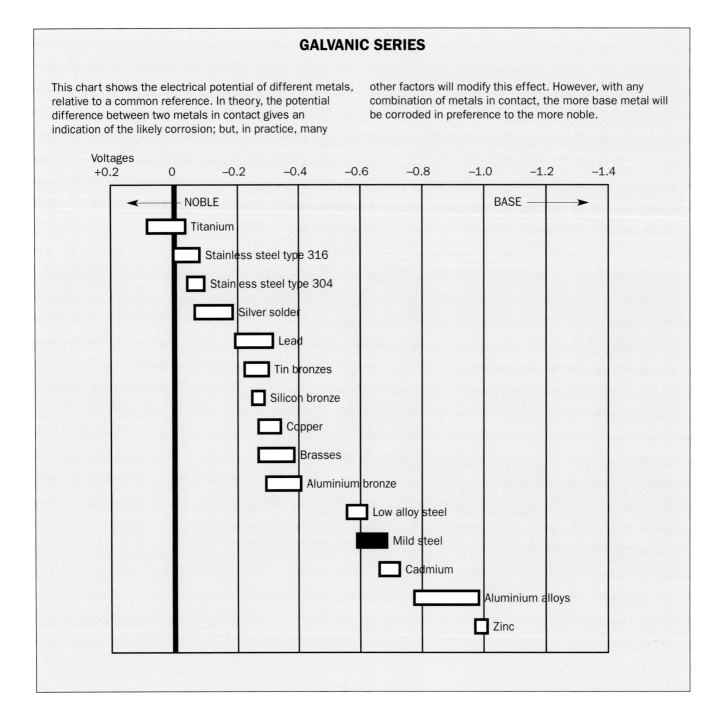

GALVANIC SERIES

This chart shows the electrical potential of different metals, relative to a common reference. In theory, the potential difference between two metals in contact gives an indication of the likely corrosion; but, in practice, many other factors will modify this effect. However, with any combination of metals in contact, the more base metal will be corroded in preference to the more noble.

Voltages
+0.2 0 −0.2 −0.4 −0.6 −0.8 −1.0 −1.2 −1.4

NOBLE   BASE

Titanium
Stainless steel type 316
Stainless steel type 304
Silver solder
Lead
Tin bronzes
Silicon bronze
Copper
Brasses
Aluminium bronze
Low alloy steel
Mild steel
Cadmium
Aluminium alloys
Zinc

Corrosion Protection

Corrosion protection depends on three strategies.

1. Design. At the design stage, it is important, where possible, to avoid water traps, crevices, hollows and other areas encouraging dirt to accumulate, water to enter or dampness to persist. This includes areas where the metalwork is in contact with brick, concrete or stonework. Be aware of possible galvanic corrosion effects. In particular, avoid the worst-case situation, like the mild steel rivet in the copper panel. Consider insulating one metal from another. Plan the kind of corrosion-resistant finishing system you plan to use, right at the outset.

2. Keeping out air. This is normally achieved in the case of architectural metalwork by protective coatings. It is worth noting that bare steel piling, driven deep into damp earth for foundation purposes, does not rust significantly, due to the lack of oxygen.

3. Keeping out water. For external metalwork, this is similarly achieved by protective coatings. The fact that bare steel workshop tools or machinery can be kept bright, using the occasional application of oil or grease, illustrates the point that a thin film of oil can repel water. It should also be noted that if iron and steel work is regularly maintained, retouched or repainted every few years, there is no need for it to rust, even in a damp climate.

COATINGS

Waxes and Lacquers

Like oiling workshop tools, forged architectural metalwork in dry interior conditions can be protected by a good initial coating of wax and some regular re-waxing. Since forge or mill scale will tend to flake off the metal over time, it is important to remove loose scale first by vigorous wire brushing, ideally using a rotary brush on an angle grinder. For a darker surface, a coating of graphite wax can be applied, diluted to a brushable consistency. After this has dried, the surface can be buffed and, if more contrast is required, areas selectively cut back with fine abrasive paper or a rubber abrasive block, to highlight them before waxing. The museum conservation wax known as 'Renaissance Wax' provides an ideal coating, which does not degrade. This may also be thinned to a brushable consistency and applied as two coats, allowing them to dry and buffing in between. Brushing enables wax to be forced deep into crevices.

Pigmented waxes and pastes can be used to bring some colour to internal metalwork.

Some of these are known as 'gilding pastes' and contain high levels of fine metal powders, offering metallic bronze, copper, silver and gold coloured surfaces. These can be selectively burnished to highlight surface texture or particular details, then waxed over for protection. The durability of this kind of finish depends on the internal atmosphere of the building, the use and location of the metalwork, and how well it is maintained. Quarterly or even annual waxing of interior ironwork may well be sufficient but in some circumstances, waxing reaches its limit. Adjacent to windows, for example, condensation can form on metalwork, degrade the wax coating and cause rusting.

Various single or two-pack, clear lacquers are available for metal finishing, using many of the same resins as paints, and may offer a glossy or matt surface. There is some advantage in using a quick drying system, to minimize the inclusion of dust in the clear layer. Lacquers can be brushed or sprayed but, because of the transparency of the coating, the process is more demanding than paint finishing, requiring careful jigging to avoid marks on the surface. Marks on paint can be over-coated, but on a lacquer surface they show. Matt lacquers can be finished with a coat of wax to provide a controlled sheen.

Rust Finishing

Colour can be given to internal metalwork by careful rusting, which provides a rich, brown finish, not unlike fine, brown suede leather. It might also be mistaken for a matt bronze surface. (*See* the opening photograph in this chapter). Fine Japanese metalwork that uses this finish is sometimes labelled 'russet finish' when displayed in a museum context, which sounds respectable but is just controlled rusting. If mild steel is shot or grit blasted, and treated with a dilute ammonium chloride or even table salt solution at about a teaspoon to 500cc (a pint), it will rust in hours. The liquid should be applied with a fine spray from a plastic garden sprayer to keep the surface damp, without allowing it to form pools, which will cause blackening. After a first coat has been achieved, loose, orange rust should be taken off with a clean wire brush, before more liquid is applied, and the surface re-rusted to deepen the coating. This cycle can be repeated until the desired degree of rusting has occurred. The surface should finally be washed down with clean water, dried quickly and waxed when it is thoroughly dry.

Preparation for Painting

As with all applied coatings, the effectiveness of paint finishing is only as good as the preparation. Stripping back to bare metal is essential. Wire brushing is not normally good enough. It is hard to remove even half the rust and scale, particularly since burnished scale looks remarkably like burnished iron. If there really is

no alternative, a traditional oil-based primer paint should be used, which is tolerant to poor surfaces. It is far better to remove forge scale entirely, by immersion in an acid pickle bath or by grit or shot blasting. Pickling metalwork on an architectural scale is only practical as an industrial process, but it does have the advantage of reaching awkward internal surfaces. My experience of using an unheated phosphoric acid bath to strip smaller items has proved very effective and economic. Components can be immersed overnight, then washed and dried to leave a matt grey surface, ideal for priming and painting.

Shot or grit blasting is offered as a service and will strip forged ironwork very effectively. Like most hand-operated processes, it is only as good as the people doing it, so developing a working relationship with your local shot blasters is well worthwhile. Shot, rather than grit, is a better preparation for direct painting, since the shot is spherical in form and produces a less jagged surface. Once the steel has been stripped in this way, it is highly reactive and will rust with remarkable speed, particularly on a wet day. So it is important to apply a coat of primer paint as soon as possible. If available, it is worth asking the shot-blast company to do this. They may well provide a complete paint-finishing service.

Since shot blasting is a line-of-sight process, it cannot strip crevices or deep internal surfaces. Some brush painting with zinc-rich paint during assembly is well worthwhile in these cases, prior to having the whole assembly shot blasted. Mating surfaces, where two bars lie in contact with each other, will benefit from coating with zinc-rich paint before assembly; this can survive even if a red hot collar is to be clinched over the top. Small abrasive guns, like a paint-spray gun, can be used to prepare these kind of surfaces for painting. Even forcing zinc-rich paint into

A railing panel with zinc-rich paint brushed in to rustproof the joints, prior to shot blasting and zinc metal spraying.

crevices after assembly can seal them and prevent the ingress of water. Any over-painting left on exposed surfaces will be stripped by the subsequent shot blasting. Waterproof silicone gunning mastics can similarly be used to seal these areas, but must be cleaned back carefully on exposed surfaces, since shot blasting may not remove thick deposits. The traditional ironwork motif of a water leaf is constructed in such a way that it traps water. This can be sealed by filling with pourable epoxy resin.

METAL COATINGS

Since zinc, cadmium and aluminium are all below iron in the galvanic series, they offer sacrificial corrosion protection as a coating. Cadmium and zinc are used very thinly in the form of electroplating, to protect screws, nuts, bolts and small fittings. In practice, the effective life of metallic coatings depends on their thickness, so the choice for architectural metalwork is either to use heavier coatings of zinc or aluminium, of which zinc is by far the more common.

Coating iron or steel with metallic zinc is a highly effective anti-corrosion protection. Zinc itself does oxidize, eventually producing a white powdery surface, but it corrodes far more slowly than steel. The zinc coating is self-healing, which means that if it is scratched through to the steel, a local cell is set up when the metal is wetted, causing the surrounding zinc to be deposited back on to the exposed steel. Zinc can be applied either by galvanizing – hot dipping – or by metal spraying. In both cases, the coating is relatively thick, in the order of 100μm (0.004in) The great virtue of these processes is that they provide a level of corrosion protection, which means that subsequent paint finishing is largely cosmetic. If the paint is chipped or worn right through, the zinc coating will still protect.

Hot-Dip Galvanizing

This is the cheaper process and is priced by weight. It can be as little as half the price of zinc spraying. Galvanizing involves the de-greasing, acid pickling and fluxing of the metalwork, before it is immersed in a tank of molten zinc. The coating is impermeable to moisture and its adhesion is excellent, because alloying occurs at the contact layer of the zinc and steel. Galvanizing has the advantage that it will either penetrate or seal hollows and crevices, so internal surfaces can be coated. Since the metalwork is heated in the zinc bath at over 400°C, there is a risk of explosion if air or moisture is trapped in voids in the assembly. For this reason, it is vital that hollow sections or tubes should be well-vented. Zinc will also coat the internal surfaces of holes intended to take

Large wall sundial with a galvanized finish, about to be etch primed and painted in the author's workshop.

Sample piece by Charles Normandale, showing a zinc-sprayed surface partly primed and finish painted.

distortion. The size of the available galvanizing tank ultimately limits the size that can be processed.

Newly galvanized surfaces are not receptive to paint, being shiny and often contaminated with a greasy flux. In Britain, several months' exposure to atmospheric weathering will turn the crystalline zinc coating to a dull grey, so the slow approach is to leave it to weather, then paint it, but this is often impractical. It is more reliable to degrease the metalwork with white spirit or a detergent solution, then use a commercially available mordant, known in Britain as 'T Wash', which contains phosphoric acid and a copper salt that blackens as a visible indication that the etch has been effective. It can be applied by brush or spray, then rinsed with clean water and allowed to dry before being primed and painted.

Zinc Spraying

This is priced by surface area. It requires the metalwork to be blast cleaned with steel grit to remove paint, forge scale and rust, leaving the surface slightly 'toothed'. The zinc spray must be applied within a very short time – hours at the most – so that re-rusting has not occurred. The process, like paint spraying, is as good as the operator and calls for conscientious blast cleaning, as well as spray application. The gun contains an oxy-acetylene flame, fed with zinc wire to spray molten zinc, which impacts the steel surface forming a series of minute, overlapping platelets. There is no alloying and the adhesion is mechanical. The surface is granular, which makes a good key for paint but, since the coating is slightly porous, it is normally treated with an etch primer, applied shortly after zinc spraying, in order to seal the pores.

There is a limit to the zinc cover that can be expected on internal surfaces, but since the particles are heavy, they will throw further than paint. This said, it is

hinge pins or internal screw threads, so these will need clearing afterwards with a drill or tap. Provided an allowance has been made for a reduction in their diameter, fixing holes are better left with zinc protecting their internal surfaces.

The initial de-greasing and pickling process is designed to remove rust, forge scale, oil and grease, but will not usually cope with paint, tar or other heavy deposits. So, reclaimed, painted steel should be flame-cleaned, paint-stripped or cleaned by shot blasting prior to galvanizing. Common defects are drips, spikes and wrinkles, or oxide inclusions in the zinc surface. These are unsightly rather than a corrosion-protection problem, but may need some time spent grinding or filing back before painting. Butt welds that have been ground flush will tend to stand out after galvanizing. More crucially, the heat of the process can occasionally create or relieve stresses in the structure, causing

SCHEMATIC PAINT FINISHING GUIDE

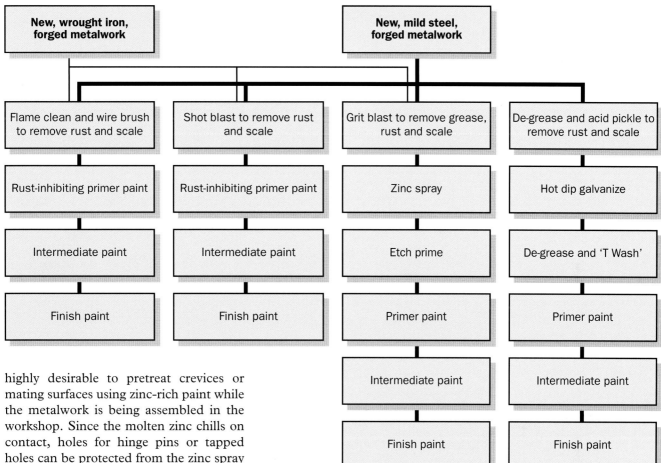

highly desirable to pretreat crevices or mating surfaces using zinc-rich paint while the metalwork is being assembled in the workshop. Since the molten zinc chills on contact, holes for hinge pins or tapped holes can be protected from the zinc spray by plugging them with plastic or wooden pegs, or by screwing scrap lengths of studding into the hole, leaving an end projecting. External surfaces like hinge pins, which do not require zinc coating, can be masked with several layers of paper masking tape.

Possible problems include: poorly covered or poorly blast-cleaned areas, overlooked by the operator; the lack of coverage of internal surfaces; and the trapping of the blasting grit in crevices. Zinc spraying is more expensive than galvanizing, but does not carry the same risks of distorting the metalwork and has no upper size limit. With a good operator, zinc spray is also less likely to obscure surface texture or fine details. Other metals can also be

applied by spraying. Aluminium is sometimes used as a protective coating in marine applications in preference to zinc. Copper, brass and bronzes can be sprayed as decorative finishes.

Paint Finishing

Paints contain of three main components:

- Pigments, which are finely divided powders providing the colour, opacity, light resistance and, sometimes, the corrosion-inhibiting qualities of the paint. Many primers contain corrosion inhibitors such as zinc phosphate, zinc chromate or calcium plumbate.

Schematic paint finishing guide. Note that intermediate paint may comprise two separate coats, to build thickness.

SOME PROPERTIES OF PAINT TYPES

Binder	Cost	Water resistance	Tolerance of poor surface	Ease of over-coating after ageing	Comments
Bituminous	Low	Good	Good	Good with same type of paint	Can soften in heat
Oil based	Low	Fair	Good	Good	Slow drying
Alkyd, epoxy-ester	Moderate	Fair	Moderate	Good	Good colour range
Chlorinated rubber	Moderate	Very good	Poor	Good	Can 'stick' during transport
Vinyl	Moderate	Very good	Poor	Good	Can 'stick' during transport
Epoxy	Moderate–high	Very good	Very poor	Poor	Liable to 'chalking' in UV light
Polyurethane	High	Very good	Very poor	Poor	Better decorative finish than epoxies

- The binder, which is an oil or resin forming the structural film, and is responsible for the main properties of the paint. Paints are often categorized by the type of binder, such as oil-based, alkyd, epoxy, polyurethane and so on.
- A solvent, which serves to dilute the binder and make it possible to apply the paint by brush or spray. Increasingly, in order to reduce atmospheric hydrocarbon pollution and toxicity, paints are being formulated using water as a solvent.

After application, the solvent evaporates leaving the binder either to air dry, dry by absorbing atmospheric oxygen or, in the case of two-pack paints, dry by a chemical reaction between the components. A lacquer or varnish is essentially a paint without pigments.

The term 'paint system' is used to describe the different coats that are required to build the necessary thickness, to provide a particular level of protection and finish. Paint systems usually comprise: a primer, which provides adhesion to the metal; one or more intermediate coats, to build up the film thickness; and a finish coat, which provides the first line of defence against weathering, protects the previous coats and provides the colour and appearance. It is crucial to any paint system that the different components are compatible and reinforce each other, rather than reacting adversely. For this reason, using the products of one manufacturer is good practice.

Asking the advice of the paint supplier – or specialist paint-finishing company – is very important. Bearing in mind that architectural metalwork is likely to remain in place for many years, maintenance considerations are as important as the initial protective treatment. Newer, more advanced paint systems are available, but may be very difficult to retouch or to re-coat on site. They may also be highly toxic and intended for specialist workshop application only. For this reason, the more 'industrial' paint finishes, along with powder coating, should be considered with a certain amount of caution.

Ten years ago I designed a piece of sculptural metalwork commissioned by the local authority of a large town in the north of England. One of the councillors who approved the commission, knew all about painting North Sea oil-drilling platforms and insisted that the metalwork was finished with the same kind of very high specification: dramatically expensive, fluoropolymer paint. To protect marine installations from the effects of wind and sea water, this was doubtless absolutely wonderful, but on a piece of metalwork in the main street – it chipped.

It is absurdly obvious but important to make the point that the top coat of paint is the one you see. Or, to put it another way, a poor paint finish can ruin an otherwise well-produced piece of work. Someone once said to me that he disliked painting, because it did not make enough noise – and I do know the feeling. After all that heroic forging, painting can seem a rather tedious necessity, but the fact is that serious attention to the finish is time well spent. Most smiths would, I think, prefer not to paint the metal at all, not so much because of the tedium but because what gives them satisfaction is a well-forged, burnished metal surface, probably highlighted with a little abrasive papering, to enhance the hammer texture. It looks like metal. Neither a syrupy gloss or a flat matt paint do much for forged metalwork.

Graphite and Figured Paint Effects

The finish that most closely resembles the as-forged surface is a black paint containing flake graphite. This can be added to alkyd and oil-based paints, in fact any paint that dries slowly enough, and is brushed or preferably sprayed on to the metalwork. Since solvents evaporate quickly as paint is sprayed, it must have

sufficient drying time to allow the paint to be applied to a large area before being burnished with a bare hand or a piece of lint-free cloth or leather. The paint must be just faintly tacky – not sticky – when this is done. Burnishing reveals the graphite, which can be polished on edges or high areas. It is crucial to burnish the paint because, left to dry without attention, the graphite will not show at all. The finish looks best with a semi-matt, eggshell or satin black paint. Since eggshell paints are more porous, it is desirable to use a less permeable gloss, intermediate coat. Flake – not amorphous – graphite can also be added to other dark coloured eggshell paints, at around two teaspoons per 500cc (a pint) of paint, diluted for spraying. Flake graphite is obtainable from locksmiths and engineering suppliers.

This kind of figured surface can also be produced by giving the work a black

Graphite paint finish, applied over a zinc-sprayed surface. Detail of a gate by the author, showing how surfaces and edges can be highlighted by selective burnishing.

eggshell finish, allowing it to dry completely, then lightly dabbing a dry, lighter colour over the top with a flat cloth, hard foam plastic or felt pad, to highlight edges and high spots. Alternatively, the metalwork can be given an intermediate coat of a lighter colour and allowed to dry completely. Eggshell black is then applied over the top, carefully wiping off the paint with a hard, flat cloth or felt pad, as spraying proceeds, to leave bright highlights on high spots and edges.

Micaceous Iron Oxide (MIO) paint finish on a church gate.

Micaceous Iron Oxide Paints (MIO)

These paints contain mica flakes and are available with different binders. The internal, lamellar structure of the paint film gives it excellent resistance to moisture penetration, so it is often used as an intermediate coat. Although the colour range is limited to greyish tints, MIO paints can provide an interesting finish for metalwork, having an essentially matt colour, dusted with minute bright particles.

Decorative Metallic Paints

Paints using finely divided metal powders as pigments are available from a number of manufacturers. Aluminium paint is widely used as an anti-corrosion and heat-reflecting finish, as well as for decorative purposes. 'Gold' paints of various colours are available in a quick drying, alcohol solvent formulation and can be used like gilding to enhance focal points and details in architectural work. Metallic aerosol paints should also be mentioned, again offering a convenient means of defining particular details.

Patinating Paints

These are water-based acrylic paints, which contain a high proportion of metallic powders. As applied, they give a metallic finish or, more dramatically, since the surface is so metal-rich, they can be patinated by applying chemicals supplied by the paint company. A patination liquid is sprayed directly after a copper paint and gives a green verdigris finish. Other effects are available that give a brown rusted finish or simulate 'antique' pewter or tin. These paints are only suitable for internal applications.

Gilding

The process of applying gold leaf to metalwork can offer a wonderful richness and give emphasis to particular details. Left to weather in situations out of reach of handling or abrasion, this can be remarkably durable, but gilding does not provide corrosion protection to the metal underneath, so it should be applied after all other finishing has taken place. Because of the risk in transporting and handling metalwork that has been gilded, it is sometimes undertaken on site. Gold leaf is available as 'books', which contain twenty-five leaves of gold, 80mm (3¼in) square. It can be bought as 'loose' or 'transfer' leaf. Loose leaf is more difficult to handle and will crumple in the slightest draught. Transfer leaf is easier to use, particularly out of doors, since the leaf is pressed on to a backing sheet of tissue paper. To apply transfer leaf, gold size – a lacquer – is brushed on to the metalwork, and when it has all but dried, just retaining a faint tackiness, the leaf is pressed on to the surface, burnished down and the backing paper peeled off. Gold sizes are available with a range of different drying times.

The purity of gold is expressed in 'carats'. Pure gold – 'fine gold' – is described as 24 carat and will not tarnish or corrode. Fine gold leaf is the most durable for exterior purposes, but 22 or 23 carat is widely used. Leaf as low as 12 carat is available, but low-carat golds risk tarnishing in industrial climates, due to their copper or silver content, which also gives them a more red or white colour than pure gold. Leaf may be finished with a clear lacquer or varnish, but this destroys its pure metallic quality. Unless the leaf is of a particularly low carat, it is likely that ultra-violet light and weathering will degrade the varnish more quickly than the gold would tarnish, if left bare.

FINISHES FOR STAINLESS STEELS

To maintain their corrosion resistance, stainless steels depend on the integrity of a thin, passive, chromium-rich oxide film.

Normally, if the oxide film is scratched, it will heal itself quickly. However, when the metal is forged or welded, the protective film is replaced with a layer containing iron oxides and, if the surface is simply left, it will corrode when wetted. Added to this, working with steel tools or grinding with contaminated discs can embed minute steel particles in the stainless steel surface, again causing rusting. It is important, therefore, either to treat the metal with an special paste to remove the local discoloration produced by welding, or to treat the entire assembly by immersion in an acid pickle tank. Specialist companies will pickle stainless steel structures to remove all traces of black oxides and carbon steel particles, leaving the surfaces clean and self protective. This leaves an almost matt white surface, which can be buffed with clean abrasive paper or Scotchbrite pads to produce the desired finish.

Sample pieces of steel rod by Charles Normandale, showing a variety of paint finishes. The bottom four are patinating paints.

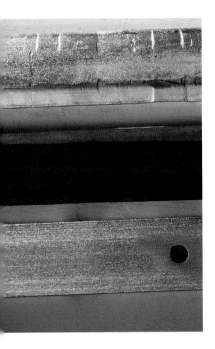

Grade 316 stainless steel flat bar, sample pieces. Centre – hot swaged to produce a handrail section. Top – similar forged bar, immersion pickled and finished with a Scotchbrite pad. Bottom – plain rolled bar with the surface similarly treated.

RIGHT: *Grade 316 stainless steel sample piece. The whole sample has been finished on an abrasive belt, then the top half only has been electropolished.*

Alternatively, the assembly can be electropolished, by immersion in an acid electrolyte, connected to the positive pole of a DC electrical supply. The process operates like the reverse of electroplating, in that the work is the anode in the circuit, causing metal to be stripped from its surface. At the same time, oxygen is liberated from the solution against the surface of the workpiece, producing a passive oxide film. The effect is to selectively remove microscopic irregularities, burrs and high spots, leaving the metal bright and clean. Sadly, however, attractive as it may sound, this is no substitute for mechanical finishing and polishing. Since it operates at such a microscopic level, scratches will not be removed, so the metal should be given the kind of surface finish required before final electropolishing. A test piece is desirable, to establish the process time needed to produce the required appearance. In my experience, electropolishing will give a clean, non-corrodible, bright, shiny surface, but it can look all too glitzy.

If a softer sheen is required, pickling and abrasive papering or pickling and glass-bead blasting will produce a more subtle effect. For interior purposes, the hammer texture of forged stainless steel can be highlighted by abrasive papering or polishing, leaving black oxide in the crevices, and finished by waxing. To achieve something of the same effect after electropolishing or pickling, black paint can be applied to the surface and immediately wiped with a cloth wrapped tightly over a block, to leave paint in the crevices and low areas.

After pickling or electropolishing, stainless steel can also be heat-coloured using a gas torch or a kiln to provide a controlled temperature. Like tempering on tool steel, these colours range from a pale straw through yellow, brown and purple to blue, with increasing heat. Colours are hard to sustain evenly over an area, even in a kiln. The better the polish, the brighter the colour.

Patterns or lettering may be applied to polished stainless steel surfaces, by first masking with two or three layers of paper tape or with specially resilient, plastic masking films. The pattern is cut through the mask and the metal surface blasted with fine sand or emery grit. Many signwriting companies use a computer-generated system to cut self-adhesive, plastic letters and can cut masks. When the mask is stripped, the pattern will be seen as a matt grey surface, which is very receptive to graphite paste or other durable pigments. These can be brushed on and immediately wiped off. The slick steel surface will wipe clean, leaving pigment in the blast-treated areas. Graphite paste used for this purpose weathers very well.

NON-FERROUS METALS

Architectural metalwork can provide opportunities for smiths to use metals other than wrought iron and steels. Many non-ferrous metals are less susceptible to corrosion than mild steel, and can be used for the beauty of their natural colour, without painting. But they do oxidize, and copper-rich alloys, in particular, will either tend to darken like old coins or weather to a blue-green colour in maritime climates. Alloys of many non-ferrous metals are commercially available in grades formulated for hot forging purposes, but all are more expensive than mild steel. Bronzes are around twenty times the price of mild steel, and titanium is more expensive still. The following is a brief summary.

Aluminium

Aluminium is light – only some 34 per cent of the weight of mild steel – soft, white and relatively weak as a pure metal, but is available in a large range of alloys of various strengths, some intended for forging, others for casting. In terms of cost, it falls between mild steel and copper alloys. Since its melting point is so low – 660°C – it shows no heat colour at a temperature suitable for forging, which is in the region of 500°C. It is very easy to overheat the metal in conventional gas or solid-fuel forges. The classic method for judging temperature is to scrape a dry strip of pine wood along the hot surface. When this readily produces a charcoal mark, the metal is hot enough. Like copper, aluminium alloys conduct heat very well, so it is usually necessary to use tongs. Aluminium alloys can be TIG welded using AC current.

Aluminium and its alloys have good corrosion resistance, due to a naturally forming, protective oxide film, which is self-healing. Since this is invariably contaminated by hot forging, aluminium forgings are best finished by hard anodizing.

This electrolytically enhances the oxide film, increasing its thickness and surface hardness, but maintains the natural silvery white appearance of the metal. The oxide film can also be dyed, offering a wide range of durable colour finishes. Not all alloys are equally suitable for colour anodizing, and the range of colours available will depend on what the anodizing company has in their tanks at the time.

Copper

Copper is some 14 per cent heavier than mild steel, with a familiar, reddish colour. It is soft and easily hot forged at a red heat, but is such a good conductor that a bar quickly becomes too hot to handle, and must invariably be held in tongs. Copper is annealed by heating to red heat and quenching in water. The metal is very soft in its annealed state, but can be work-hardened to some advantage by cold hammering. Due to its softness, copper can be awkward to drill or machine cleanly. It can be silver soldered to iron and steel, and with sufficient current will TIG weld very readily to itself. The use of copper in architectural work is limited by its lack of structural strength, but its rich colour offers decorative possibilities. Left unprotected, copper will tarnish in exterior situations, becoming a dark brown. With continued weathering, a powdery green, self-protecting patina can eventually develop and prevent the metal corroding further. This, and a variety of other patination colours, can be achieved chemically, but only the green verdigris patina is stable out of doors. Since the patinated surfaces are porous, wax finishing is very effective in preserving patination colours for interior use.

Copper Alloys

Copper alloys include brasses and bronzes. Brass is traditionally defined as an alloy of copper and zinc, while bronze is an alloy of copper and tin. But, like the

Copper and brass sample pieces, treated with different chemical patination solutions. The distinct texture of the two circular samples is achieved by packing them in sawdust, damped with the chemical solution.

terminology of iron and steel, these definitions have become blurred, to a point where they now mean very little. Perhaps because historically it was widely used for cheap ornaments, 'brass' has somehow never acquired the kind of semi-precious quality invested in the word 'bronze'. So copper alloys tend to be called bronzes, even if they contain no tin at all.

Copper and nickel form another family of alloys. Cupro-nickel is a malleable, silvery alloy of some 75 per cent nickel and copper, which provides the familiar 'silver' coinage in Britain. Monel is an alloy that originated as the product of smelting a naturally mixed ore, containing some 67 per cent nickel, 28 per cent copper with iron and manganese. This is a silvery, corrosion-resistant material, which forges like mild steel and was popular for architectural and decorative metalwork in the art deco period, before being supplanted by stainless steel.

Forging copper alloys calls for far more careful temperature control than is required for mild steel. The heat colour may be so low that some brasses can only be forged at a heat that is just visible in the shade under a forge hood. Care must be taken to hammer only when and where the metal is at the correct heat. As a general rule this means that when a bar is heated, only the further two-thirds of the heat should be hammered, leaving the third nearest the parent bar untouched, to act as a shock absorber. Brasses and bronzes will oxidize and tarnish, some very much more slowly than others. Copper/tin and copper/zinc alloys respond very well to chemical patination treatments, offering a wide range of coloured and textured surfaces for internal use. Protected by waxing, in areas where they are not abraded, these can be very stable.

Brasses

Brasses have a red-gold or yellow-gold colour, depending on their zinc content. They are all stronger, harder and more rigid than copper and generally cut, file and machine very well. They are categorized as alpha brasses, which have up to 37 per cent zinc and are intended for cold working; and beta brasses, which contain more than 37 per cent zinc and are intended for hot forging. Brasses containing up to 20 per cent zinc are called gilding metals. A malleable, reddish gilding metal of 90 per cent copper and 10 per cent zinc is widely used by silversmiths for cold forming, fabrication and subsequent plating. An alloy of 60 per cent copper and 40 per cent zinc is a yellow brass, known as Muntz metal, and is a good, hot forging metal, working at a dull red heat.

Brasses polish very easily and retain their colour with fairly minimal maintenance but, left alone, will tend to blacken, particularly in industrial climates. Brasses respond well to chemical patination treatments and, after waxing, can be used very successfully in interior situations.

Bronzes

Bronzes embrace a large family of alloys, some intended for hot working, others for cold. They vary in colour from an almost copper red, through to a greenish gold. Bronzes containing tin, phosphorus or silicon usually weather to a green or black patina, while aluminium bronzes tolerate weathering far better, tending to retain their colour.

The classic sculpture bronze – a 90 per cent copper and 10 per cent tin alloy – is used for casting. Close to this is 'admiralty gunmetal', containing 88 per cent copper, 10 per cent tin and 2 per cent zinc, used for casting marine components. Some bronzes suitable for hot forging contain no tin at all. The reddish coloured silicon bronze forges well at a low red heat. This contains 95 per cent copper, 3 per cent silicon, 1 per cent manganese and 1 per cent zinc. Aluminium bronzes are stronger materials. Those containing 10 per cent or more aluminium, are suitable for hot forging at red heat and have a pale gold colour. Nickel aluminium bronze (NAB) has a brassy colour, contains 75 per cent copper, 10 per cent aluminium, 5 per cent nickel and 5 per cent iron. Manganese bronze is really a high-tensile beta brass, containing around 58 per cent copper, 39 per cent zinc, and 1 per cent each of aluminium, iron and manganese. Many bronzes will respond to chemical patination, but those containing higher percentages of aluminium may be little affected.

Titanium

Titanium is a silvery grey, high strength metal, with a high melting point of 1,668°C and is some 56 per cent of the weight of mild steel. It is available in a range of alloys, some more suitable than others for hot forging, but all of them very expensive. It forges very well at temperatures similar to those for forging mild steel, but will tolerate higher temperatures. Care must be taken, however, since at high temperatures there is considerable grain growth in the metal, which can result in a crystalline or granular surface. Like stainless steels it is naturally protected by a thin, very adherent oxide film, which renders it almost inert in terms of weathering, and superior to high grades of stainless steel in maritime climates. When cold, it is hard and springy, and can be worked much like stainless steel, grinding with an unmistakable white spark. Forging leaves a thick oxide on the surface, which can be removed by abrasive papering, to leave the metal with its natural oxide film.

Titanium may also be coloured by heat or, far more predictably, by anodizing, which microscopically increases the thickness of the oxide film to produce interference colours similar to, but more vivid than, temper colours on steel. The anodizing process can be controlled very accurately to produce a specific and even colour.

Lead

Lead is a familiar, very soft and heavy metal, some 45 per cent heavier than mild steel. Silvery white when first cut, it soon develops a dull grey protective oxide coating. It is far too soft for structural purposes, but is of interest to blacksmiths for 'leading in' – grouting with molten lead – to fix railings or hinges into masonry. It is a toxic metal and can be absorbed through the skin, so gloves should be worn when handling lead, and great care taken when heating it, to avoid inhaling vapours.

12 INSTALLATION

PLANNING

Fixing metalwork is perhaps the most stressful phase of any project. Until that point, the work has been undertaken in a familiar workshop environment where, should unforeseen problems arise, the necessary tools and equipment are at hand. Fixing demands planning, in order to anticipate possible problems and to ensure that they can be solved. The key is to plan the installation right at the outset, as an integral part of the design process. If you know that you are going to have to transport, lift and fix it all in place, it is clearly a design decision to consider the size of particular components, how they can be handled, what kind of fixings are going to be required and how they should be placed. Whatever the nature of the metalwork, once on site with the work off-loaded, the procedure resolves itself into moving it into position and setting it up, level, vertical and in line, before placing fixings and securing it.

There are a number of important organizational concerns, which must be resolved before you start work on someone else's property, and these are dealt with at the end of this chapter.

TOOLS AND EQUIPMENT

Working on site, however carefully planned, is invariably to some degree a step in the dark. It is never a bad thing to assume the worst and bring more tools than are strictly necessary, in case you lose a drill bit down a crack in the paving, break a tap while clearing out a threaded hole or hit an unexpected reinforcement rod when drilling concrete. Even the electric tool you checked in the workshop the day before, will suddenly need new motor brushes, out there in the rain, after all the shops have closed. The lesson is to bring spares and bring tools to maintain tools. A hammer drill or angle grinder may be rendered inoperable for lack of a small electrical screwdriver, and this might just be the angle grinder you need to sharpen a blunt drill. 'Equipment' should also include odd items like string, adhesive tape, cardboard or sheeting to deflect grinder sparks, and some stiff wire to hook out masonry cores after drilling or to fish around down a crack for that drill bit. Pieces of steel and timber packing are almost always required, and preparing proper pairs of wedges by sawing diagonally across short lengths of timber is well worthwhile. Sweeping brushes, a dustpan and a vacuum cleaner, fitted with a small-diameter extension to suck the dust out of drilled holes, are all essential. Pieces of clean rag, touch-up paint, brushes and thinners are also crucial items. On top of all this are things like ladders, step ladders, timber to sit them on if the ground is soft, an old blanket or folded piece of carpet to pad the ladder against the paintwork, a bucket to carry water, a crowbar, tapered steel drifts for aligning bolt holes, and so on. If in doubt, take it.

Despite protesting that I was not a locksmith, I was once persuaded by an architect to visit a medieval church where a beautiful, old iron-bound chest had been slammed shut and could not be opened. I spent well over an hour packing every conceivable hand and electric power tool into the back of my car and drove forty miles,

OPPOSITE PAGE: Fixing railings at the National Youth Theatre, Holloway Road, London.

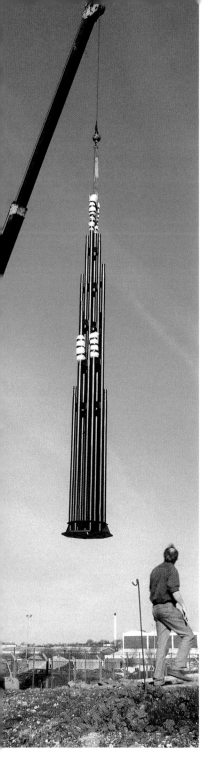

The core structure for a piece of public art being lifted on to its foundation on an earth mound, by a crane sited some 15m away on a roadway.

to be met by the church warden who handed me a huge iron key and walked off while I contemplated the problem. The chest was clearly jammed solid and the key would not turn in the lock. Having reluctantly reached the conclusion that I was probably going to have to start drilling out rivets in the lid of the chest, it dawned on me that the blade of the key had been twisted out of alignment with the shaft, so I gripped it in a heavy vice in the tailgate of the car, hit the blade twice with a large copper mallet and the job was done. The chest opened smoothly and I drove away thirty minutes after arriving. The lesson of the story is – do not begrudge transporting that unnecessary hundred kilos of equipment, because you just never know.

TRANSPORT

Transporting finished metalwork calls for some care, most of all in securing and protecting the work, whether it is in a car, van, pick-up, trailer or large truck. In all cases it must be securely tied down in and, where appropriate, wedged into place so that there is no risk of movement. The metalwork should be laid on padding and the ropes or ratchet straps should all be well-padded where they pass over the metal, to avoid chafing. Any movement can result in the strap wearing the paint back to bare metal in just a few miles. Pieces of carpet make very effective padding and can be obtained from carpet fitters as off-cuts, or even in neat rectangles from carpet shops as last year's samples.

While padding protects the metalwork, it is crucial to consider what protects you. Although we are all highly responsible drivers, it is important to remember that, if the metalwork is being carried in a car or van, you are in there with it. In a traffic accident, a small window grille or a box of tools can turn into a lethal missile. We have all seen video pictures of an unsecured dummy child being carried over the front seats and out through the windscreen. Well – try a gate. Give this some thought while you load the vehicle and lash things down. Make sure you arrange lengths of steel or a heavy crowbar to go to one side of the seats, rather than straight though them, should someone drive into the back of you. Put heavy tool boxes low down, in the foot well if possible.

Depending on the nature of the metalwork, the journey and the amount of handling or storage expected on arrival, it may well be worthwhile packing everything in bubble wrap, skinfoam, industrial cling-film or other wrapping material. With some kinds of paint there is a risk that plastic films can stick, so this should be checked. Wrapping the work can prevent damage during transit and handling, and on site it may be advisable only to expose necessary areas, so that the wrapping can be left in place while fixing, to prevent accidental damage. If work is still continuing on the site, the metalwork can be left protected from plaster, paint or collision, and only removed later by others, when all the work has been completed.

If you hire a truck and driver, particularly a truck with an integral hydraulic crane, I would suggest leaving the loading to the driver. By all means be involved, but leave the initiative to him or her. It is your responsibility to ensure that the appropriate timber frames or special packing are available if the work needs supporting in a particular way, but most drivers are very adept at working out the best way to fit and balance the load. At the end of the day, it is the driver's responsibility to deliver it to the right place, at the right time, in the same condition as when it was loaded.

ACCESS

The problems of moving metalwork into position vary considerably depending on the scale and location of the project. There

Skates, simple workshop-made devices with wheels or castors, for moving pieces of work.

is a major difference between taking a small window grille out of the back of your car and tucking it under an arm to carry it to its position and hiring a crane to lift a tonne or two into place over a wall; these two extremes are at least clear-cut – either you can lift it comfortably or you cannot. More difficult decisions arise with pieces that are barely possible to lift alone, but seem too small to justify heavy lifting equipment. It is a question of whether to pay for help, find volunteers or employ some kind of mechanical assistance. The decision may well depend on the location, because, for example, there is probably no alternative to simply manhandling a section of balustrading up the stairs. It makes a difference whether the particular location is in a building or outside, whether the approach is over hard paved surfaces or soft ground and whether it is level, stepped or sloping. Lifting vertically is the real problem.

Short of a crane, there are a number of alternative ways of moving pieces of metal-work horizontally, or over shallow gradients, all of which reduce the need for manual lifting. They need a hard surface on which to work effectively, so on soft ground, sheets of building plywood or lines of timber planks will need to be laid down. These methods also require that the

metalwork be stood up on one edge and held in balance while being pushed along, with perhaps the occasional assistance of a lever. The crudest method is to use plain rollers – odd lengths of round bar or heavy tube – which might be used in the work-shop to move a piece of equipment. These need some kind of carrier on which the metalwork is placed, not least since, if they are allowed to roll directly under the item being moved, they will damage the paint-work. By placing a padded edge of the metalwork in a length of light steel channel section, or a timber trough, it can be rolled along without damage.

Using one or two 'skates' in the same way, may be a better alternative. These can be made in the workshop from a piece of board and substantial wheels or castors. Heavy-duty skates are available commer-cially and are used by machinery movers. These consists of a series of steel rollers fit-ted like caterpillar tracks round a small steel shoe. Having tools of this kind to take the weight while you concentrate on bal-ancing the load, steering and pushing,

CASE STUDY

A sequence of photographs illustrating the installation of a pair of very large and heavy steel and stainless steel gates and side panels, designed by Alan Evans and Matthew Fedden, and made by Alan Evans and Simon Hunter, securing the access to a large truck loading bay at the rear of a building at Bigg Market, in the centre of Newcastle.

ABOVE: *One post and side panel is already fixed, as the other is manoeuvred into place.*

ABOVE: *Detail of the bearing housing on the bottom of the back stile, the race and mounting.*

LEFT: *The front corner of the right-hand base-plate, showing a self-levelling laser device being used to set the top and bottom bearing positions vertically in line. The laser throws a spot vertically up and down, registering here against the side of a small hole marking the centre of the bottom bearing, and similarly at the top bearing position. The base-plate level is adjusted on jacking screws through small plates under the base-plate, one of which is visible at the corner. The four short pillars lift the bottom bearing to compensate for the sloping ground on this side of the gateway.*

CASE STUDY

ABOVE: Detail of the top bronze bush and bearing housing.

ABOVE: Lifting the left-hand gate into place. The man at the left, wearing a white helmet, is operating the crane on the truck, through a radio remote control unit.

ABOVE: The bottom bearing mounting, held temporarily by a plastic tie, being delicately manoeuvred into place. The lift is under the control of the man at the left through his remote unit.

ABOVE: The top bearing being located on its bolt holes.

RIGHT: The gates almost complete and ready for the base-plates to be grouted up underneath and the automatic opening equipment to be fitted. A powerful piece of city centre metalwork and a rhythmic symphony of punched holes. Alan Evans and Lesley at the left.

makes life a little easier. Even using a sack barrow, well-padded to take the weight at one end of a panel of metalwork, while pushing from the other, can offer worthwhile help. Depending on the size of the panel and the width of the access, a steerable four-wheel trolley may allow metalwork to be laid flat on suitable padding and moved in that position. A pallet truck offers far better load-carrying capacity and manoeuvrability, but again the work needs to be supported vertically. If the metalwork is to be fixed at ground or floor level, it is only necessary to remove it carefully from its support and manhandle it a short distance into place.

LIFTING

Many pieces of metalwork – a horizontal balustrade panel, for example – may need lifting a short distance to meet its fixing points. At the simplest, this can be accomplished by hand-lifting one end at a time and inserting timber packing at each end, until the correct level is reached. Where

access is restricted, or with heavier panels, the same kind of manoeuvre can be accomplished using a crowbar or jack, and padding it against the metalwork. The balance of the panel is clearly critical and it is essential to stabilize it in some way; for example, by temporarily clamping timbers at either side of the posts or masonry to box in the metalwork, allowing it only limited sideways movement. If space allows, angled timber props can be used from either side.

More serious lifting will need a portable crane. Small hydraulic – even folding – cranes on castors are used by garages to lift out engines. These are available with capacities up to 2 tonnes and are relatively cheap to buy or can be hired. They are designed with legs projecting forward to fit under a vehicle and may, for some purposes, need a short extension to the jib, to ensure that it projects beyond the legs, allowing say a window grille to be fitted without the legs fouling the wall. It may be necessary to ballast the other end of the crane to achieve this. I used one of these to fix four large internal window grilles in Portsmouth City Museum, which needed to be held securely with the top of the grille some 3m (10ft) off the ground, while fourteen bolt fixings were drilled and placed (*see* Chapter 5). The ability of this kind of crane to be moved while carrying a load, and to provide small vertical adjustments, is very helpful, allowing a fixing bolt to be placed at one side, then the height of the grille adjusted fractionally to level up its other side.

Sheerlegs – a tripod carrying a pulley block – is an ancient lifting device. Sheerlegs today consist of steel tubes linked loosely by a heavy steel cross bar, so that the legs can be folded into a flat bundle for transport, or splayed to provide stability when in use. It can lift vertically but cannot be moved under a load, which calls for careful placing. Unlike a crane with a jib, which lifts in front or to one side of its own

Sheerlegs in use by Bill Cordaroy to lift and fit a pair of gates. (Photo: Bill Cordaroy)

footprint, the configuration of the tripod requires that it be able to straddle the working area. The legs need to be planted on a firm, level surface and secured by long steel pegs driven into the ground or by a tension rope, so that they cannot slide. For work such as gates or heavy railings, where a straight lift is required to bring the metalwork up to the fixings, it provides a simple, portable and effective answer.

In many instances, both delivery and the lifting required to fix the work can be achieved by a flat-bed truck fitted with a hydraulic crane. These are becoming very sophisticated in their control systems and can lift increasingly heavy loads. If a truck is needed in any case to transport the work, the additional cost of one equipped with a crane is not large. Well maintained, these cranes can move work with great precision but, like most equipment, are only as good as the operator. Modern machines have a remote control system, enabling the driver to carry a control panel wherever required, for a clear view of the lifting operation. This makes for far safer working and, to a large extent, removes the need for possibly ambiguous hand signals. It is important with any kind of crane to ensure that soft nylon slings are used in contact with the painted surface of the metalwork, rather than hooks or chain slings.

A hired crane is the expensive but ideal answer for heavy lifting, or perhaps more often where reach is the problem. Heavy lifting needs heavy equipment, so access and the load-bearing capacity of the ground or paving may present a problem. Rather than plywood or planks, a heavy crane may need its approach to be covered with railway sleepers. It is not only the dead weight of the metalwork that determines the need for, or the size of, a crane, but also the horizontal distance over which the load must be lifted. Since the load capacity of a crane diminishes with the reach, a sizeable crane may be needed to

lift a relatively modest weight over a long distance. The long jib and cable of a crane allows work to be lifted over obstructions. The long drop of the cable to an extent 'cushions' the movement of the crane jib, allowing work to be guided into position very easily. Crane drivers are invariably experienced people with real concern for precision and safety.

Various other machines are worth considering. A fork-lift truck can be fitted with a crane hook for lifting and is a very effective tool, provided it can be brought to, or is already available, on site. Although not essentially intended as load-lifting equipment, a farm tractor fitted with front loading arms, or a diesel hydraulic excavating machine (JCB), is more mobile than a fork lift and can provide controlled lifting. Hydraulic and electric work platforms – cherry pickers – should also be mentioned. These are available for hire in a wide variety of configurations, from a small folding device that can be towed behind a car, to a high-reach platform mounted on a diesel truck. The work platform itself may be intended for one person only, or be large enough to carry two or three. The electric platforms usually run on low-voltage battery power and can be used inside buildings. Others for outside use, run on petrol or diesel engines. Although they are more expensive,

Gates, already hung as a workshop assembled unit, being lifted into place by a hydraulic crane on the delivery truck. A clever design by Brian Russell for Whitehaven Football club. (Photo: Brian Russell)

they provide far better access and man-oeuvrability than a fixed scaffold tower, as well as providing the capacity to lift and carry tools and small components.

SETTING UP

Having moved the metalwork into place, setting up – levelling, checking, aligning and fitting – is a small but very crucial phase of fixing. At this point the piece is usually poised in a faintly precarious state, wedged or propped with pieces of timber, or perhaps still held on the hoist or crane, but not secured in place. For this reason it is tempting to rush into drilling and placing fixings as quickly as possible. However, this is the one point in the whole operation when standing back for a minute is time well spent. The need to take care in setting up the metalwork illustrates the inevitable compromise required when fitting an accurate workshop-made component into a rather less accurate building. Like the old workshop adage of measuring twice and cutting once, this is the time to take a careful look and be sure that everything is as it should be; to check

dimensions and be sure, for instance, that this is the right panel in the right place, and there is nothing fouling the edge or caught underneath. The panel can then be checked with a level and adjusted as necessary until it is set on line, truly vertical, with its top edge horizontal or at the required angle. Again it is worth spending time to do this, checking carefully after each adjustment to ensure that one alteration has not disturbed another, and that the readings are correct in each plane. Keeping in mind each separate plane is an important discipline.

At the end of the day, it is question of what looks right, and this may go back to the design of the metalwork. If, for example, a window grill is designed with an external frame to fit snugly in the window opening, the accuracy of the opening is crucial. There is little point in struggling to fit an accurately squared panel, truly horizontal and vertical, if the window reveals are out of square. Metalwork does not often need to be fitted in this way. Substantial spaces are usually allowed all round a balustrade or railing panel, grille or gate, so that if the wall is not vertical or the floor is not horizontal, the discrepancy can be lost in the gap. The narrower the gap, the more it shows. The clearance between two leaves of a gate is dramatically obvious if it is not parallel, but if the gap tapers between the back stile and the brick pillar to which it is hinged, this is far less visually disturbing.

Wedges, packing pieces or clamps need to be fitted tight while fixings holes are marked or, more particularly, if they are to be drilled through. The vibration of a hammer drill can disturb metalwork very easily unless it is held very securely. It can help to centralize the drill through the hole in the metalwork by using a temporary sleeve made from plastic or rubber. Short lengths of plastic plumbing pipe can be split to reduce their diameter, if necessary. Rubber or flexible plastic hose provides some cushioning from the vibration. Thick-wall tubing like old propane or oxy-acetylene hose, or flexible, vehicle brake tubing can be useful in locating a smaller pilot drill on centre, through a larger hole in the fixing plate.

Where lugs or studs have already been placed – for example, lugs set into masonry piers to secure railings – setting up may only consist of dropping bolts in the holes, checking with a level and, where necessary, adjusting heights by inserting packing washers before tightening up. Where railings or grilles are grouted into masonry at either side, the fixing holes are marked out level, then drilled or cut. The holes cut on one side are made twice the depth of those on the other, so that the tails on this side of the panel can be inserted and the panel pushed in at an angle, sufficiently for the tails on the other side to clear the window reveal. The panel can then be squared up and these tails inserted in their holes. The grille can then be centralized in the opening, and levelled by packing up as necessary with fragments of stone, brick or concrete before grouting in place.

FIXINGS

There are fundamentally two kinds of fixing: those where a tail or lug projecting from the metalwork is directly built in or grouted into a hole; and those that use some form of mechanical screw or bolt fixing. Grouting may require more site work, drilling larger holes and possibly mixing grouting material, but it has the great advantage of leaving a 'clean' connection with no projecting bolt, screws or nuts. In consequence it is not open to the kind of vandalism that removes the odd fixing bolt just for fun, or more serious attack aimed, for example, at removing a window grille in order to break into the building.

Grouting

Grouting in metalwork requires that it be set up in place, the positions of the tails marked, then the panel moved, so that holes or pockets can be cut to accommodate them. The panel can then be finally located in place and packed up to the correct level. If the holes are vertical, it is a straightforward operation to pour in, or inject, the grouting material. There are three different types of material suitable for fixing metalwork: molten lead, cement-based and resin-based grouts; all have their advantages and disadvantages. The advantages of grouting as a method are that it eliminates the need for fixing plates, flanges or the problem of what to do with bolt heads or nuts. It also provides some built-in adjustment, in that the holes are necessarily larger than the tail to be fixed, in order to allow room for the grout. This means that, for example, a gate can be set up with the tails of the hinges tucked in drilled holes or pockets cut in the masonry, while the gate itself is wedged or propped in position, truly vertical and with all its correct clearances. In a sense, what you see is what you get. The operation of grouting in the hinges puts no strain on the metalwork, and does nothing that might vibrate or disturb its position.

ABOVE: *Leading railing uprights into masonry, as part of a major restoration commission at Blickling Hall Mausoleum in Norfolk. Bill Cordaroy maintains the bar vertical, while his assistant pours in the lead. (Photo: Bill Cordaroy)*

RIGHT: *The restored railings with a new top rail, also leaded to the uprights. After much research Bill Cordaroy discovered that silicone putty, sold as a temporary adhesive for tacking papers to a wall surface, provided the best material to hold the lead in the joint while pouring. (Photo: Bill Cordaroy)*

Grouting with Lead

Securing metalwork with molten lead is called 'leading in'. The stone, brick or concrete should be dry, as far as possible. Prior to pouring in the lead, a squirt of oil into the hole is essential to prevent residual moisture causing the lead to spit. Quite how this works is obscure, but presumably it has some fluxing effect and, understood or not, works very well in calming the lead. Greasing the metal tail has the same effect. Because of the risk of the lead erupting, it is essential to wear a face shield and gloves. The lead should be melted in a steel ladle, close to the working position, to avoid having to carry it any further than is necessary. Lead can be melted over a coke or charcoal brazier, but a propane ring burner is ideal. Always wear gloves to handle lead, avoid overheating the metal and breathing the fumes. Once molten, the dross should be skimmed off and the lead poured in smartly without stopping, because it solidifies almost immediately and, if you hesitate, it can freeze in a narrow gap, blocking the flow. Holes should be filled well proud of the surface, because the metal must be hammered in or 'caulked' to consolidate it, and it is important to leave the exposed lead angled to shed water. Caulking requires 'caulking irons', which resemble cold chisels but with a narrow flat end, about 25 × 6mm (1 × ¼in), usually dog-legged to enable them to work close to the metal when driven by a hammer. Caulking is essential both to tighten the lead against the metal tail and the walls of the hole, and to dress the joint surface to shape. The metal is so malleable that small scraps of lead can be caulked in cold to fill any voids. Watertight, spigot and socket joints in cast-iron pipes used to be made cold, by caulking with lead wool.

ABOVE: *Leaded joint grouting in the upright of a balustrade by Steve Lunn (see Chapter 7). Note how the lead is caulked up proud of the surface to avoid a water trap.*

LEFT: *The extraordinary Blickling Hall Mausoleum, showing the finished railings. I understand that during the work, the occasional spooky cup of tea was taken inside on rainy days. (Photo: Bill Cordaroy)*

Horizontal tails or hinges can be leaded in by making a pouring cup – unlikely as it may sound – from 'plasticine' modelling clay. This is pressed in place so as to stick to both the masonry and seal around the metal being fixed, leaving a funnel-shaped opening at the top. The cup must be shaped to provide a good flow and it is important to clean the masonry to remove any powdery surface, to ensure that the plasticine adheres. The shape of the cavity in the plasticine must leave enough lead projecting from the finished joint to allow it to be caulked in. It is better to err on the side of leaving too much, since any surplus can be cut off with a sharp chisel. The plasticine in contact with the molten metal will degrade rapidly used in this way, but it is cheap. A more durable alternative is silicone putty, which is more expensive but will last longer. The great advantage of using lead is that it freezes almost immediately after pouring, can be caulked up solid and is load-bearing within a few minutes, no matter how hot or cold the weather.

There is an account of the securing of thirty-six heavy, vertical wrought iron bars to a rock, as part of the foundations of the Eddystone lighthouse by John Rudyerd in 1706. This was built on a reef in the sea, fourteen miles south of Plymouth, which was only exposed at low tide. The iron uprights were in two parts, forming a dovetailed end, so that fitted side by side in an undercut hole in the granite and bolted together, they could not be withdrawn. With waves threatening to fill the holes, Rudyerd devised the idea of mopping out as much water as possible, then filling the holes to the brim with boiling tallow – animal fat – to drive out the remaining moisture. Once set solid, this sealed the holes. At the next low tide, the ends of the irons were heated in a coal forge and each bar plunged into a hole, melting its way through the tallow and displacing most of it. Molten pewter was finally poured in, replacing the tallow, and

grouting the iron to the rock. The tallow presumably also had much the same fluxing effect as the squirt of oil, noted above. A thought for a particularly rainy day.

Cement-Based Grouts

These are usually available in powder form to be mixed with water, and may dry quite rapidly – in as little as fifteen minutes – or may take several hours. Even rapid-setting cements usually take several hours to fully cure and achieve their maximim load-carrying capacity, although this may not matter a great deal when grouting into a floor surface. Some grouts may be mixed to a highly fluid consistency and poured into a hole from a plastic jug, like thin cream, or they can be mixed to a thicker consistency and injected with a mastic gun. As described above, a cup can be made – in this case even from potter's clay – to allow a semi-liquid grout to be poured into a horizontal joint. The fluidity of these grouts can be very useful to ensure penetration of the fixing hole, but may also find voids in the masonry. When the liquid fails to fill in the hole, it is probably flooding somewhere. It may be that leaving the hole alone for a while will allow the material already in there to clog the leak, or making up a thicker mix and packing grout into the joint may provide an answer. At the worst it may mean removing the metalwork and preparing the hole by lining it with damp newspaper, or ramming a wad of newspaper down to the bottom.

Thicker mixes can be injected using a re-cycled mastic cartridge and nozzle as a syringe, or by folding a triangular piece of sheet polythene into a cone, like a pastry cook's icing bag, and securing it with duct tape. The pointed end can be cut to the required diameter. This only will survive half a dozen fillings, but it is cheap to make and can be improvised on site should the need arise. The advantage of cement-based grouting materials is their price, compared with resins. They can be

A combination of bad siting, poor grouting, water penetration and rust has caused the bottom socket bearing of this gate to break out of the masonry.

very fluid, enabling holes to be filled quickly and easily, and they can be tinted to match the stone, so their appearance can be very sympathetic. As water-based cements, their drying speed will vary to a degree, depending on the dryness and porosity of the masonry. Very dry and absorbent masonry may require damping before the grout is used.

Resin Grouts

Resin grouting is now a familiar process for securing screw fixings in drilled holes, but can, of course, be used to grout in the tails or lugs of pieces of metalwork, as described above. It is expensive, so for many purposes it may be too expensive, compared with cement grouting. Grouting in a bolt requires a relatively small amount of resin, but using this kind of material to, say, grout in the ends of vertical posts for a balustrade or railing will require considerable volumes. Using resin to grout in the hinges of a gate may be another matter, since the strength of resin and the simplicity of the system can outweigh the time required to set up lead- or cement-based systems, as described above.

Resins are available either as bulk material to be dispensed through a gun, or as individual capsules, specifically for fixing bolts. The gun system is more flexible and uses a disposable foil pack of resin and hardener, which are brought together and mixed in a special disposable nozzle and dispensed in measured amounts. Once used, the nozzle remains full of the resin and hardener mix, and becomes useless once this has set. The long nozzle enables resin to be injected fairly deep into holes, and extensions can be added to make this even deeper. Specific formulations of polyester and epoxy resins are available for fixing into different materials, such as stone, concrete, brick or blockwork. The resin is viscous enough to be injected horizontally or vertically into cavities without running back out, and may contain quartz fillers,

which give it a very high pull-out strength when applied to bolts.

Despite being quite expensive, the advantage of the sytem is its convenience, strength and reliability. Like so many things, it needs some understanding to use it efficiently. The time needed for the resin to set fully is a function of temperature. It can be conveniently quick on warm days, but very slow on a cold day. On a hot day it can be almost too quick. To make the best use of this requires several joints to be set up and ready for the resin before it goes solid in the nozzle. It can be very frustrating to run out of something as trivial as a plastic nozzle. However, the newer resin-capsule systems are reputed to be unaffected by temperature.

Bolt and Screw Fixings

Mechanical fixings in masonry offer two basic alternatives: a projecting threaded stud; or a flush-fitted, internally threaded socket. The choice depends on a number of factors, which include: the visual quality of the finished result; the need for adjustment; and whether you are prepared to move the metalwork to drill oversize holes. If the base-plate for a gatepost or railing is to be buried under the ground or paving, its appearance is not a great concern. Having threaded studs projecting from the foundation surface allows for good height adjustment and makes it possible to fit nuts under the base-plate as well as above, to jack it level and into position, and to lock it in place. On the other hand, threads projecting through nuts do not look very sympathetic at eye level, securing the hinges of a gate. Some stud fixings can be placed by drilling directly through the fixing holes in the work, while socket fixings, being internally threaded, are always larger than the fixing hole and require a large hole to be drilled in the masonry.

The appearance of fixings is very important in forged architectural metalwork. We go to a lot of trouble to make beautiful forms, surfaces and details, and take time to head up a neat rivet. So the same care and attention should be given to screw fixings. Hexagon bolt heads, nuts and odd ends of thread always stand out like the proverbial sore thumb – engineering components – which are out of context in a piece of artist blacksmithing. Forging a bolt head to a more suitable shape or making special cap nuts may take a little time but is well worth the effort. Even forging hexagon heads square looks somehow more like blacksmithing. Hexagon socket heads are less obtrusive and countersunk screws of this kind will sit in flush. With a short piece of hexagon key in a fly press, you can even hot punch your own sockets, to adapt or make bolts with socket heads.

Fixing into timber also calls for some care with the use of screws. Now that plain steel screws are virtually unobtainable – they are all zinc or cadmium plated – left to themselves these can stand out like a rash of silver spots. Painting the head, or heating it to burn off the plating and waxing them for interior use, does not take a lot of time. More irritating still, in my view, is the fact that coach screws with square heads seem to have become obsolete and all now have hexagon heads, in a pointless imitation of machine bolts, and require more forging to put them right.

An important concern with some exposed fixings is not only appearance but security. Particularly in public places, the issue of vandalism may require that fixings be used that cannot be unscrewed by some passing idiot, often simply to see if it can be done. Security or 'prison' nuts and bolts are available where the drive section shears off after tightening, to leave a smooth tamper-proof fixing in place. Others have heads, designed on a ratchet principle, which can only be rotated inwards using a special key and cannot be removed except by drilling out, or by taking other drastic measures. Short of these, special bolt heads can be devised and made in the workshop, which match special drive wrenches. Or the sockets of hexagon socket head screws can be drilled and a small pin inserted in the centre, preventing a normal hexagon wrench from entering the cavity. A hexagon wrench can then be adapted by annealing it and drilling a clearance hole in its end, so that it will fit over the pin, then re-hardening and tempering it for use. Even fitting hexagon socket countersunk screws and filling the cavities in the heads completely flush with polyester resin car body filler, painted over, will act as a deterrent. Similarly, cylindrical bolt heads or cap nuts can be made, with two drive holes like those in an angle grinder nut. The holes may be drilled so they do not match a standard angle grinder spacing and a wrench made to match. Again these holes can be filled with resin.

Whatever the kind of fixing, it is always worth considering the use of stainless steel. This is more expensive but stronger,

Various screw and bolt fixings. From left to right – two steel expansion studs, a plastic expansion sleeve and bolt, a large stainless steel sleeve anchor, a small cadmium-plated sleeve anchor, hammer-in expanding anchor with modified stainless steel countersunk hexagon socket bolt, expanding anchor without bolt, square-head coach screw and plastic plug, small square-head coach screw, coach screw reforged to provide a countersunk hexagon socket head, coach screw reforged to provide a round hexagon socket head.

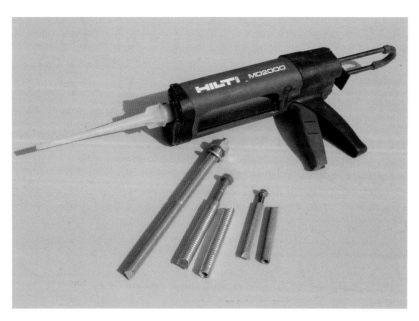

Above, a typical gun for injecting resin from disposable cartridges. Below, resin anchor bolts, from left to right a stud anchor, a sleeve anchor with and without bolt, and a small sleeve anchor with and without bolt.

and the benefit of considerable corrosion resistance may be well worth the cost. In fact, as part of the budget of an average commission, the additional cost of a handful of stainless steel fixings is small. During fixing, these are the one component of the whole carefully finished project that is attacked with a wrench or socket spanner, often damaging their paint finish and requiring them to be re-painted afterwards. Stainless steel fixings may still need painting, but it is purely cosmetic, and you are not left with that nagging feeling that they may start rusting away, the moment your back is turned. For some applications, it may be worth considering the use of stainless steel 'tails' welded to a mild steel structure, to prevent corrosion where metal is grouted into a possibly damp, ground-level foundation.

Resin Anchor Fixings
As described above, these have become a routine way of fixing architectural metalwork. Their great advantage is in providing a means of fitting a stud or internally threaded socket, without putting any stress into the masonry itself. They are literally glued into place. In consequence, they can

be set in softer stone or brick and, where necessary, placed closer to an edge than would be desirable with expanding fixings. A wide variety of stud and socket fittings is commercially available. To fix these, a hole is drilled to a specific diameter for each screw or socket size, as listed by the manufacturer. The dust must then be cleaned out with a special brush, or sucked out by fitting a suitable piece of tube to the end of a vacuum cleaner nozzle. With a resin-dispenser gun, the required number of squirts of resin are placed in the hole, initially with the nozzle near the bottom to ensure proper filling. Then the stud or socket is pushed into the hole, embedding itself in the resin, which is displaced to fill the hole. When using this system, it is good practice to place a small squirt of resin on a piece of card, immediately after injecting a hole, as a control sample to indicate when the resin has hardened.

Using the resin-capsule system, the hole is similarly drilled at the manufacturer's specified diameter for the size of stud or socket. The related size of capsule is inserted and the fitting rotated in the hole, using an adaptor fitted to a SDS hammer drill, to break up the foil capsule, mix its contents and distribute them around the stud or socket. Commercially available studs and sockets are expensive but convenient. Small quantities, or special sizes, can be made more economically in the workshop. Studs can be made by simply cutting up lengths of studding (all thread), while sockets can be machined and tapped from bar; or use large-diameter studding to provide the external key, drilled and tapped with a smaller internal thread.

Expanding Bolts
There are many forms of bolt and anchor fixings, which rely on expanding the shank of the fitting to lock it in position. Many of these are intended for use in concrete and are only effective if the material is sufficiently strong to resist the sometimes considerable

bursting or jacking pressure exerted by the fixing. It is a matter of judgement when to stop tightening the nut or bolt head. For this reason they should not be used on soft stone or brick, placed in joints or close to edges. Some studs and sockets expand the shank by pulling a conical wedge upwards as the fixing is tightened, and can be removed if necessary. Other sockets use a wedge driven downwards by a setting tool and an initial blow with a hammer to hold the fixing in place, where it is retained by the tail of a bolt or stud, once this has been screwed in. Once fitted, these sockets cannot be removed. Other expanding bolts, sometimes called throughbolts, provide a stud whose diameter is only marginally larger than the nominal thread diameter, so the work can be set up, holes drilled through, and bolts fitted without any need to move the metalwork.

Plugs and Cavity Fixings

Despite the advent of more sophisticated systems, plastic wall plugs and large wood screws can be effective for fixing metalwork in the right application; for example, handrails, small window grilles or balustrades. Plastic plugs are available that can take large coach screws. They will not cope with the heavy pull-out loads that resin anchors can sustain, but they can still be very useful for fixing in applications where the load is sideways to the fixing, in shear rather than tension.

Beyond these are a wide range of specialist dry wall, plasterboard and cavity fixings, none capable of taking heavy loads, but which might occasionally be needed, for example, to provide a wall fixing at one end of an internal balustrade.

DRILLING

A conventional, hand-held electric drill is all that is needed for drilling holes for fixings in timber. Or with a carbide-tipped drill bit, it can make holes in plaster and brickwork, to fit plastic plugs for wood screws. However, for drilling harder masonry and larger holes, more specialized equipment is required. A rotary hammer drill can make holes in brick, stone and concrete, and is the workhorse for a great deal of site fixing. Depending on its power, this kind of hand-held drill can conveniently provide holes in masonry up to a maximum of perhaps 25mm diameter (1in) with carbide-tipped drills. This capacity covers a large range of stud and

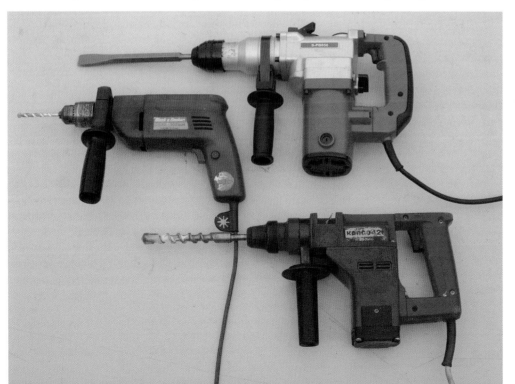

Hand electric drills for site fixing. Top, single-speed hammer drill, capable of hammer drilling, rotary drilling and chisel cutting. Middle, two-speed rotary drill with percussion setting for light masonry drilling. Bottom, variable speed hammer drill.

Terry Clark, wet diamond drilling concrete, to provide fixings for Alan Evans' Bigg Market gates in Newcastle.

socket anchor sizes, but is not very large if posts or tails are to be grouted into masonry. Hammer drills are effective in masonry and concrete but can kick or jam if the drill bit hits a steel reinforcement rod. Newer types of tipped drills are claimed to be able to cope better. For larger holes, core drills are far more efficient. Carbide-tipped core drills are available that will extend the range of a hammer drill up to some 90mm (3½in) in soft stone or lightweight concrete block. Core drills in general are more efficient for larger hole sizes, because they are only making a narrow cylindrical cut. The bulk of material in the hole remains as a solid core, which may need to be snapped off and fished out of the hole with a piece of bent wire or a vacuum cleaner, or occasionally assisted by a chisel. Some hammer drills also have a 'hammer only' setting, which allows chisels to be driven, so that

holes can be opened out into square or slotted shapes, or an odd projection in the masonry can be removed.

In hard stone or concrete, diamond core drilling is required. A diamond drill bit can be used dry and hand-held in a conventional, low-speed hand electric drill, for drilling a few holes. For drilling large numbers of holes and providing accurate alignment, a dedicated diamond-drill machine on a stand is far more effective. This is like a compact, low-speed version of a workshop bench drill mounted on a base, which can be either held down with weights, temporarily bolted to the surface being drilled or more usefully held in place horizontally or vertically by a vacuum. The base-plate has a soft rubber sealing gasket all round its edge and is attached to a vacuum pump, which sucks it tight to the wall or floor. Depending on the material being drilled and the situation, diamond drills can be used wet or dry. Wet drilling is very effective, keeps the drill cool and removes the dust as a slurry. It requires a special attachment to feed water from a pressurized container through the core of the drill and out at the tip, where in many situations it can be allowed to run to waste. For working inside a building, additional equipment is required to intercept either the dust produced by dry drilling or the slurry produced by wet. Because of their cylindrical shape and cutting action, diamond drills can be used to make overlapping holes – like a figure of eight – to provide slots for grouting in flat bars or rectangular posts.

INSURANCE

Needless to say, all insurances are hedged about by exclusions and conditions, which require careful reading. Most conditions are reasonable and common sense, but you need to know what they are, to ensure you are fulfilling them. For example, in relation to requirements when using gas torches or electric welding on site, my insurance calls for fire safety checks to undertaken regularly for at least an hour after completion. So three-quarters of a hour is not enough.

Public Liability Insurance

No matter what risks you might be happy to take in your own workshop, insurance is utterly essential when you work elsewhere. Most local authority clients and large contractors will not allow you on site unless you can show evidence of a specific level of public liability insurance. This provides cover against injury to other people and the costs of damage to property. From your own point of view, whether required by the client or not, this kind of cover is crucial. It is also important to ensure that any specialist contractor you have hired to assist with the installation also has the appropriate level of insurance cover, particularly if they will be on site while you are, since you may be deemed to be responsible for their activities. These people might include the delivery truck driver, crane driver, the people laying the concrete foundation, making good the paving or paintwork or undertaking electrical work.

Product Liability Insurance

This is usually included alongside public liability insurance and provides cover for damage or injury caused by the metalwork itself, after it has been installed. If someone is injured by catching their hand in a railing, or if a gate falls off its hinges and damages a vehicle, you are covered. However, since you will only be covered so long as this kind of policy is still in force, it is important to consider how long after you cease to work as a blacksmith, you might still need to maintain the policy. This is legal territory. Presumably at some future point in time, the gate falling off would cease to be your fault, and fair wear and tear, or lack of maintenance, would be more likely to take the blame.

Employer's Liability Insurance

Quite separate from risks to third parties, is employer's liability insurance, which provides cover should an employee be injured. Regular employees will doubtless already be covered by this kind of insurance, but it is important to remember that – as often happens – if extra people are brought in specially to help with the installation, even if only for a day, they will also need to be covered. It is a routine matter to have additional names added to the policy for just a day or a week, and this is not normally a large expense.

Contents Insurance

Goods in transit is usually a clause in the workshop contents insurance, and provides you with cover should the metalwork be damaged while being moved on a vehicle, or while it is being loaded or unloaded. Feeling that your metalwork is essentially indestructible may be dramatically put to the test, should a traffic accident take place or the whole thing be dropped by a crane. The hired truck or crane may well carry its own goods in transit insurance, but you are well advised to have your own.

METHOD STATEMENTS AND RISK ASSESSMENT

Increasingly it seems that local authorities or large contractors require the submission of method statements and risk assessments, before allowing you on site to install the metalwork. A method statement is no more than a description of what you are going to do, and you will have considered this anyway in preparation for fixing the work, but you may not normally write it all down for others to read. Preparing a written, step by step description of the procedures you have planned can be seen as a bit of a chore or as a useful exercise. At the very least it prompts you to visualize every detail of the operation and consider exactly what tools and equipment you need. It can also serve to remind you of points that the client must undertake beforehand, to enable the work to proceed.

A typical method statement, which was written for the National Youth Theatre railings (*see* Chapter 8), begins:

1. Arrive on site, clean out post holes and top of concrete foundation blocks.
2. Set up dumpy level central in car park and sight each post hole to check and note levels.
3. Identify highest concrete level, fit steel packing pieces in other holes, as necessary, to match levels.
4. Two hours later, truck to arrive, park in Holloway Road tight to kerb, and begin unloading and placing post units in position, using integral hydraulic crane. Posts fronting the road and side posts up to the reach of the crane, will be set directly in place. Others will be off-loaded as close as possible to their positions and manhandled into place.
5. Once posts are off-loaded, the railing panels will be unloaded and stacked close to their positions.

NOTE that the crane will be working across the pathway and consequently safety barriers will be needed to block the path and route pedestrians around the truck, using portable barriers sited in the roadway. These will be needed for a maximum of two hours.

6. Once all posts and panels are unloaded, the truck can leave the site, and pedestrian barriers can be removed.
7. Set out string lines and position and adjust alignment of post units.
8. Drill 4 × 18mm diameter fixing holes through each post base-plate into concrete foundation, using 110V hammer drill.

And so on...

A risk assessment is usually presented as a table – a form to fill in – listing all the procedures and kinds of tools likely to be employed in the work, identifying the hazards associated with their use, ascribing a level of danger to each hazard and describing the measures taken to reduce or manage them. There is no fixed format, so far as I am aware, and you may express the hazards and controls put in place, as you wish. Some forms also ask for details of the numbers of people put at risk, and who they are; for example, the operator, other workers nearby, everyone in the area, the general public and so on. The purpose of these documents is to demonstrate that you have considered the risks involved and have put in place appropriate safeguards.

Just as hired specialist power tools usually carry some form of check and test label, it is important not simply to check and maintain your own pieces of equipment. Your insurers will love you if you undertake this on a regular basis and keep a record of the date when it was done. Similarly, safety equipment like harnesses and hard hats will have their own manufacturer's certification. Quite apart from being good practice, this kind of record backs up the phrase 'in good working order' on the risk assessment form. In reality it may be hard to escape the thought that these forms are simply providing food for filing cabinets, to satisfy a bureaucratic requirement. Although, in the event of an accident or insurance claim, the existence of this kind of written evidence may become very important. Once established, many of the items will be applicable to each new commission and will only require re-editing to meet the needs of the particular situation.

If (as it should be) safety is an integral part of your normal working discipline – in or out of the workshop – it is initially quite difficult to set down all the hazards in writing, not least because you have spent a working lifetime learning the dangers and developing the instincts to avoid them. In

TWO EXAMPLES OF RISK ASSESSMENT FORMS

Form 1

Operation	Hazard	Level of risk	Risk	Control measures	Final risk class
Use of electric tools	Electrocution	Death	Medium	1. Suitably qualified operatives 2. Suitable protective clothing, boots and gloves to be worn by all 3. Hearing protection to be worn by all 4. Eye protection to be worn by all 5. All tools 110V, checked to insure they are in good working order, and guards are properly in place 6. Proper supervision 7. Warning signs to be displayed to ensure others on site do not disconnect essential supplies	Low
	Entanglement with moving parts	Minor to serious injury	Medium		Low
	Flying debris	Minor to serious injury	High		Low
	Noise	Minor to serious injury	Low		Low

Form 2

Hazard	Controls in place	Hazard 1 = Minor injury 2 = Serious 3 = Major/Fatal	Risk 1 = Improbable 2 = Possible 3 = Probable	Rating Hazard x Risk 1-2 = Low 3-4 = Medium 6-9 = High	Further risk reduction measures Low = No action Medium = Monitor to reduce risk High = Stop activity until risk reduced
Use of angle grinders	Trained operator, gloves and eye protection to be worn. Temporary shields used to deflect sparks where necessary. Flammable material removed from the working area, before work starts. 110V equipment, in good working order. Ear defenders to be worn by operator.				
1. Risk of injury from moving disc		1	2	2	
2. Fire risk from sparks		2	2	4	Careful supervision at all times to minimize risks
3. Risk to people from sparks		1	2	2	
4. Electrocution – cutting power cord		2	2	4	
5. Noise hazard		1	3	3	

this sense 'training' is a very important point to make, in describing measures put in place to minimize hazards. Blacksmiths are used to working safely with hot metal, heavy weights, explosive gases, power hammers, noisy power tools and so on, which might appear to other people to constitute an extremely hazardous working environment. So it may be no bad thing, once in a while, to be reminded of this, by the need to think about safety before you work on site.

ARRANGEMENTS BEFORE ARRIVING AT THE SITE

Beyond all the paperwork detailed above, there are a number of down-to-earth, practical arrangements that need to be made to enable you to operate safely and efficiently when you arrive to install the metalwork. These are the kind of details that might need no more than a phone call, if you are installing a small window grille in a private house, but could call for a great deal more planning if the project is large, heavy and in a public place. It is crucial to ensure that the preparatory work has been undertaken before you arrive, to allow your work to proceed smoothly, particularly if it is a day's drive away. Listing these things on paper is far better than trusting a phone call.

The following points are an indication of the kind of questions that need to be considered, but are not intended as an exhaustive list. In no particular order:

- Are there any existing structures that need demolition, removal or maintenance before the work can be fixed? These should be specified in detail, and the work scheduled for completion at least a week ahead of the time agreed for fixing. These items might include removing the old railings, removing obstructing masonry, clearing tree branches to allow crane access or ensuring that decorative work is completed above the site of your metalwork, rather than risking paint being dripped all over it.
- Has all the work been completed in direct preparation for fixing? This might include the provision of concrete foundations, the completion of stone cladding work, building in the hinge or fixing points for gates, railings and so on. Crucially, time must have elapsed to allow, for example, concrete or paint to cure thoroughly.
- Ask for an assurance that there are no electric power, telephone or other cables, water, drainage or gas pipes in the area where drilling will take place to provide fixings. Ask for the line of any services within the work area to be indelibly marked on the site.
- Notify your needs for specific electric power supplies and water, where required.
- If there is a need to park a vehicle or crane where it obstructs the flow of traffic:

  – Is police permission required?
  – Is a permit or waiver required? and if so who will obtain it?
- Describe the dimensions and weight of any heavy delivery vehicle or crane and ask for an assurance that the ground surface or paving is capable of sustaining such a load.
- Establish the identity of the person to report to on arrival – name, role and telephone number.
- If the working area needs to be partitioned off with screens or safety barriers, for reasons of public safety, establish who will arrange for these to be put up.
- If work is to be fixed inside a building, make sure that the entire access route will be clear of furniture, wall hangings, carpets or other obstacles.
- Where you are fixing through delicate or vulnerable surfaces – fabric-clad internal walls, marble flooring – ensure that, if any temporary protective covering is already there, then it is left in place or, if not, make arrangements to provide it.
- Are there any restrictions to working days or hours on the site? If so, what?
- Is there a secure area where tools and equipment can be left overnight?
- Notify the number of vehicles needed to transport people to the site, for which parking arrangements will be required.

Some of these items may well be considered as part of the original contract, and agreed at the outset. Preparatory building work, demolition, the provision of foundations, ensuring clear access, seeking a police permit to unload a vehicle and providing public safety barriers are the kind of concerns that might reasonably be provided by the client, builder or site agent. All these are easier and better arranged by someone with local or specialist knowledge. Laying concrete, for example, is, in my view, far better undertaken by people who do it every day.

GLOSSARY

Arris The sharp edge or corner, where two surfaces meet. A square bar is described as being set 'on the arris' if it is placed at 45 degrees, so that a corner rather than a face is presented to the viewer.

Back stile The heavy upright bar of a gate to which the hinges are attached.

Balustrade The uprights, the infill and handrail guarding a drop.

Fuller A round-ended tool either fitted in the hardie hole of the anvil or a top tool with a handle driven by a sledge-hammer

Fullering Notching, stretching or spreading metal with a round-ended tool called a fuller, or with the cross-pein end of a hammer.

Grout Liquid cement or resin, used for fixing.

Grouting-in Fixing metalwork by locating a fixing plate or tail in a pocket cut in masonry and filling this with a liquid resin or mortar.

Heel The often heavily upset end of a bar, integral with a tenon joint, in the frame of a gate or other structure. The heel provides a wide shoulder to the tenon, ensuring rigidity.

Heel bar A bar with a heel, usually the bottom horizontal rail of a gate.

Jig Strictly a device that holds the work and guides the tool working on it, such as a jig for drilling a particular pattern of holes. But in common usage, any specially made tool to position components for assembly or, for example, to allow numbers of bars to be formed to the same shape.

Journal bearing A bearing in which the load is at right angles to the axis of the shaft.

Leading-in Using molten lead to grout metalwork into masonry.

Micron (μm) One-thousandth of a millimetre, $25\mu m = \frac{1}{1000}in.$

MIG Metal Inert Gas. An arc welding system using inert gas shielding and a wire feed to provide filler metal.

Mortise *See* tenon.

Pein The opposite end of the hammer head to the face.

Pillow block *See* plummer block.

Pin or pintle The shaft on which a hinge revolves.

Plummer block The concave block that forms half a split journal bearing, in which a shaft can rotate. The other half is the cap or strap. Often used as the fixed part of an upper gate hinge.

Reamer A parallel or fluted cutting tool used to refine the diameter of a drilled hole.

Reveal The side surface of an opening or recess.

Riser The upright part of a step.

Standards The fixed uprights supporting the panel of a balustrade.

Stringer or string The sloping members of a stair, which carry the ends of the treads and risers.

Studding Threaded rod, all thread.

Swage A semi-circular or other concave tool, either fitted in the hardie hole of the anvil, a top tool driven by a sledge-hammer, or a pair of tools joined by a spring and aligned by pins for use under a power hammer.

Swaging Shaping hot metal to a particular form between swages.

Tenon Projecting tongue usually forged on the end of a bar to fit a corresponding hole (a mortise), creating a mortise and tenon joint. The tenon is usually riveted over to secure the joint.

TIG Tungsten Inert Gas. An arc-welding system using an inert gas shielded tungsten electrode and a hand-held filler rod.

Wreath The curved part of a handrail, which changes plane to link two flights round the well of a stair.

FURTHER READING

Andrews, J., *The New Edge of the Anvil* (Skipjack Press, 1994)

Ayrton, M. and Silcock, A., *Wrought Iron and its Decorative Use* (Dover Publications, re-published 2003)

Baboian, B., Cliver, E.C., and Bellante, E.L., *The Statue of Liberty Restoration* (National Association of Corrosion Engineers, 1990)

Bealer, A., *The Art of Blacksmithing* (Castle Books, 1995)

Campbell, M., *Decorative Ironwork* (V&A Publications, 1997)

Chatwin, A., *Into the New Iron Age: Modern British Blacksmiths* (Coach House Publishing, 1995)

Dunkerley, S., *Robert Bakewell* (Scarthin Books, 1988)

Geerlings, G.K., *Wrought Iron in Architecture* (Dover Publications, re-pubished 1983)

Gordon, R.E., *Structures or Why Things Do Not Fall Down* (Da Capo Press, re-published 2003)

Hawkins, D., *Art Metal Forging* (A & C Black, 2002)

Her Majesty's Stationery Office, *The Building Regulations 2000,*
– *Approved Document K, Protection from falling collision and impact*
– *Approved Document M, Access to and use of buiding*

Hughes, R. and Rowe, M, *The Colouring, Bronzing and Patination of Metals* (Thames & Hudson, 1991)

Jeynes, J., *Practical Health and Safety Management of Small Businesses* (Butterworth-Heinemann, 2000)

Krier, R., *Architectural Composition* (Academy Editions, 1991)

Meilach, D.Z., *The Contemporary Blacksmith* (Schifer Publishing, 2000)

Parkinson, P., *The Artist Blacksmith* (Crowood, 2001)

Polley, S., *Understanding the Building Regulations*, 2nd edition (Spon Press, 2001)

Starkie, G.J., *Ironwork, Part 1. From the Earliest Times to the End of the Medieval Period* (V&A Publications 1927, re-published 1978)

Starkie, G.J., *Ironwork, Part 2. Continental Ironwork of the Renaissance and Later Periods* (V&A Publications 1930, re-published 1978)

Starkie, G.J., *Ironwork, Part 3. The Artistic Working of Iron in Great Britain from the Earliest Times* (V&A Publications 1922, re-published 1978)

Pracht, K., *Gelander, Gitter und Zaune aus Metall* (Charles Coleman, 2000)

Pracht, K., *Stadtraum-gestaltung mit Elementum aus Metal* (Charles Coleman, 2001)

Salvadori, M., *Why Buildings Stand Up* (W.W. Norton & Co, 1990)

Smith, R., *An Introductiion to Perspective* (Dorling Kindersley, 1995)

Templar, J., *The Staircase – Vol 1, History and Theories* (Massachusetts Institute of Technology, 1992)

Templar, J., *The Staircase – Vol 2, Studies of Hazards, Falls and Safer Design* (Massachusetts Institute of Technology, 1992)

Warren, N., *Metal Corrosion in Boats* (Adlard Coles Nautical, 1991)

INDEX

aluminium 149
Anhoj, Gunvor 102, 132
assembly 27–37
  curved panels 30–31
  flat panels 29
  jigs 31–32

backstays 95
balustrades 74–87
  fixing 82–85
  regulations 80
  structure 77–79
Bennie, Elspeth 102
bolts *see* fixing
brass 150–151
British Standards 64–65,
    73, 80, 87, 97, 131
bronze 151
Building Regulations
    64–65, 72–73, 80, 87,
    105, 131

Clark, Terry 89, 96, 113,
    116, 118
copper 149
copper alloys 149–151
Cordaroy, Bill 66, 107,
    156, 162
corrosion 136–139

design 49–65
  concept and design 50
  problem-solving 58
  sources 51–52
  strategies 52–57
  terminology 52–57
design considerations:
  balustrades 76–82

fences 89–95
gates 108–125
grilles 100–103
handrails 67–70
railings 89–95
screens 100–103
dog bars 107, 108–110,
    128
drawings:
  engineering 58, 60–62
  layout 27–29, 58
  presentation 58, 62–63
  sketch 58, 59–60
  survey drawing 39–40,
    42, 58, 59

Evans, Alan 27, 48, 53,
    67, 70, 88, 92, 97, 99,
    154–155

Fedden, Matthew 119,
    154
fences *see* railings
finishing 136–151
  for iron and steel
    136–147
  for non-ferrous metals
    150–151
  for stainless steels
    147–148
  galvanizing 141–142,
    143
  paint finishing 143–146
  zinc spraying 142–143
fixing 153–172
  bolts and screws
    164–167
  drilling 167–168

expansion bolts 129,
    162–163
  grouting 161–164
  lifting equipment
    158–160
  method statements 169,
    170–171
  resin anchor bolts 129,
    166
  risk assessments 169,
    170–171
  tools 153
forges 13–14
forging 13–25
  bending 24
  fullering 15–17
  hot cutting 20
  power hammer 14–17
  punching 20–22
  swaging 17
  tapering 18
  twisting 23
  upsetting 19–20

galvanizing 141–142, 143
gates 106–131
  design 108–125
  fixing 125–131
  hinges 117–121
  latches 121–125
  locks 121–125
  regulations 131
  structure 110–112
gilding 146–147
grilles 98–105
  design 100–103
  fixing 104–105
  regulations 105

handrails 67–73
  design 67–70
  making 70–71
  regulations 72–73
Horrobin, Jim 6, 10, 12,
  26, 31, 32, 79, 102,
  126–127

installation 153–172
  see also fixing
insurance 168–169
Ironhorse Studios 49

Johnson, Phil 16, 24, 28,
  29, 33, 61, 86–87,
  118, 119, 129

Kranenborg, Robert 77,
  114, 118

lead 151, 162–163
Lunn, Steve 7, 16, 25, 33,
  82, 93, 160

Margetts, Paul 103, 106,
  131
materials 133–136,
  149–151
method statements
  see fixing
model-making 63–64
mortise and tenon joints
  32–35

Normandale, Charles 15,
  31, 96, 101, 110, 142,
  147

paint finishing 143–146
pin joints 37
protective clothing 7–9

Quirk, Andy 8, 77, 118

railings 88–97
  design 89–95
  fixing 95–97
  regulations 97
regulations:
  balustrades 87
  gates 131
  general 64–65
  handrails 73–73
  railings 97
  screens 105
risk assessments see fixing
riveting 32–35
Rowe, Andy 103
Russell, Brian 52, 55, 69,
  100, 112, 159
Russell, Oliver 124

safety 7–9
screens 98–105
screws 35–36
stairs:
  balustrades 74–87
  spiral 73, 85–87
  terminology 76, 83
steel 134–136
  alloy 135
  carbon 134–135
  corrosion 136–139
  mild 134

stainless 135–136,
  147–148
  weathering 135
surveying 39–47
  angles 43–44
  curves 44–46
  drawings 39–40, 42, 58,
    59
  equipment 40–41

templates 47
Thomas, Shelley 54, 81,
  84, 93, 103, 108
titanium 151
Topp, Chris 22, 110
transport 154–155
Tucker, David 33, 56, 57,
  62, 80, 128

wedges 37
welding:
  arc welding 34–36
  fire welding 24–25
  gas welding 34
  MIG welding 35
  TIG welding 35
Wilson, Avril 53, 91
workshops 10–11
wrapping joints 37
wrought iron 133

zinc spraying 142–143